Deliver Us from Addiction

Confessions of an Alcoholic's Wife in the Word of Faith New Apostolic Reformation

Ariel Abornski

Christian Touch Publishing

Deliver Us from Addiction
Confessions of an Alcoholic's Wife in the Word of Faith New Apostolic Reformation
Ariel Abornski

Christian Touch Publishing
Printed in the United States

Print ISBN 978-0-578-42386-9

Cover Design by Fajar Wahyu

Dedicated to my mother, Patricia, 1943-2015

Table of Contents

Author's Note

The Word of Faith (WoF) movement is a worldwide faction within Christianity that claims to access spiritual power through thoughts and confessions of faith or fear. The New Apostolic Reformation (NAR), with its emphasis on dominion, prophets, and apostles, brings the WoF teachings to another level of supernatural experience and revelation. Though these movements began in Pentecostal and Charismatic denominations, their teachings on health, wealth, success, and dominion, as well as the techniques of positive confession, visualization, and spiritual warfare are making headway in mainstream Christianity.

This book draws from my experiences in several Pentecostal churches that I attended over a period of 24 years. The churches that taught the WoF/NAR message have been consolidated into one church in this story, and the corresponding WoF pastors into one pastor. I've also eliminated characters / families by combining several into one composite person / family.

To the best of my memory, the sermons, teachings, and conversations bear close resemblance to what was said. Because some of my characters / pastors / churches are composites, please be careful not to assume that the specific person, pastor, or church has done and said everything exactly as attributed to his/her character or congregation. Most names are fictitious. Any resemblance to names of people or churches is purely coincidental. Minor details have been changed to protect the privacy of the people involved.

Some of the advice I followed, and many of the religious concepts I endorsed early in my life were erroneous. Before accepting information about medicine, theology, or addiction, please research the subjects thoroughly.

Prologue

"When did the gunshot occur?" asked the middle-aged, female police officer. The shiny badge on her uniform caught my eye as it mirrored the light from above, briefly reflecting a beam of light onto a clipboard she was preparing to hand to me.

"About 7:00 PM last night." My voice caught in my throat, and I felt my right eyelid twitching. The small, windowless room—devoid of pictures and decorations—felt suffocating, and I could barely focus as Officer Smith slid the clipboard and pen across the table to me.

"I need you to fill this out."

My trembling hands could hardly grasp the clipboard as I tried to recall the events that had transpired after I'd walked out of the bathroom the previous night...

"**B**ut I don't...wanna leave. Can't I stay here tonight?" Kevin was slurring his words, as usual.

"No Kevin."

"C'mon. I just wanna...be a...family again," Kevin pleaded, wiping a tear from his eye. He hiccupped, buried his face in his hands, and started sobbing.

I felt no sympathy, only annoyance that he was breaking his promises. Again. He was supposed to be sober when he came over for visitation with our children, not inebriated. "I'm calling Bubba to come get you. You're drunk."

"Dammit! You don't care a thing about me! I should just end it all!" This was not the gentle man whom I'd married. Kevin hurled several choice expletives toward me.

My chest tightened, and my breath caught in my throat. I wished Tyler and Amber didn't have to hear harsh, abusive language, but couldn't think of a way to diffuse our situation.

Though people often do terrible things when intoxicated, I took a gamble that Kevin wouldn't follow through with his threats and decided not to give in to his manipulations. (One should never call the bluff of someone who is talking about suicide, especially when that person is drunk or high. Human life is much too valuable to take chances with, and I hope others won't follow my example in this). Blinking back tears, I turned my back to him and headed to the bathroom.

"Mom!" Amber called to me through the bathroom door.

"Can't it wait until I'm out?" I blew my nose, wishing I had more patience, yet needing a few moments alone. The pleasant melody of tree frogs drifted through my open bathroom window, filling the country air with song as I leaned against the wall, trying to find peace. I took a deep breath in and slowly exhaled...

"But Dad just walked through the house with a shotgun!" Amber's voice was shrill, and her words frantic. "And he cocked it on the way out the door!"

When the bullet exploded from the barrel of Kevin's rifle, a burst of heat surged through my entire body, starting at my feet and exiting through my head. *What was that?! Did I literally feel Kevin's spirit leaving our world?*

The tree frogs became silent. Amber screamed! Rushing to the kitchen door, I grabbed the doorknob, then halted. *What might I find?*

Terrified, I opened the door and looked toward the garage.

1 The Influence of Companions

Do not be deceived: "Bad company
corrupts good morals.
1 Corinthians 15:33 NASB

If you're a blonde woman, you know what it means to be called a 'blonde', just as a Polish person in Wisconsin knows what it means to be called a Polack. Mom was as blonde a Polack as you could find. In her fervency for the Lord, she unabashedly told everyone about Jesus and had given out tapes which explained the baptism of the Holy Spirit to our staunch Catholic relatives.

"To think that Trish was in the convent in high school, and now she's abandoning the Catholic church. For shame! For shame!" One can almost see my great aunts wagging their fingers in disapproval. Though most of them rejected Mom for her change in religious direction, there was one special aunt who had a completely different reaction.

Aunt Sharon was a rotund, grandmotherly Charismatic who bubbled over with enthusiasm for Jesus and the Holy Spirit. When she heard that Mom and I had given our lives to the Lord, she immediately invited us to Bible studies in her spacious, country home where she shared hearty hugs, and warm, hand-sized sugar cookies. She gave me a gift which had the power to impact every area of my life, from the company I would keep to the moral choices I would make. Although I read my Bible every day after school, my faith in the Scriptures was to be shaken to the core within the year.

My seventh-grade science book, with pictures depicting organisms which allegedly transitioned from a single cell into all the various plants and animals over millions of years, introduced me to the theory of evolution. If I had known that each of the missing links portrayed in my textbooks, such as Java Man, Piltdown Man, and Nebraska Man would eventually be disproven, life might have gone quite differently for me.

As it was, I looked at the drawings of apes progressing into man and couldn't reconcile the story of evolution with the biblical account of creation. This caused me to question the validity of the Bible and whether my Christian faith could possibly hold any real value. That answer came from my religious instructor.

"The Bible is mostly made up of stories and is not meant to be taken as literal truth," said Mrs. Herman. "When Moses wrote the first five books of the Scriptures, he wanted to give the Israelites an idea of how the world *might* have begun."

I wish I'd known then that God's Holy Word has a perfect record of predicting historical events, including hundreds of detailed prophecies which have been precisely fulfilled to the smallest detail, sometimes hundreds of years in advance.[1] Additionally, a continuity between themes flows through all 66 books, even though they were written by different men—including kings, philosophers, fishermen, poets, shepherds, statesmen, scholars, a physician, a rabbi, etc. Throughout 40 generations over a span of 1500 years, these books were written on three continents, in three languages, and during times of peace and times of war, addressing hundreds of controversial topics. Despite these wide variations, there is perfect harmony throughout one unfolding story: how people can be redeemed from sin and go to Heaven when they die.[2]

King David, who penned many of the Psalms, explained who the true Author of the Scriptures was.

The Spirit of the LORD spoke by me, And His word was on my tongue. 2 Sam. 23:2 NASB

The Apostle Paul attested to the fact that the Scriptures came from the mind of God.

> *"All Scripture is inspired by God and profitable for teaching, for reproof, for correction, for training in righteousness; so that the man of God may be adequate, equipped for every good work." 2 Timothy 3:16-17 NASB*

The Apostle Peter tells us,

> *So, we have the prophetic word made surer, to which you do well to pay attention as to a lamp shining in a dark place, until the day dawns and the morning star arises in your hearts. But know this first of all, that no prophecy of Scripture is a matter of one's own interpretation, for no prophecy was ever made by an act of human will, but men moved by the Holy Spirit spoke from God. 2 Peter 1:19-21 NASB* (Emphasis mine)

In my opinion, a book authored by the God of the universe deserves to be trusted as the final authority on spiritual issues. Unfortunately, my demise commenced when I placed my Bible on a bookshelf, accepting the position that it was false, and that evolution was fact. The foundation for my moral basis was gone, and the choices I was about to make would impact my life for many years.

Though I went with my parents to their new church, worldly attractions crowded out most thoughts of living by biblical standards. Because I had previously said the 'Sinner's Prayer', I thought I would go to heaven when I died, if God was real.

One must question, however, if a person should depend upon a broken commitment that couldn't sustain itself when the pleasures of the world were able to entice that person away. Biblical experts may debate this subject, and it is not within the scope of this book to determine that answer, but serious error in our belief system could lead us to think we are saved when we might very well be lost. If I had truly turned my life over to Jesus, my choices should have reflected His Lordship.

Though it may seem ludicrous for an individual to allow her heart to placate herself for even one transient day of this temporary life, the natural tendency of teenagers is to allow their heart's desires to preside over logic. The mature soul, however, can realize that any amount of pleasure in this world could never be worth giving up an eternity of enjoyment with our Creator, and that everlasting torment and suffering should be avoided at all costs.

Yet what we suffer now is nothing compared to the glory he will reveal to us later. Romans 8:18 NLT

And what do you benefit if you gain the whole world but lose your own soul? Mark 8:36 NLT

"**M**om, I picked up these forms to enroll at the public high school." I stood in the kitchen and stated it as a fact, rather than asking permission.

"You did?" Hunched over her sewing machine, with the pedal to the medal, Mom was sewing as fast as her Singer could go. The machine fell silent as she looked up at me.

"Yes," I said. "Will you sign them so I can drop them off at the guidance counselor's office tomorrow?"

"Are you sure you want to change schools?"

"I do. The public school has a swimming pool and more class options."

Most of my Catholic instructors were excellent teachers, and Mom knew I was receiving a fine education, but she may have been relieved that I was leaving my parochial high school. Since Mom had begun to read her Bible in earnest, our Catholic traditional beliefs quickly came under her scrutiny, and she took every opportunity to feed me facts that she had been discovering.

Over the course of the previous year, she had told me, "Praying to the saints and worshiping Mary alongside of Jesus is *idolatry," and "The Bible doesn't say Mary ascended into heaven, nor does it say she was a virgin forever. In fact, the Bible says Jesus had brothers."

I didn't understand why these points mattered or what idolatry was, but I was glad for the opportunity to switch schools.

*Idolatry–the worship of idols or excessive devotion to, or reverence for some person or thing. —Webster.

"**H**i Ariel, how's it going?" Aunt Annie, Dad's youngest sister, was one of the only people I recognized on my first day in the public high school. One year older than me, and more like a cousin than an aunt, Annie was completely genuine inside and out. She could get away without makeup because her olive colored skin was flawless. Her green eyes were a similar almond shape and color as mine, and we were about the same height: five feet, five inches. We could have passed for sisters, except her hair was light brown and wavy, while mine was dark brown and straight.

"Not good," I replied. "The combination for my locker doesn't work, and I've been having a hard time locating my classes." I held back tears.

"Oh? Maybe I can help." Annie seemed to care more about me than her own schedule. From the school office, we were sent to the janitor, and within the hour, all was taken care of.

"**I**f you love me, you will let me..." It was my senior year in high school, and I'd been dating Mark for more than a year. He'd spoken these words often, indicating he was thinking of his own self-gratification. Besides providing hard liquor, Mark pressured me a lot. Perhaps this was partly due to his father's stack of pornographic magazines in their bathroom.

If a man really loves a woman, he wouldn't coerce her, but I can hardly place all the blame on Mark's plate. I had little idea how strongly a man is tempted by what he sees, and I could have worn more modest clothing. When I was inebriated, my physical desires overcame my principles as I rationalized, we were going to get married anyway. Shortly after committing to the relationship fully, another side of my boyfriend began to surface.

"Stop looking at the guy on the other side of you!" Mark demanded, as we sat at a round table in one of our favorite bars.

"Which guy? What do you mean?" I didn't remember looking in the other direction.

Ten minutes later, we were outside, and he had me pinned in the doorway of a vacant store, yelling at me.

Though he was becoming possessive, physically abusive, and jealous, I had my ideals that I would sleep with only one man in life. I blamed myself for his behavior, believing our relationship was stunted because I'd made him wait too long for sex.

I didn't realize that those of us who are codependent are always evaluating ourselves to see where we might assume fault when relationships deteriorate. We think that if we can become more perfect, our companions won't be so inclined to abuse us. We do not comprehend that other people should be held accountable for their behaviors and that their mistreatment of us is the result of their own character. For instance, we might do something which makes another person angry, but he makes the decision as to whether he will react in an abusive manner or respond with maturity of character.

"Don't even try to get out of here!" Mark's dark eyes flashed with anger as he stood between me and his bedroom door. We'd been playing pool in the basement rec room when he'd lost his temper and forced me into his room, shoving me onto the bed.

I turned away from him, determined not to let him see the tears. I needed to use my wits, like the time he had locked me in the car with him on a dead-end road. That time, I convinced him to open a window, telling him I was too warm. I then managed to get my torso out the window and kicked against him until he let go and exited his own door. I raced toward home, one-half mile away. When he caught me and threw me on the ground, stars swirled in my head. Though I'd broken up with him after the incident, he kept saying he loved me, promising it would never happen again.

Here I was, in a similar situation. *Think, Ariel,* I told myself. I pretended to relax a moment, then took a blanket as though I was going to cover myself. When I tossed it over his head and attempted to get around him, he went ballistic, throwing me back on the bed and punching a hole in the door.

"Is everything okay down there?" Mark's oldest brother called from the stairwell. Thank goodness Tim was home.

Mark turned from his splintered bedroom door, holding his fist. "I'm sorry, Ariel."

"I'm not sure I want to marry you, and I don't want to do anything physical outside of marriage, not even kiss. It makes me feel guilty."

Not long after that, a situation arose in which Mark did something where I knew the facts beyond a doubt. Wanting to convince me that I was the guilty one, Mark grabbed my Bible off the bookshelf and gave me his made-up version of what happened, capping it off with, "I swear to God, Ariel, I'm telling the truth."

My parents had a marriage built on faithfulness, trust, and sacrifice, and in that pivotal moment, I realized that Mark treated me in ways my dad would *never* have treated my mom. I'd remained in the traumatic relationship for several years trying to make it work, but this was the straw that broke the camel's back.

Mark had sworn on God's Word several times in the past, assuring me of his faithfulness. Not that I held the Bible in high regard, but because I couldn't trust him, I took the Scriptures from his hands. "I don't ever want to see you again."

"I'm sorry. I shouldn't have done that. I could never sleep with another woman." One liners came tumbling out of his mouth. "I can't even be turned on by another woman. If you break up with me, I'll kill myself."

I pictured him crossing the bridge on the way to his parent's house and worried he might follow through, but didn't cave in. Luckily, Mark was only bluffing.

Suicidal threats seem to be a common way addicts try to manipulate others to continue riding their merry-go-round of selfish craziness. While we should take such warnings seriously, we must not succumb to coercion. We can contact a suicide hotline, call the police, and tell friends and family members if someone claims to be suicidal. Professional help is critical.

Now that I'm older, I realize the sooner one begins to live by God's standards, the less trouble a person brings upon oneself, for we choose our companions, spouse, and entertainment according to those things we value. I had idolized popularity and adventure more than I valued the Lord. How I wish I could go back in time and turn my life to God at that point, because it could have saved me many sorrows!

We live in a time and society where addictions to drugs, alcohol, and pornography are reaching epidemic proportions, and suicide is a leading cause of death in the USA. It is difficult to turn on the news without seeing headlines about opiate addictions, riots, school shootings, and sex trafficking. These are symptoms of a society where materialism, power, and selfishness prevail over a relationship with God and intimacy with family. Our destructive ways of coping with emotional pain and handling stress are exhibited to our children, and the cycle continues from one generation to the next.

In an article titled *Religious Dysfunction*, Reverend David Henke says, "There are three areas of legitimate human need and desire that often are not met sufficiently (by the measure of the one in need), or quickly enough, to satisfy. So, the temptation may be to fulfill their need by an illegitimate means. Those three areas include the sense of being in control, having significance, and having money. Let's call them Power,

Prestige, and the Purse. These are the root motivations out of which flow a behavior pattern of the misuse of power, the seeking of prestige, and the coveting of money."[3]

The empty void in my soul cried out for true love as I wiped the dust off the Book with the answer to my greatest need. I thought about my evolutionary instruction in science class and recalled what my religious instructor had said about the Word of God. Then I placed the wisdom of the wisest Being there is back on the bookshelf...and wondered, *What if I am pregnant?*

2 Today's Choices, Tomorrow's Consequences

For the ways of a man are before the eyes of the LORD,
And He watches all his paths. His own iniquities will
capture the wicked, and he will be held with the cords of
his sin. He will die for lack of instruction, and in the
greatness of his folly he will go astray.
Proverbs 5:21-23 NASB

"Did you hear who's pregnant?" Monica giggled as she added a French fry to the hot oil in the pan on my stove top. Five-foot-two, eyes-of-blue, with strawberry-blonde hair that reached her shoulders, Monica's freckled cheeks were flushed.

"No, who?"

"Mark's girlfriend!"

"She is? Well, at least *I'm* not." I felt my chest tighten. Sometimes, just seeing a tall man with dark brown hair and eyes would cause me to have shortness of breath and heart palpitations.

"Why are you shaking?" Monica asked.

"I don't know. Maybe it's because we're talking about Mark."

"I hope you don't mind that I invited my brother to join us," said Monica.

"Of course not. My mom said that Kevin seems like a good guy. Whenever she brings your mother home from shopping, he comes out to help unload the groceries without being asked." Taking a swallow of my wine cooler, I continued frying hamburgers on the next burner as Monica tossed another fry into her pan of oil. It had been years since I'd watched Mom make French fries, and I wasn't sure we were doing it right.

The oil foamed up slightly in the pan with each fry Monica added, causing her to shriek with delight. Apparently, she had never made French fries either. It was easy to see that my best friend had drunk her first wine cooler too fast. She added another potato wedge, squealing again as the oil came yet higher. It sizzled to the very top edge of the pan. One more potato slice would be too much.

"Stop!" I shouted, as Monica grabbed another fry. It left her hand and dived into the oil.

"Whoooeee," she whooped again. One would have thought she was on a toboggan slide coming out of the chute. The bubbling oil came up over the edges of the pan and down onto the burner, igniting immediately. Fire flared up the sides of the pan, catching the contents within and blazing up toward the hood of the stovetop. Smoke quickly filled my tiny kitchen as I grabbed a box of baking soda out of the cabinet. Though it took only a moment to put out the flames, the whole apartment was filled with smoke.

"Oh my gosh, Sandy's going to kill me." My roommate, who was away for the weekend, had plastic wrap on all the windows to save on the heat bill. Since we couldn't open them, Monica opened the door into the hallway to get rid of the smoke. The corridor alarms started shrieking.

Shortly after that, Kevin showed up with a 12-pack of Miller beer in his hand. He smiled and looked at the floor.

"Come in," I said. At five feet, eight inches and 150 pounds, Kevin shared Monica's small nose and freckles, but not her fair skin or her gaiety. Carefully avoiding eye contact, he seemed like a broken kitten who needed to be loved. *I can help this man to have a higher self-esteem,* I thought. My codependent heart wanted to reach out and fix the man who crossed the threshold into my life.

"**I** hate you! Why can't you leave me alone?!" I dug my nails into Mark's side, seething with anger. It was a terrible thing to do, and I'm sorry for it now, but that seemed to be the turning point where Mark stopped following and harassing Kevin and me. He'd been showing up at Kevin's parents' house, at my apartment, and at several bars I frequented. Everywhere I went, there he was, demanding to talk to me. To keep him from finding me, I moved to a different location, changed my phone number, and stopped going to my favorite dancing bars.

Unlike Mark, when Kevin drank, he became happy, never angry. Though he was always gentle-natured, I had frequent nightmares in which he turned into Mark and became abusive. Since I believed Mark mistreated me because I made him wait too long for sex, I allowed these subjective experiences and ideas to guide my morality. I should have followed the objective instructions of the Bible, which is outside of ourselves and is not distorted by the heart's desires.

True love is sacrificial, and willingness to wait for sex until marriage builds self-control. Those who can deny their bodies begin to forge the strength of character needed for a solid marriage. They develop stronger will-power, which makes them less prone to addiction.

"Will you marry me?" After two years of dating, Kevin handed me a velvet-covered jewelry box. Sitting side-by-side on the couch in my parent's living room, I opened my gift. The recessed ceiling lights shined down on us as my sister, Amanda, and her boyfriend, Jerry, shared in our special moment.

The clear, sparkling diamond shimmered as it refracted a rainbow of colors. "Yes, I will." I didn't let the fact of Kevin's drinking concern me. Certain that he would never let me down and would quit drinking shortly after our marriage, I believed we would live happily ever after. We were married in the month of October during my first year of college.

"I promise to be true to you in good times, and in bad, in sickness, and in health. I will love you and honor you all the days of my life." Kevin looked directly into my eyes, pledging his heart to me. I'm certain he meant his promises to the extent that he was capable, as much as a person can when their heart already belongs to alcohol.

I regret I cannot change my past choices, but I learned a valuable lesson that I desire to share with other women before they get married. If a man cannot give up his bad habits and turn to the Lord in his actions <u>before</u> marriage, one should not expect the addictions and selfishness to get better after the ceremony. Once a person is married, like a hunter who has bagged a buck, the effort to please almost always diminishes. The companions we choose to keep, whether drinking buddies, church friends, or the Lord, will affect the decisions we make today. Later, we pay the consequences.

3 Worldview Matters

Envision a teeny-tiny speck of dust called Time within a magnificent, rapidly expanding universe called Eternity. At the outermost edges, this cosmos is explosively enlarging in all directions faster than 186,000 miles per SECOND, which is the speed of light. As you watch, the particle of dust called Time almost appears to shrink while Eternity expands.

On this tiny grain of sand in the realm of Time are small creatures who possess temporary lives. These little beings become so focused on what happens there—whether they've experienced unfairness, whether they've gotten what they've wanted while residing there, or whether they agree with the moral rules of the Creator of the Time—that they lose sight of Eternity.

—Ariel Abornski

In the first two years of our marriage, I was in college and discovered such complexity, order, and design within cells, plants, and animals, as well as within the processes of life, that my belief in evolution began to waver. The critical thinking skills I lacked in junior and senior high school began to grow, and I started to analyze the information in my science textbooks in a new way.

'There HAS to be a Creator.' The realization hit me when I studied the intricate, complicated order of the human dentition. The sensitive nerve and blood vessel (pulp) of each tooth is shielded by a layer of dentin, which is covered with enamel. (An evolutionary random process might have placed the nerve on the outside, making it too painful to eat). Ameloblasts, specialized cells that make enamel, complete their work from the top of the tooth down so the

erupting portion of the tooth is protected before it is exposed. Cementum, a special coating for the roots of teeth, enables perfectly ordered periodontal ligaments to anchor teeth to bone. The incisors, designed for tearing food, are ideally situated in the front of the mouth, and the molars, superbly fashioned for grinding, are positioned in the back. The artistically engineered grooves and fossas on the roots of the teeth give perfect shape for maximum strength and stability. Though my textbooks attempted to give natural explanations for all of life's processes—**excluding** the possibility of a supernatural God—the evidence for an intelligent Designer seemed unmistakable to me.

If God was out there, I wanted to find Him, but I had entertained the idea that all religions led to Heaven. I needed to determine whether religious pluralism, a Hindu concept that is oppositional to Christianity, was a viable option. To demonstrate what pluralism is, I'd like to pose two multiple choice questions. You may pick one or more answers.

1.) Which set of animals belongs the mammal family?

A. Birds and fish only
B. Cats and dogs only
C. Frogs and alligators
D. None of the above
E. All the above

If I told you the answer was E, I would be making an illogical claim because a few of the answers (A, B, and D) are exclusive, and all the answers contradict one another. The correct answer is B.

2.) What happens to a person after he dies?

A. His soul goes to heaven or hell, depending on whether he surrendered his life to Jesus. (Christianity)
B. His soul goes to hell forever or to purgatory until the penalty for his sin is paid, at which point he passes into heaven. (Catholicism)
C. He stays in the grave because he doesn't have a soul. (Atheism)
D. He waits to be reincarnated into a different body for another chance at life. (Hinduism, Buddhism, New Age Spirituality)
E. All the above

Religious pluralism suggests that E is the answer. However, several of the answers are exclusive in nature, and all the answers contradict one another. Logic tells us that these can't all be right at the same time.

There are several faiths which claim exclusivity to God, as though their religion is the only way to Heaven. Christianity, while it is inclusive in the sense that a person from any race can become a member, is exclusive when it claims to be the only way to God. Jehovah's Witnesses, Mormons, and Muslims are a few others which allege exclusivity to God. Which path should a person pursue? In my quest for truth, I didn't want to give allegiance to my subjective feelings, but preferred to follow the objective evidence, wherever it would lead.

"Why do you think the Bible is true?" As my newborn baby, Tyler, was nursing, I took a sip from my water glass while Mom and I sat in her spacious living room.

"Well," she began, "if you and I wrote a book about parenting, and we wrote our chapters separately, would the book be perfectly consistent throughout?"

"Not likely," I replied, shaking my head. I believed (like many young people), that I knew several areas where my parents had made mistakes when they raised me.

"You see, Ariel, though we come from the same home, we couldn't possibly agree on everything. Imagine the inconsistencies if we were to include women from several different time periods and cultures, allowing each to write a chapter of our book."

"There'd be a lot of disagreement, but what does that have to do with the Bible?"

"Forty different authors wrote about many topics in the Bible without contradicting one another."

"Really?" I set my water glass on the end table, hopeful that my thirsty heart could find a source in which to trust.

"Yes, and there are common themes that thread their way throughout the books of the Bible, pointing to one Author. The Old Testament has hundreds of prophecies telling about a Messiah who would be crucified so we could be saved. The New Testament shows how Jesus fulfilled those specific prophecies exactly as foretold."

"Wow. I always thought faith was believing without having evidence."

To realize that we have access to the thoughts and wisdom of our Creator was astounding to me. As I began reading the Scriptures, one of the first things I noticed was that *none* of the writers promoted getting to heaven by doing good deeds or by living an admirable life, but rather by accepting the atoning gift of Christ's innocent blood, which was poured out on our behalves.

Is there another 'holy book' or tradition of man that can compare? My Bible would never again take up space on a bookshelf, gathering dust.

"Can't I even take a shower without you crying?!" I peered out from behind the shower curtain at my colicky baby. Tyler was sitting in his bouncy seat and didn't seem to notice my complaint. In that moment, I realized my life could no longer revolve around me. My son was unable to meet his own needs, and it was up to me to comfort him, even when it was inconvenient.

A week after my conversation with Mom, I heard the whisper of God, ***"You may let your own soul slip into eternity without Me, but you need to think about Tyler's afterlife."***

As I looked at my infant, I considered the fact that he needed me to show him the way to heaven. I thought of the agony which God the Father endured when He watched Jesus go through the tortuous crucifixion. As a parent, I couldn't imagine allowing my child to make such a sacrifice for the sake of those who might reject him. How would God feel, then, if I continued to choose my own way through life, refusing to accept the high price He paid?

"There are many different Christian denominations," said Pastor Bill, a short, stocky man with kind, blue eyes and light brown hair. "Each one has slight variations in their beliefs. For instance, some Christians are ***cessationists***. They believe that the gifts of the Spirit ***ceased*** with the original twelve apostles. Our church is a Charismatic church. We are ***continuationists*** because we believe the Holy Spirit gifts ***continue*** today."

"When you are baptized in the Spirit, He gives the ability to speak in tongues, which can include another human language or a heavenly, angelic language. Some people receive the gift of discernment and can distinguish between God's Spirit and evil spirits. Others have the gift of healing and can lay their hands on sick people so they recover. Those who have the gift of prophecy can often tell the future ahead of time."

Pastor Bill seemed to have a genuine heart for the Lord and could quote many Scripture passages from memory. I listened carefully to his messages, taking notes throughout each sermon, trusting him completely.

As I began to know God, my ways started to change, but not without pain. Slowly, He began to break the me-centered thinking of my youth. I remember the first time God directed me to see an argument from Kevin's point of view.

I had furiously slammed the door on the way out of our 2-bedroom apartment and headed for my gray Dodge Omni hatchback. Revving the engine for good measure, I angrily gripped the icy steering wheel in one hand and the stick-shift in the other, jamming it into first gear. If I hadn't been in a parking lot, I would have squealed the tires to show Kevin just how ticked off I was!

How could he be so inconsiderate as to leave his greasy, black hand marks all over my perfectly straight hand towels?! The empty toilet paper roll and the dirty socks lying on the bathroom floor put me over the edge.

The nerve of that man! Does he think I am his maid?

Ariel, you are being the more difficult one to live with. You should be grateful that he changed the oil in your car.

What?! If he would get his act together, we'd have a great marriage! I fired back at the intrusive conviction.

Think about it from his point of view.

His point of view? What about me?! It never dawned on me that I could be at fault for any part of our marital struggles. Now that I'd truly decided to turn my life over to God, He began giving me a new perspective on many things. While it was my heart's desire to know the Lord and to live my life in a way that honored Him, it was killing me to die to myself!

Kevin was probably astonished when I arrived home a few moments later and apologized.

"No, I haven't had a drink since the day I decided to quit." Dad's Bible was lying open on the lamp table next to his Lazy Boy recliner, and he massaged one of his aching feet as he answered me.

I looked at the most faithful, honest, and hardworking man I knew. Dad's black hair didn't cover the shiny olive colored skin on the top of his head as well as it used to, so he left a shock of it long enough that he could comb it up over the top to the other side.

"Thanks for the good example you set, Dad. I hope Kevin will quit drinking someday, too."

My father, a truck-driver, was gone at least 70 hours a week and still managed to do maintenance on other people's cars, projects on our house, and jog five miles every other day. He began developing an increasingly positive attitude since he gave his life to Jesus. Even so, he was a firm believer that Murphy's law worked better for him than for anyone else. The mosquitoes liked him more than other people, and if there was a bone in the fish, he was sure to get it.

Oh, the agony of the Christian walk. I believed God was telling me that blaming had become a way of thinking for me, a mindset as natural as breathing. Deep in my heart, I had often found myself inwardly accusing Kevin, rather than considering where I might have been wrong. I always had one person or another to blame for my difficulties and bad moods. I felt like God was holding my heart above a fire of purification, asking me to look honestly inside of myself to see where I was guilty.

As I listened to God, He was changing me from the inside out, and I was learning that everything in life wasn't all about me and my own distorted, self-centered viewpoint. Rather, I needed to understand God's view of the world, obtaining His worldview.

4 Introduction to Cults and New Age Spirituality

A cult is a religious perversion. It is a belief and practice in the world of religion which calls for devotion to a religious view or leader centered in false doctrine. It is an organized heresy. A cult may take many forms but it is basically a religious movement which distorts or warps orthodox faith to the point where truth becomes perverted into a lie. A cult is impossible to define except against the absolute standard of the teaching of Holy Scripture.[4] —David Breese, deceased Christian pastor and theologian.

s we prepared lunch together one Sunday after church, Mom said, "The Jehovah's Witnesses met with me again on Friday."

"Oh? How did that go?" I reached for the loaf of homemade, whole wheat bread on Mom's countertop.

"Not good. It's hard to open a closed mind." Mom brought out the lunch meat, mayonnaise, and cheese, and set them on the counter next to me.

"What do you mean by a 'closed mind'?" I asked, opening the jar of mayo.

"A person with a closed mind is not willing to accept the possibility that their beliefs may be wrong. Their minds aren't open to any information that contradicts what they've chosen to believe."

"But how do we know that others, like the Jehovah's Witnesses or Mormons, aren't the ones who are right?" I began spreading mayo on each piece of bread.

"Well, Ariel, one of the signs of a *cult is that they base their main doctrines on **extra**-biblical information that can't be proven, like the visions Joseph Smith—the founder of the Mormons—had."

"I suppose a vision might be one's own imagination."

"Sure, or an evil spirit, posing as an angel of light. Either way, when new revelations undermine what the Bible says about Jesus—that He is God and that salvation comes through Him alone—they can't be from the Lord. God's Spirit will never give visions that contradict His Scriptures, and we must not add to or take away from the Bible." Mom headed to her dining room table, which had several Bible versions lying open on it. She picked up her tattered NIV and began turning the pages.

"Here it is." Mom began reading Revelation 22:18–19. *"I warn everyone who hears the words of the prophecy of this scroll: If anyone adds anything to them, God will add to that person the plagues described in this scroll. And if anyone takes words away from this scroll of prophecy, God will take away from that person any share in the tree of life and in the Holy City, which are described in this scroll."* She looked up. "Even though these words are written about the book of Revelation, the principle applies to the entire Bible."

Mom then turned to Proverbs 30:5-6 and read, *"Every word of God is flawless; He is a shield to those who take refuge in Him. Do not add to His words, or He will rebuke you and prove you a liar."*

"When you call Jehovah's Witnesses a cult, do you mean a mind-control cult, like Jim Jones with cyanide-laced Kool-Aid or the Branch Davidians in Waco, Texas?"

"No," Mom replied. "I'm not talking about a social cult, where one thinks of brainwashing, animal sacrifices, and mass suicides. Theologians define the word cult as a religion which claims to be Christian but deviates from one or more essential Christian doctrines."

"So, you believe Mormons and Jehovah's Witnesses are cults then?" I began layering cheese and meat on the bread.

"Yes, they are. Christian cults share common deceptions, claiming Jesus is not Almighty God, and salvation isn't by faith alone. Jehovah's Witnesses promote salvation by works. They claim we can't get to heaven apart from their Watchtower organization, as though the Bible isn't enough. On top of that, the New World Translation Bible was written by their own translators and contains serious errors which reduce the divinity of Jesus, making it look like He is not equal to the Father."

"How do we know our translators are right, and theirs are wrong?"

"Well, *every* Bible translation, except the Jehovah's Witness Bible, is in full agreement on key passages about Jesus' deity. We know the academic credentials of those who translated all Bible versions, but those who did the

New World Translation are kept anonymous. How can we know their qualifications or hold them accountable for error when they won't reveal who these people are?"

"It sounds like they have something to hide."

Mom began slicing a watermelon while I cut the sandwiches diagonally and arranged them on a plate.

"Several times in the past, the Watchtower prophesied the end of the world would come in specific years, which have come and gone. The Bible instructs that if a prophet's predictions do not come to pass, that prophet has not been sent by God, and we should not fear them."

"I guess if their predictions are wrong, it makes sense we shouldn't give too much credibility to anything else they say." I began clearing Mom's pile of books, pamphlets, and mail from the table.

Mom set the watermelon on the lunch counter. "If the Bible was the only book we ever read, we could discover the one way to spend eternity with God. Cult leaders, though, expect their followers to place trust in their organization for salvation *in addition to* the Bible."

"I see."

Mom handed me a book called, *Kingdom of the Cults*, by Walter Martin. "You can borrow this. The better we understand cults, the less vulnerable we will be to their deceptions."

After church one day, Mom gave me two books by Frank Peretti: *This Present Darkness* and *Piercing the Darkness*. These books sparked my interest in New Age Spirituality (NAS), and I began to research it in depth. NAS is derived from Neo-Paganism (new or revived witchcraft), Hinduism, Taoism, Gnosticism, Spiritualism, and Theosophy. It is a diffuse network of thousands of churches and organizations with widely varying beliefs that are based in mysticism and ancient eastern spiritism (the communion with evil spirits). These groups are interested in enlightening people about an alleged astrological Aquarian age (which is supposed to put an end to the Christian era), forming a new world order, and ushering in a world leader (the antichrist). New agers often claim to be 'spiritual, not religious'.

In opposition to Christian beliefs, NAS redefines Jesus' unique position as God by lowering Him into the same category as people who have 'realized their own godhood'. This antichrist doctrine claims that Jesus was only one of many people who have reached Christ-consciousness, which is in stark contrast to the Bible. The Scriptures teach that Jesus is **the** Christ, the sole Anointed One of God.

A parallel concept promoted by NAS and other occult religions is the divinization of man, promoting people to godhood. Humanity has an affinity or desire to be powerful and to be like God, which may be why it is popular within new age circles to say, "I am," or "I am god," and why there are so many books about the power of those words.

The actress Shirley Maclaine wrote an autobiography which became a short mini-series on TV in the 1980's. The title, *Out on a Limb*, represents being out on a branch of the Tree of the Knowledge of Good and Evil, taking in the forbidden 'knowledge' offered by the serpent in the Garden of Eden. When one partakes of the fruit of enlightenment from the father of lies, however, it leads to blindness.

God gave Adam and Eve all the knowledge they needed. They spoke with Him daily and could have asked whatever they desired to know. Satan seduced them, offering deceitful mystical knowledge. He appealed to man's desire to be his own god, to put himself first, and to obtain power.

> *Now the serpent was craftier than any beast of the field which the LORD God had made. And he said to the woman, "Indeed, has God said, 'You shall not eat from any tree of the garden'?" The woman said to the serpent, "From the fruit of the trees of the garden we may eat; but from the fruit of the tree which is in the middle of the garden, God has said, 'You shall not eat from it or touch it, or you will die.'" The serpent said to the woman, "You surely will not die! "For God knows that in the day you eat from it your eyes will be opened, and you will be like God, knowing good and evil." Gen. 3:1-5 NASB*

In *Out on a Limb*, Shirley addressed reincarnation, eastern meditation (the mind-emptying/self-hypnotizing way to achieve an altered state of consciousness, which opens oneself to the spirits), and channeling spirit guides (allowing other spirits to operate through one's body). She also promoted the belief that we should worship the god within ourselves. To demonstrate her divinity in the film, she stood on a beach proclaiming, "I am god."

The two words, 'I am,' are very significant here. YAHWEH—the name God gave Himself, means 'I am' or 'I am who I am.' These are the very words Jesus used to proclaim His divinity on multiple occasions. When He came to them walking on the water, they were fearful.

*But he said unto them, **I AM**; be not afraid. John 6:20 Jubilee Bible 2000*

Responding to the crowd one day,

*Jesus answered, "I tell you the truth, before Abraham was even born, **I am**!" At that point they picked up stones to throw at him. But Jesus was hidden from them and left the Temple. John 8:58-59 NLT*

According to the Old Testament, if a mere man equated himself with God, or claimed to be God, he committed blasphemy. The Israelites, whom Jesus was speaking to, were God's chosen race, the nation to whom the Scriptures were given. They knew exactly what Jesus meant when He used the phrase, 'I am,' and because they didn't believe He was God, they wanted to kill Him.

Satan means adversary. Christians have given this name to the evil entity which deceived Eve in the Garden of Eden. He has several distinguishing characteristics. First, he is prideful. He thinks he knows better than God. Second, he wants to be the one on top. He sought to promote himself to godhood, to ascend to the highest throne, and to be ruler of the universe. Third, he is rebellious. He would rather go his own way, shaking his fist at the Creator, than to bow his knee and submit. Fourth, he offers knowledge/gnosis that is contrary and antagonistic to the Word of God.

Throughout history, occult doctrines have been offered by demons who pose as deceased relatives in séances, by way of mediums who channel spirit guides, and with divination tools, such as the Ouija board. Just as Satan—the father of lies—told Eve, 'You shall be like God,' these spirits encourage people like Shirley Maclaine to use the phrase 'I am' regarding self. Whenever we see pride, self-promotion to godhood, rebellion, and knowledge that is pitted against the Bible, as we find in NAS, we should consider whether we are dealing with satanic (Satan-like) influences.

New age literature promotes Lucifer, the name thought to belong to Satan before he rebelled against God. Walter Martin, a world-renowned expert on cults and occult apologetics, said "The god of the New Age movement is Lucifer, light-bearer, adversary, prince of darkness, who moves through religion, politics, and economies with one purpose in mind: integrate, unify, and then destroy. And the destruction is aimed at the Church of Jesus Christ."[5]

David Spangler, a mystic author who helped found NAS tells us, "Lucifer stands at the door of a man's consciousness and knocks...If a man says, 'Come in,'... he [Lucifer] becomes the being that carries that great treat, the ultimate treat, the light of wisdom."[6]

Russian occultist, Helena Blavatsky, was a medium (witch) who channeled evil spirits and claimed to have received knowledge from these entities during trances. She incorporated Hinduism and the information from her demonic sources into her writings. Helena founded the *Theosophical Society with the goal of uniting all world religions and eliminating Judaism, Islam, and Christianity.

*Theosophy – divine wisdom, the religious knowledge of the goddess Sophia, who is considered by Gnostics to be Lucifer. (According to Gnostics, Sophia fell from the galactic core and became the mother earth, Gaia. She channeled herself through the serpent in the Garden of Eden to enlighten Eve. This is a seductive spin on the historical account which we find in the Bible. It is designed to make people believe that Sophia/Lucifer was a luminous goddess who came to deliver mankind from Yahweh).

The teachings of the Theosophical Society, based on Hinduism and other occult religions, eventually gave birth to New Age Spirituality, with the hidden agenda of uniting all world religions under one banner. As we shall discover in future chapters, NAS has been infiltrating the church for decades, slowly introducing heresy—deviation or false teaching which opposes the main Christian doctrines. NAS is one movement through which Satan is integrating paganism with Christianity so he can unify all world religions and destroy mankind.

Helena, considered to be a matriarch of NAS, said this about Lucifer: "In this case it is but natural — even from the dead letter standpoint — to view Satan, the Serpent of Genesis, as the real creator and benefactor, the Father of Spiritual mankind. For it is he who was the "Harbinger of Light," bright radiant Lucifer, who opened the eyes of the automaton created by Jehovah, as alleged; and he who was the first to whisper: "in the day ye eat thereof ye shall be as Elohim, knowing good and evil" — can only be regarded in the light of a Saviour."[7]

Lucifer's lies are intriguing and might cause us to question whether we have the truth. Those who promote gnostic myths about Lucifer/Sophia, however, are not able to make accurate predictions or to tell the future with 100% precision. The Lord tells us how we can know that He is God, the authentic One. He says,

I make known the end from the beginning, from ancient times, what is still to come. Isaiah 46:10 NASB

A mantra of luciferians (those who worship Lucifer) is, 'Become a living god', which is the aim of NAS. Though NAS demotes Jesus and elevates man to godhood, it is technically not a cult. It is much worse, with far reaching implications, as we will discover in later chapters. While we would expect Satan to come against Christianity from the outside, most Christians do not realize that the luciferian teachings of NAS are invading the church from within. We need to be aware of its main doctrines so we can avoid being taken in by its deceptions.

"**M**y drinking has never hurt you," said Kevin. "I haven't had an accident or gotten a DUI." Kevin often stopped at taverns after work, so he always had a few beers under his belt on his 35-mile commute home.

At 1:00 AM one morning, when he was pulled over for swerving between the lanes, he told the police officer, "My wife and I had a fight, but I only had a few beers."

"Go home and make up with your wife." The officer let him off the hook, which was unfortunate. Consequences can teach a powerful lesson.

Another night, he was driving drunk and plowed into a snowbank, which stopped his car from smashing into a tree. Though Kevin seemed to evade consequences thus far, I realized that serious fallout would eventually occur if he continued to live a lifestyle of disobedience toward God's Word.

5 Subtle Deception, Testing the Spirits, and Spiritual Warfare

Within the theological structure of the cults there is considerable truth, all of which, it might be added, is drawn from biblical sources, but so diluted with human error as to be more deadly than complete falsehood.[8]
—Walter Martin

"Thank you for the ride," I said.

"You're welcome," Pastor Bill replied as he opened the bus doors to let everyone off. It was the anniversary of Roe V. Wade, and Pastor Bill drove the bus that brought the participants back to the starting point after the annual walk was over. Our pastor lived a life of integrity that demonstrated his convictions. He wasn't afraid to put his neck on the line for his beliefs, portraying an earnest desire to please the Lord.

We had several church members who had given up alcohol and/or drugs, and I felt proud to be part of a congregation that seemed to be on the cutting edge of Christianity. People were regularly *slain in the Spirit, our members often testified that they'd been healed of disease, and prophecies were frequent occurrences. In my eyes, these signs proved God was with us.

**Slain in the Spirit* – when a person is overcome by spiritual power and loses the strength to stand, usually being caught by other church members as he falls backwards. The person often lies on the floor, as if asleep or in a hypnotic trance.

"Pastor Bill is teaching about tithing and giving again," said Mom.

"Yes," I replied. "It's good to be learning principles which help us achieve health and wealth."

"I like how he takes us from one book of the Bible to another, linking verses together into newly emerging themes of Christianity."

Our church was also learning about divine health, positive confession, taking dominion over the earth, and our power to battle spiritual forces in high places. From select verses in Ephesians 6, Pastor Bill began teaching us a prayer formula to put the armor of God on ourselves. Here is an abbreviated version:

"I take the helmet of salvation upon my head, and I put on the breastplate of righteousness. Next, I take the belt of truth, the Gospel shoes of peace, the shield of my faith, and the double-edged sword of the spirit."

Each morning, and throughout the day, I incorporated these new prayers into my routine so the devil wouldn't have a chance to harm my family.

One day, when I was in our walk-in closet rummaging through boxes of winter clothes, quite a few empty beer cans were hidden away. A growing stash of cans was in the bathroom closet behind the towels, and another pile was accumulating beneath Kevin's side of the bed. I was always coming across them when I put clean clothes in Kevin's drawers and when I looked for tools in the garage.

There was no such thing as a sober evening or weekend. The real Kevin was hidden behind glazed eyes, preventing true intimacy, and while he pursued alcohol, I chased spiritual excitement.

I read Benny Hinn's book, *Good Morning Holy Spirit,* and quickly devoured his next book, *The Anointing*. He seemed to have found the key to the *anointing and power of the Holy Spirit. If only I could love God as much as Benny did and follow his teachings, I could help others receive miracles that would change their lives.

*Anointing–to have the Holy Spirit poured like oil over a person.

(Many people in the WoF movement desire to please God and yearn to be close to him. We place a high value on supernatural experiences and want our families, friends, and neighbors to be touched by God's power).

I began reading a book from the church bookstore called *The Believer's Authority* by Kenneth Hagin, the father of the WoF movement. It confirmed Pastor Bill's teachings and helped me understand some of the concepts that had been confusing me.

In the book, Ken spoke of his vision where a spirit, which called itself Jesus, was teaching him a lesson. A monkey-like demon began causing a commotion, and after a while, Ken commanded the demon "In the Name of Jesus, you foul spirit, I command you to stop!" Then, the 'Jesus' spirit said, "If you hadn't done something about that, I couldn't have," The apparition gave Ken this Bible verse:

Jesus came and told his disciples, "I have been given all authority in heaven and on earth..." Matthew 28:18 NLT

'Jesus' continued, "but I immediately delegated my authority on earth to the Church, and I can work only through the Church..."[9]

Wow! I puffed up with confidence. *We believers have a lot of power!* I didn't realize these teachings were in direct contrast to Christian doctrine. Though Jesus gave authority to Peter and the disciples, the Bible does not say Jesus relinquished supreme control. A king who delegates authority to an ambassador will still maintain sovereignty (rulership) over his domain.

Though I was familiar with the following Bible verse, I never thought to test a televangelist.

Dear friends, do not believe everyone who claims to speak by the Spirit. You must test them to see if the spirit they have comes from God. For there are many false prophets in the world. 1 John 4:1 NLT

My carnal nature was excited about the new revelation. I loved to read WoF books rather than analyze the Word of God. It would have been better if I had studied Bible commentaries which were written by theologians—experts in the languages of the Scriptures, the culture of the Israelite nation, and the history of biblical times. These men know how to interpret Greek, Aramaic, and Hebrew correctly, how to keep the meaning of the Scriptures in context, and how to discern the intended message of the Author of the Bible.

Our WoF teachers tend to read into the Scriptures what they want us to believe. They tell us God lost dominion over the earth when Adam sinned, as if, in doing so, Adam gave his authority to Satan. We are told that the Holy Spirit needs man's permission to work on earth, and without man, God can do nothing here.

Do the Scriptures teach that God has no authority on earth, or that He is not in control? No. To the contrary, in the book of Job, we discover Satan admitting that God's hedge of protection kept him from harming the righteous man. (Job 1:9-10) After Satan tested Job, he returned to speak with God, and we discover he needed permission to test Job further. (Job 2:4-6)

Throughout the Old Testament, we see God sovereignly taking charge wherever He wills. Using His prophet's mouths, the Lord urges His people to obey Him and promises rewards for obedience. He gives warnings of terrible consequences for rebellion, and we see His prophetic words coming to pass based on whether the people chose to obey or whether they decided to rebel. If God had no authority and was on the outside looking in, how could He promise blessing or threaten consequences?

By accepting this pride-inducing new revelation, and by thinking more highly of ourselves than we ought, we are in rebellion against the wisdom in God's Word. We can choose to recognize a fraudulent spirit, or we can become more like Satan: proud, rebellious, and bearing false knowledge. This may sound harsh, but to be like Satan is to be satanic, and the practice of being like Satan is satanism (though I do not mean the spiritual religion of satanism).

"**W**e have more truth than the other churches in our area," Pastor Bill stated one week. "We have new revelations that the Holy Spirit has given to anointed men of God in these days."

The WoF understanding of health, wealth, and positive confession was different than that of the writers of the New Testament. I wondered if the apostles and martyrs might have avoided poverty, dungeons, and execution if they had known our prosperity teachings.

One afternoon, I walked into Mom's spacious, well-lit kitchen where she was bent over the kitchen sink, rinsing off a raw chicken.

"What are you making?" I asked.

"Chicken soup," Mom straightened up slightly and pulled her shoulders back. A hair net covered her wavy, blond hair, and her lilac colored shirt had several water splatters on the front. With a fair complexion and blue eyes, Mom would've been five feet, six inches tall if not for the kyphosis in her upper spine. At 130 pounds, she looked fit and healthy. "Would you chop some carrots and celery for me?" she asked.

"Sure." Taking out a cutting board and knife, I began working alongside her. "Mom, do you think Aunt Sharon will die of cancer?"

"I hope not," she answered, adding a quick prayer and inserting Aunt Sharon's name into Psalm 118:17. "Thank you, Jesus, that Aunt Sharon shall live and not die, and she will declare the works of the Lord."

"Can we assume she's going to live?" I asked. "I mean, what if God plans for her to die soon?"

"It's never God's intention for a believer to die of sickness." Mom repeated what she had learned in church. The phone rang, and she plopped the raw chicken in the sink, wiped her wet hands in a towel, and picked up the receiver. "Hello?" She paused to listen. "Alright, we'll see you around 4:00." Mom walked back to the sink, grabbed the chicken, and placed it into her largest soup pot. "That was Annie. She and Jeff left Green Bay a few minutes ago. They'll be here in an hour or so. Now, where were we?"

"We were talking about prayer." I stopped chopping carrots to look at Mom. "Doesn't God have different plans for each of us? Can we insert any Christian's name into healing verses?"

"Well, when the Holy Spirit gives us a personal 'rhema' word, we can apply it to ourselves." Mom rinsed off some celery and brought out a bag of *kluski* noodles, a Polish staple food, from her cupboard.

"A rhema word? What do you mean?'"

"The Holy Spirit may give us a feeling when we're reading a Bible verse so we know it's a word just for us."

"I see."

Several hours later, as our family enjoyed dinner together, Annie asked, "Can you please pass the soup?"

"Sure," her husband obliged.

"Oops." Annie's eyes danced with merriment as she pretended she was going to spill a ladle full of soup on Jeff's lap, rather than in his bowl.

Quick to react, he scooted his chair backwards to get out of the way.

"Fooled you," laughed Annie.

Jeff's dark-brown eyes flickered with amusement while Annie filled his bowl. Two could play the same game, and the overgrown kid in Jeff had to get even. He tossed his buttered bun up into the air, intending for it to land on her plate. "Have a roll, Hun!" With a splash, it plopped into her full bowl of soup.

Built like a muscle man, Jeff strongly resembled a taller version of Sylvester Stallone from the Rocky movies. Born and raised on a farm near Green Bay, Wisconsin, his skin was deeply tanned. His short, black hair had a few gray strands, probably a result of Annie's mischievous antics.

"How about if we call it a truce?" Annie patted him on the shoulder...and slipped an ice cube down his back.

On my way to work the next morning, I listened to a Kenneth Hagin tape. He was healed of heart problems when he was a young man and said our bodies should never wear out with age. I thought, *If it's possible for a person to walk in enough faith, we may start seeing people who never die.* I felt empowered by the teaching, believing my prayers and faith would help Aunt Sharon receive a miraculous healing. I also hoped to achieve a level of faith strong enough to stop all sickness and death in my own body.

"**I**n the name of Jesus, we bind powerless the spirits of sickness and disease," the prayer leader called out. "We bind you spirits of divorce, pornography, lust, and poverty. We command money to come to our church. We demand all the tithes that have been held back over the years to come into our storehouse. We rebuke you, Satan, and bind you powerless. You may not keep money from coming to this church!"

(According to our beliefs, when we speak words such as, "I bind you powerless" to an evil spirit, it becomes impotent, as if it were tied up).

It was our Tuesday night prayer meeting in the church sanctuary. We had been learning to do spiritual warfare in an authoritative manner, and our church members were applying prayer techniques like those used by the fictional characters in two of Frank Peretti's novels, *This Present Darkness* and *Piercing the Darkness*. Though the Bible didn't include names for evil spirits—like alcohol, lust, poverty, sickness, cancer, greed, and so forth, we named the demons according to various afflictions and sin problems that we were fighting against.

The microphone was passed to me.

"Thank You, Jesus, for the Bible. Thank You for what You're doing in our church. We ask for a hedge of protection to surround our families, and we command evil spirits to stay away from our members." With each sentence, my voice rose in volume. "Thank you, God, that we can stand on Your Word because You keep Your promises. Thank You for divine health for our members. Thank You for deliverance from addictions." I was practically shouting as I commanded, "We lift up our families and tell you Satan, KEEP YOUR HANDS OFF OUR HOUSEHOLDS! In the name of JESUS! AMEN!"

"AMEN!" shouted our circle of intercessors.

Afterwards, several people told me what a great prayer warrior I was, and Church Leader Judy approached me with a prophetic word.

"God is saying your marriage will be a light to those in darkness. He's going to use you for His glory, and you will have a ministry that helps others in their marriage struggles. The Lord says that you are not too young, and He wants to begin using you soon."

Judy handed me a book called *Spiritual Authority* by Watchman Nee and said, "I would like this book back quickly so I can pass it around to other members."

As was often the case, I left church feeling on top of the world.

When a class on spiritual authority was offered during the Sunday school hour, I learned about the importance of understanding one's position under his or her pastor. According to spiritual authority teachings, we are to submit to our pastor without question. We shouldn't try to discern whether our pastor might be wrong because he is under God's authority, and he answers to the Lord.

Shortly after I read the book and took the class, one of Pastor Bill's sermons confirmed the spiritual authority teachings.

"Miriam became leprous as a result of speaking against Moses, the anointed man of God," taught Pastor Bill. "When she consulted with Aaron to criticize Moses, God's anger burned against her. If you speak or gossip against anointed spiritual leaders, something bad could happen to you."

"**T**yler and I need you to be sober," I said, as Kevin and I stood in the kitchen one evening. "I'm afraid if you wait too long, you won't be able to quit drinking."

"Don't worry. I can quit anytime." Kevin opened the refrigerator and grabbed two cans of beer, sneaking one into his coat pocket.

"Then why not now?" I asked.

"Because I like it. Besides, I'm too young to quit."

In my prayers earlier that day, I'd heard a warning from God, which I shared with Kevin. "If you keep choosing alcohol over Jesus, you're going to lose everything. Your health and your brain will be affected. You could have an accident, and we might lose our home." I pleaded with him to turn to the Lord before it was too late.

The door banged shut behind Kevin as he headed for the burning barrel in our backyard. He didn't seem to realize that he was on a train ride, heading for a wreck, and I wondered how Tyler and I would be affected when he paid the consequences for his rebellion.

In my loneliness, my mind turned to his sister, Monica, my best friend. I thought back to the time she came with me to church while we were in high school, before Pastor Bill's time. The worship leader had us singing in tongues for about five minutes, which felt like an eternity. I was sure Monica thought we were crazy, for it sounded like those around us were babbling like infants. I dared not look her way as it continued, on and on...

There is a reason why the Bible says,

Therefore, if the whole church assembles together and all speak in tongues, and ungifted men or unbelievers enter, will they not say that you are mad? 1 Corinthians. 14:23 NASB

After the sermon, there was an altar call, and I lined up with others to be prayed on by the pastor. As each person was being prayed for, he/she would fall backwards into the ushers' waiting arms, apparently slain in the Spirit. When Pastor Frost came to me, he placed one hand on my forehead and began to pray, forcefully tilting my head backward. The aggravated nerve in my neck started to burn. I didn't feel supernatural power, but the compliant side of my nature dared not resist. Two ushers placed their hands on my back, so I let myself be pushed over. As I lay alongside all the others, I worried, *What is Monica thinking? Will she ever come back to my church again?*

Though she never came back to church with me, Monica and I remained close friends for several years. Now, as I washed the supper dishes and looked out my kitchen window toward the burning barrel, hot, salty tears spilled down my cheeks. I prayed for Monica and Kevin, wondering how much time remained before one of them would crash and burn.

I could see the smoke rising from Kevin's fire as I began praying. "Kevin will not be like most addicts. I claim his deliverance from alcohol this day! You vile spirit of alcohol, take your tentacles off my husband right now!"

To me, spiritual warfare against the enemy and prayer to God could be intermingled. The majority of my 'prayer time' was spent rebuking demons, binding them with my 'faith-filled' words, and ordering them to leave my husband.

WoF 'prayer' is a mix of positive confessions, Bible verses, binding the spirits over our territory, rebuking demons, and "loosing" God's Spirit. The following is a redefinition of prayer from the late WoF preacher, Myles Munroe, a favorite of our church.

"Prayer is man giving God permission or license to interfere in earth's affairs. In other words, prayer is earthly license for heavenly interference."[10]

The pain in my neck was often unbearable, and neither Tylenol or aspirin products brought noticeable relief. There were times I really didn't want to live. In my studies of New Age Spirituality, I knew of several occult techniques that could possibly bring relief, such as psychic healing, Reiki, acupuncture, and the use of crystals. However, if it wasn't the Lord's will to heal me by His own hand, I would not knowingly turn to the hand of demons.

In church, Pastor Bill was teaching us to quote certain verses of the Bible to bring forth the blessings we needed and/or desired. If we wanted a healing, we found Bible verses about health and were encouraged to quote them over and over. In like manner, if we needed money, we sought verses about wealth.

The materials I purchased from our church bookstore and from guest speakers solidified the prosperity message. It seemed as if many biblical passages could be interpreted to be about health and wealth if a person thought about the verses from various angles. Our WoF preachers took liberties with the Word of God, using **eisegesis**—reading into the Scriptures and pulling out confirmation of their biases, pre-held agendas, or presuppositions. Many of us in the congregation followed their example. It was always exciting to glean what we needed, or wanted, from God's Word.

The practice of **exegesis**—to get to the original intended meaning of Bible passages by using critical analysis—was not normally practiced or promoted in our church. As far as I can recall, Bible commentaries weren't referred to in the sermons.

Because you will come across exegesis and eisegesis again, I've devised a simple way to remember the meanings. The twisted S in ei**s**egesis reminds one of the serpent, who twists the Scriptures. The X in e**x**egesis is made with straight lines, which can stand for straight (orthodox) teaching and correct meaning.

New Year's Eve journal entry—

I've begun letting go of small frustrations rather than ruminating on them. If I find a mess that Kevin left behind, I try to think of something positive about him. Over the past year, God has exposed several dark areas in my life that needed to be changed. Without His guidance, I wouldn't have discovered these weaknesses.

At the New Year's Eve service, Kevin's breath smelled like alcohol. When Pastor Bill greeted him, I felt certain he would notice. After the sermon, Pastor Bill appeared to be moving in the charismata, the gifts of the Spirit. He called Kevin to the altar and said. "God has a word for you for the New Year. God wants you to know He's going to deliver you, and you are going to experience some freedoms that you've never had. It's going to be better than it was before. Yes, it's going to be better than it was before."

My sister and her husband, Jerry, were also called to the altar. A tall, lean, dairy farmer with straight, dark-brown hair and big brown eyes, Jerry stood slightly behind my sister. He was wearing his normal attire: blue jeans, a button-down western shirt, and cowboy boots.

Amanda, quite a bit shorter than Jerry, had wavy, brown hair with blonde highlights. Her soft, purple angora sweater accentuated the slight curves of her pencil thin figure.

Placing one hand on Jerry and the other on Amanda, Pastor Bill began prophesying about their deepest desire. "The Lord has remembered you, and He's heard your requests. Don't think for a moment that He has forgotten you. In fact, the Lord says, 'you will be holding your first baby before the year is over.'" (This prophetic dialog is a close paraphrase which I quoted often in my prayers over the following year).

We had several reasons to trust these prophecies. First, God is not like fallible men, who might lie. In the book of Isaiah, He says,

> *For I am God; there is no other. I have sworn by my own name; I have spoken the truth, and* ***I will never go back on my word:*** *Isaiah 45:22b-23a NLT (Emphasis mine)*

Second, a pastor who is filled with the Holy Spirit would've been able to discern which spirit spoke through his mouth. Third, we presumed to be in a sanctuary full of 'Spirit-filled' Christians. If they had discernment from God's Spirit, like the Apostle Peter did when he perceived Ananias and Sapphira were lying (Acts 5:1-11), they would have recognized when a false prophecy was given. No one protested to the prophetic word which came from Pastor Bill's mouth.

At home, I listened to the tape recording of Kevin's prophecy and transcribed it into my special notebook. I was hopeful that my husband would be sober and that Tyler would have a cousin before the end of the upcoming year.

6 Positive Confession, Visualization, and Thought Power

"Occultists have long known that the most powerful way to tap into the spirit dimension is through visualization..."[11]
—Dave Hunt & T.A. McMahon

e need to be able to visualize ourselves healthy and wealthy. When we create a picture in our mind, it helps our faith," said Pastor Bill.

Using creative visualization to tap into supernatural power sounded new age to me, and I'd read that these ancient, eastern religious practices were antagonistic to Christianity, but I trusted my pastor not to teach us an occult method. I tried to imagine my neck healed and to envision a sober husband.

"The words we speak are powerful," continued Pastor Bill. "They go forth to accomplish what we proclaim. God spoke creation into existence with words, and because we are made in His image, our faith-filled words have a creative force that manifests in the physical realm. If we speak forth perfect health, our words will attract wellness. We have the authority to destroy cancer, sickness, addictions, and poverty. When we insert our names into Bible verses, God watches over His words to confirm them."

I was a little confounded. What does one do with the passages of the Bible that say negative things? I could quote the verse telling us that the wealth of the wicked is stored up for the righteous (Prov. 13:22), but could I read aloud Proverbs 23:4-5, where we are told that wealth makes itself wings and flies away? I could say part of the verse in Job 1:21, "The Lord giveth...," but I was afraid to say the other half of the same verse, "and the Lord taketh away."

Then, there was this passage from Mark.

> *"Yes," Jesus replied, "and I assure you that everyone who has given up house or brothers or sisters or mother or father or children or property, for my sake and for the Good News, will receive now in return a hundred times as many houses, brothers, sisters, mothers, children, and property—**along with persecution**. And in the world to come that person will have eternal life." Mark 10:29–30 NLT (Emphasis mine)*

I could claim part of the above verses, but must I omit the second part that says, 'along with persecution'?

"**W**here are Aunt Mae and Uncle Pat lately? I haven't seen them in church."

"They decided to go to Evangelical Free Church," Mom replied.

"Why?"

"I don't know. Mae didn't say."

It seemed that those who were sincerer in their faith often left our church to attend elsewhere. Another married couple had recently said that we were a name-it-claim-it-church and left our congregation. I couldn't understand why that bothered them or why they wouldn't want to attend a church with so much truth...

Amanda and Jerry entered our row just as the sermon began. She hadn't mentioned the prophecy about having a baby this year, and I didn't want to bring it up.

"God's Word is living and sharper than a double-edged sword." Pastor Bill's sermon broke into my thoughts. "There is tremendous power when we quote God's words out loud. God wants us to recite verses of the Bible that are positive so they bring good things to us. In fact, we are supposed to speak against sickness, suffering, and poverty. We are never supposed to be sick after we get saved. Amen?"

"Amen," echoed the congregation.

"Sickness came with the curse, but Jesus took our punishment. He took our infirmities upon Himself, exchanging them for His divine health, which is part of our salvation. Divine health is ours to claim, but we must have enough faith, and speak only positive words about our constitution.

"We should speak those things which are not as though they are. Then, we will become spiritually healthy, which will manifest in our physical bodies."

It felt so wonderful to learn to be overcomers and conquerors by the power of our words and faith that I didn't consider the inconsistencies, such as the fact that cancer took Aunt Sharon's life.

"Because our words carry creative force, we should be careful what we speak," said Pastor Bill. "We shouldn't say aloud, 'This dessert is to die for,' or 'My back is killing me.' To speak those words would open the door for death to come in. Amen?"

"Amen," a chorus of members repeated.

"If someone says, 'Your child sounds like he is sick,' their words can bring it to pass. If a person states, 'You will always be poor,' their words have power to accomplish what is spoken. When we hear negative words spoken about our lives, our situations, or our loved ones, it is important to immediately negate those destructive words. Make a positive confession to reverse them."

It is true that the words we speak can bring destruction to reputations, and our tongues can either build people up, or tear them down.

The tongue can bring death or life; those who love to talk will reap the consequences. Proverbs 18:21 NLT

While the words we speak can cause hurt feelings and low self-esteem, the Bible doesn't say that our tongues have supernatural force to **attract** life or death, and the Scriptures do not claim that our words carry a creative power that is like the words of God. The above passage has been twisted (eisegesis) to confirm the *Law of Attraction*, which is a demonic doctrine promoted in the occult. I'll explain the origin of the *Law of Attraction* in a later chapter.

After the sermon, I began to cringe whenever people would say things like, 'My child is rebellious,' or 'My child is catching a cold'. I thought the words they spoke were going to attract rebellion or disease in their children. I also considered how the WoF teachings implied that others possessed the power to bring bad things into my life by the words they spoke. I worried, *What if I don't hear a negative statement someone speaks about me or my family? How can I cancel it out?* I didn't realize that the Bible doesn't advocate focusing on the power of our thoughts or words, nor the words of other people. Rather, our faith is to be in the power of our God and in His Word.

"Do you know why there are sick and insane people in nursing homes?" Our guest minister—a young pastor with brown hair, dark eyes, and a medium build—spoke about the divine health doctrine. "People perish for a lack of knowledge. Ignorance of God's Word can kill you." With his chest out and his chin up, Pastor Know-Better stood tall, thrusting his Bible into the air as one would brandish a sword. "Mental illness and physical disease result when people don't know the spiritual laws that govern our world."

Setting his Bible on the podium and scanning the audience, Pastor Know-Better declared, "It is crucial we claim good health and confess that we have sober minds. Never say things like, 'I must be losing my mind.' Speaking such words can open the door to insanity.

"If people allow the enemy to destroy their minds," Pastor Know-Better shook his finger, "and steal their health, it is their own fault."

Is it true that people in nursing homes have allowed dementia to take their minds because of their ignorance? If our WoF premises were true, Pastor Know-Better had come to the proper conclusion. Absolute health, through the correct application of supposed spiritual laws, doesn't mean a person might be healthy. It means a person will be healthy, **without exception**. Therefore, those who are sick and feeble-minded can be blamed and judged for their condition. After all, because of their ignorance, they didn't apply the spiritual laws.

When we begin with a false premise—one that leads to vain conceit and strips us of loving compassion, we will come to a wrong conclusion. This way of thinking could cause us to lose our sympathy, empathy, and respect for the infirm. And the Bible tells us,

> *Since God chose you to be the holy people He loves, you must clothe yourselves with tenderhearted mercy, kindness, humility, gentleness, and patience. Colossians. 3:12 NLT*

7 Seeds of Money, Harvests of Greed

A servant of God has but one Master. It ill becomes the servant to seek to be rich, and great, and honored in that world where his Lord was poor, and mean, and despised.[12] *—George Mueller*

Most people believe Jesus was poor, but He was actually rich. Turn to your neighbor and say, 'Jesus was rich.'" Pastor Bill paused a moment while we obeyed.

It always seemed like Jesus was poor and lowly when I was reading my Bible, and though I couldn't yet speak the words, 'Jesus was rich,' that time would soon come.

"Jesus was given gold, frankincense, and myrrh from the wise men," Pastor Bill continued. "His seamless robe was so valuable that the soldiers cast lots for it while He hung on the cross. On top of that, He needed a treasurer, which means He had a lot of money to manage."

While I was just beginning to consider a life of self-sacrifice as a Christian, I discovered that Christians were to have the best of both worlds. Not only do we get to go to Heaven when we die, but we're entitled to everything good while living here on earth!

On the narrow path that leads to Heaven, it is imperative that we not allow ourselves to get sidetracked, veering to the right or to the left, and we must put to death all that belongs to our lower nature, such as greed.

Do not turn aside from any of the commands I give you today, to the right or to the left, following other gods and serving them. Deuteronomy 28:14 NIV

Set your minds on things above, not on earthly things. Put to death, therefore, whatever belongs to your earthly nature: sexual immorality, impurity, lust, evil desires and ***greed, which is idolatry****. Colossians 3:2,5 NIV (Emphasis mine)*

Unbeknownst to me, my heart was about to receive an inoculation of narcissism, or me-centeredness. This frame of mind would hinder my Christian walk, taking my focus off loving Jesus for who He is and placing it on following Him because of what was in it for me. This stunted the fruit that might have otherwise grown, kept my roots in shallow ground, and affected my witness for the Lord.

"Being content with the money you have is actually a sign of selfishness," continued Pastor Bill. "It indicates a heart that is only thinking of itself. After all, we should want more money so we have more to give away. Amen?"

"Amen," we bounced back.

The following Sunday, Pastor Bill prompted us to be generous givers toward the church debt. "God's Spirit told me that our church needs to pay off our mortgage *and never go into debt again*."

At the end of the sermon, Pastor Bill had the ushers pass out pledge cards for us to fill out. Next, there was a special offering to reduce the debt. While I wrote out the check, I couldn't stop thinking of my three favorite dental patients, Mary, Misty, and Sandy, stay-at-home moms who seemed to have time for the most important things in life—Bible study, their husbands, and their children. I wished to be like them, but with all the calls for money at church, it didn't seem affordable to work less than I was.

"**I**f you do not give 10% of your income to church, you are under a curse," said Pastor Bill. "Position yourselves to receive God's blessings by paying your tithes and giving above and beyond what you think you can afford. With the measure you give to God, He will return it back to you."

When I first heard some of Pastor Bill's messages, they baffled me because they appeared to contradict the main messages of the Scriptures. For instance, the Bible says we are no longer under a curse once we turn our lives over to Jesus. Will God's curse come upon us again if we don't adhere to the law exactly? Over the following weeks, rather than respecting Kevin's desires, I pestered him until he agreed to tithe.

"**J**esus told a parable about a farmer who sowed seed on the ground," stated Mr. Guest Speaker. "Do you know what we can learn from this parable? We can apply the same principle to our finances as a farmer who sows seeds in his field. If we need money, we should sow financial seeds into good ground, such as ministries that are pleasing to the Lord. Then, we will reap a harvest that is 30, 60, or 100 times what we've sown. We can't earn that kind of interest at a bank!"

Thus far, Mr. Guest Speaker had spoken about his passion, turning the seed (God's Word) into money. Next, he told the story of the widow who gave a few mites (pennies) into the temple offering. "Jesus commended her because she didn't give out of her excess, but out of her poverty.

"I'd like to share an astonishing testimony with you," Mr. Guest Speaker continued. "In the back of a congregation where my friend was preaching, a woman held her infant, which had no arms or legs. The mother planned to use her last few dollars to buy baby formula, but God's Spirit directed her to put the money in the offering. She decided to be obedient, and before the eyes of everyone, her child grew four new limbs. Somebody, give the Lord a praise offering!"

Our congregation burst into applause and loud cheering. Though the story was third-hand and unverifiable, I'm sure I wasn't the only one who believed it. Miraculous stories like this were a common phenomenon, often told by guest speakers and at conferences, though these kinds of miracles were never witnessed in our church.

"You may only have a small amount to give," continued Mr. Guest Speaker, "and you might need the money to pay a bill tomorrow, but if God's Spirit is convicting you, you could be on the brink of your long-awaited miracle.

"Jesus took our poverty so we could become rich. Your gift of $100 today, increased 100-fold, could bring a you a return harvest of $10,000. Think about that." He paused a moment. "And your gift of $1,000 could bring you $100,000. Imagine what you could do with that money!"

Pastor Bill and our church elders were agreeing with Mr. Guest Speaker, giving credibility to his words. If only I'd spent more time in God's Word, rather than on the exciting books and CD's that proclaimed what I wanted to hear, I might have recalled this verse:

You see, we are not like the many hucksters who preach for personal profit. We preach the word of God with sincerity and with Christ's authority, knowing that God is watching us. 2 Corinthians 2:17 NLT

"**G**ood morning." The greeter at Evangelical Free Church shook my hand. The pleasant aromas of freshly brewed, hazelnut coffee and cinnamon sweet rolls beckoned us further into the foyer. We had come to see a baby dedication at Aunt Mae and Uncle Pat's church.

"Did you notice people talk about what they value and treasure most?" Pastor Doug began his sermon with a question. "The treasure of a person's heart is at the forefront of his mind and is what comes from his mouth. Some people enjoy sports, and whenever they get together with others, they begin talking about the most recent game. Young mothers like to discuss their children and parenting, and young men talk about sports and women."

The congregation laughed.

"What sets you on fire? How often do you find your conversation turning to the Lord?

"In the Book of Deuteronomy, chapter 11, verses 18–20, the Lord instructed the Israelites saying, '*Fix these words of mine in your hearts and minds; tie them as symbols on your hands and bind them on your foreheads. Teach them to your children, talking about them when you sit at home and when you walk along the road, when you lie down and when you get up. Write them on the doorframes of your houses and on your gates.*' (NIV)

"Do you know why Jesus spoke about the Scriptures so often?" asked Pastor Doug. "The Word of God was always on His mind. Jesus was passionate about the Scriptures." (It was evident that Pastor Doug treasured the Bible, also).

We learned about the parable of the farmer who sowed seed on various types of ground. I was surprised that the seed, which represented the Word of God, was not turned into an opportunity for the church to make money.

After the service, the cozy, gas fire flickered in the stone fireplace of the church cafe' as we sat around a table relishing the warm fellowship of Uncle Pat and Aunt Mae, which was better than the treats from the coffee and dessert bar. Tyler, however, savored the cookies!

"Why did you leave Word of Faith Church?" I asked.

"Well," said Uncle Pat. "For one thing, the music was so repetitive and soothing that it seemed like it could almost put you in a trance."

Uncle Pat was one of the wisest people I knew, but I felt he was amiss about the worship at Word of Faith Church.

"**T**hink of this book as an investment. God wants to bless your finances so you can be a blessing to others and to His kingdom." Pastor Bill held up a copy of a booklet called *The Miracle of Seed Faith* by Oral Roberts and proposed we purchase the book from our church bookstore—which had recently been moved into the sanctuary.

"I want you to pay close attention to this verse," said Pastor Bill. "*But people who long to be rich fall into temptation and are trapped by many foolish and harmful desires that plunge them into ruin and destruction. For the* ***love of*** *money is the root of all kinds of evil. And some people, craving money, have wandered from the true faith and pierced themselves with many sorrows. (1 Timothy 6:9 NLT, emphasis by Pastor*)

"So, you see," said Pastor Bill, "money itself is not the root of all evil, but notice the verse says, 'the *love* of money is the root of all evil.' You can *have* money, as long as you don't love it, as long as money doesn't *have* you."

At our midweek service, a female preacher took the podium. "The Lord told Abraham He was bringing him to a land flowing with milk and honey." Mrs. Preacher had hundreds of shiny, black braids encircling her head, dazzling earrings, and a glamorous, purple dress. "When God promised land flowing with milk and honey, He was promising to bless *the business transactions* of Israel. Milk and honey represented the commerce of the Holy Land. You see, Israel was located on a trade route where people traveled from one nation to another."

Several weeks later, we had another guest speaker in church. "When you pray, never say, 'If it is Your will' to the Lord," said Mr. Televangelist. "Those are faith destroying words. It gives God pleasure when we command Him. Our confidence to boldly demand the promises in His Word demonstrates that we know what the Scriptures say."

Normally, one would think it is disrespectful to order our Heavenly Father around by speaking in demands and commands. Would we speak that way to our parents, or would we allow our children to order us around? I didn't contemplate those questions, but rather, I relied on what I was told and adjusted the way I prayed.

In my dream, a crowd of people stood around the throne, bringing many requests to God. Everyone was asking for something. "Lord, I need..." and "Father, I want..." or "Lord, Your Word promises..."

Then, God spoke. "**The one who has My attention is the child who is simply saying, "I love You.**"

8 Health and Wealth

You ask [God for something] and do not receive it, because you ask with wrong motives [out of selfishness or with an unrighteous agenda], so that [when you get what you want] you may spend it on your [hedonistic] desires. You adulteresses [disloyal sinners—flirting with the world and breaking your vow to God]! Do you not know that being the world's friend [that is, loving the things of the world] is being God's enemy? So whoever chooses to be a friend of the world makes himself an enemy of God. James 4:3-4 Amplified Bible

e know God wants us to be in good health and to prosper in all things," said Pastor Bill. "Turn in your Bibles to the book of Third John, chapter two, verse two."

I looked at the familiar text.

<u>The elder to the beloved Gaius</u>, whom I love in truth. Beloved, I pray that in all respects you may prosper and be in good health, just as your soul prospers. 3 John 1:1-2 NASB (Emphasis mine)

Taken in the context of the meaning which the original author had in mind, one would naturally assume John intended the greeting specifically for Gaius. In this passage, John commends Gaius' good reputation, which evidenced his soul's maturity. Gaius displayed the virtuous fruits of hospitality, generosity, kindness, and compassion toward the servants of Christ.

"In other words," continued Pastor Bill, "if our soul is prospering—if we are growing in the ways of God and developing Christian character—God promises us health and wealth."

I briefly wondered if we were taking an interpretive leap of logic when applying the verse to ourselves.

"Next," Pastor Bill continued, "I'd like you to turn to the book of First Peter, chapter two, verse 24."

I read the verse in my Bible.

> *"He himself bore our sins" in his body on the cross, so that we might die to sins and live for righteousness; "by his wounds you have been healed." 1 Peter 2:24 NIV*

Since the verse speaks about salvation from sin, it seems to say that our souls are healed from our iniquities.

"By Jesus' stripes, the marks of the Roman whip on His back, our bodies are healed of every physical disease the enemy tries to inflict on us," asserted Pastor Bill.

He reviewed several Bible passages that addressed God keeping His people in health, all of which were written to particular people at specific times.

> *He said [to the Israelites], "If you listen carefully to the LORD your God and do what is right in his eyes, if you pay attention to his commands and keep all his decrees, I will not bring on you any of the diseases I brought on the Egyptians, for I am the LORD, who heals you." Exodus 15:26 NIV*

> *Then they cried to the LORD in their trouble, and he saved them from their distress. He sent out his word and healed them [the Israelites]; he rescued them from the grave. Psalm 107:19-20 NIV*

> *Then Jesus said to the centurion, "Go! Let it be done just as you believed it would." And his servant was healed at that moment. Matthew 8:13 NIV*

Our congregation was taught that we could demand the promises of these verses, as well as many others, directly for ourselves.

The central focus in my husband's life was his compulsion to drink. As a result, my life began to revolve around the yearning to see Kevin set free from his obsession. There were times when his addiction seemed to swallow me up, consuming my thoughts and keeping God from the center of my life. The desired outcome to my prayers became my all-encompassing fixation, an idol of sorts. Jesus became a means to an end, the formula for a successful marriage, with the Lord Himself on the peripheral edges of my devotion.

"We need to confess—speak aloud—that we are healed *before it actually happens*," said Pastor Bill. "Our faith-filled words, like containers of power, will reach into the spiritual realm and bring our healing toward us."

Might others be claiming healings that haven't yet manifested in order to bring the desired miracles toward themselves? I wondered.

My neck pain was excruciating most of the time. The husband and wife in front of me had a baby with Spina Bifida, and across the sanctuary was a man who was paralyzed from the waist down. Like me, these others were listening raptly to the message.

"You see, Jesus took our sickness and disease upon Himself," said Pastor Bill. "When we are saved, an exchange takes place. Our diseases are removed from us, and God's divine health is given to us. However, we need use our faith-filled words to claim it."

After the service, supernatural power began to manifest, which seemed to validate the teaching.

"There's somebody here who has had pain on the left side of your neck for a long time." It seemed as if Church Elder Jake had a *Word of Knowledge* (a spiritual gift in which a person receives revelatory information from God that he or she wouldn't otherwise have known, as defined by Pentecostals). "If that's you, come to the altar."

I headed to the front of the sanctuary.

"There's someone who's been suffering with headaches recently," continued Church Elder Jake. "If that's you, God wants to heal you today." Several people lined up next to me.

One after another, various afflictions were named until there was a line of people extending from one side of the sanctuary to the other.

While I waited in line, clapping and joyous shouting would break out every few minutes as Pastor Bill moved from one person to the next. Finally, he came to me, clasped my hands, and began praying. It felt like my right hand was being pulled forward as my torso twisted to the left. Then my left arm was being drawn forward as my trunk turned to the right. I resisted, assuming Pastor Bill was causing the movement.

"I'm not doing that Ariel," he stated.

Since his hands were barely touching mine, I realized he wasn't causing the movement. The midsection of my torso was twisting and stretching, and the action seemed to come from within my muscles, as if an invisible therapist was re-adjusting my back and neck.

After the service, I discovered that two other church members had experienced the same phenomenon. Their healings had taken place before mine, so they could not have been imitating me.

A young man approached me and said, "Be aware that Satan will try to take away your miracle. Don't let him convince you that you aren't healed."

When I found Tyler in childcare, he repeated the words I'd spoken so often. "Mommy can't pick me up. Her neck hurts."

Unable to contain my elation, I captured him, hoisted him up, and danced in a circle. "Mommy got healed in church today! I **can** pick you up!"

Unfortunately, the following morning, something popped in my neck and part of the pain returned. I assumed the 'father of lies' was trying to convince me to take the affliction back into my life. I couldn't understand why it should be so hard to maintain a healing. In the Bible, were the miracles of Jesus and His disciples ever rescinded? Equally troubling was the fact that perfect health was supposed to be part of my salvation. If my faith wasn't strong enough to bring about divine health, could I trust that I was saved?

I went home for my lunch break and found that I could tap into the same energy force which I'd experienced in church. I spent about 20 minutes allowing my body to be stretched and pulled, seemingly of its own accord, taking on various yoga-like poses. I should never have allowed the invisible force to manifest itself in my body, but I assumed that I was experiencing the healing power of God.

"**S**atan would like us to believe that suffering comes from God because it makes us mature," Pastor Bill taught. "In fact, suffering comes from the devil, and we shouldn't tolerate it once we are saved. Amen?"

"Amen," I called out along with many others.

"God doesn't need to use diseases to teach us lessons. Would you give cancer to your child to train him?"

"No." Many of us shook our heads from side to side.

"Believe it or not, some people don't want to be healed," explained Pastor Bill. He told us a story about a disabled man who wanted to remain in his diseased state. "People become familiar and comfortable in their incapacitated role."

I'd been wondering why some people didn't get healed, especially those in wheelchairs. But what about the baby with Spina Bifida and the other young children who hadn't been healed in church?

"I'm going to impart some keys of wisdom to you," said Preacher Wisdom, our guest minister.

We listened to a story about Preacher Wisdom's foolish friend, who refused to accept his financial teachings and remained in poverty.

"Poverty mentality is a sin. I have books and tapes full of wisdom that will help you overcome poverty mentality, if you are wise enough to purchase them." Preacher Wisdom held several tape sets over his head.

He had counted *56 types of blessings in the Bible and offered a special set of tapes for the price of $56, as if it was a magical number. We were asked to take out our checkbooks and wallets and hold them up while he led us in prayer. Then, he instructed, "Sow a $56 seed to reap all 56 types of blessings in the Bible. Within 56 days, you'll have your miracle! You should have a testimony service in two months to declare the miracles you receive."

It seemed slick that he told us to donate while our pocketbooks were held in the air, like an offering to God. This man operated like a clever con-man seducing the crowd.

*56 was not the exact number.

"She's beautiful," said Amanda. "May I hold her?" My sister brought an armload of gifts, as she did whenever anyone had a baby.

"Here you go." I gently placed my infant, Amber, into her arms.

"Look, she curled her little hand around my finger," Amanda looked into the eyes that were looking right back at her and blinked quickly several times. "I cry every month when I find out I'm not pregnant. If our baby is to be born this year, I should be pregnant by now."

I wondered if Pastor Bill's prophecy in December had been misspoken. Maybe the baby would only be conceived, rather than being born, by the end of the year.

"A prophet may give you a *conditional* word," said Pastor Bill. "The prediction will only come to pass if you meet the requirement. For instance, a prophet may say, 'If you keep focused on God, you will be financially blessed this year.' If you don't keep your focus on God, don't blame the prophet when his prediction doesn't come to pass."

I thought back to a recent prophecy that Amanda had received from Prophetess Deb, a woman well-known for her anointing. "I see two children in your womb," she had said. There had been no conditions or recommendations. All that remained was the fulfillment.

December 31 journal entry—

God has been opening my eyes to dark areas within my heart. Blaming others has been a pattern of my mind that He is bringing to my attention and helping me overcome. The Lord is teaching me to treasure my time with Kevin and Tyler more than I value having an immaculate house, and He is showing me that I don't have to be in complete control of everything. If I thought that I was close to perfect last year, I'm even closer now, and I seriously doubt there is much more to improve upon. (The human heart can be so blind!)

As the year ended, it was discouraging that Kevin was still drinking, and Amanda wasn't pregnant.

Though the neck pain returned, it wasn't quite as bad as it had once been. I believed the symptoms were a lie of the enemy and diligently continued to proclaim my healing. Several times per week, I would go into my bedroom, close the door, and be receptive to the 'power' which moved my body. Strangely, the sessions never made me better and occasionally exacerbated the pain.

9 Cross Examination

The first to speak in court sounds right—until the cross-examination begins. Proverbs 18:17 NLT

"But Mommy, I don't want to get dropped off at daycare. I want to be with you." Tyler's words weighed heavily on my heart as I left him. Now that we were tithing and giving extra money to church, it seemed I'd have to add another workday at the office each week. Yet the harvest of wealth that was coming upon our pastor seemed to confirm that God blesses those who are faithful.

"We could sell our home and buy a smaller place near your sister in Kentucky," I suggested to Kevin. "If we have less assets, we won't need to work so much."

"I'll think about it," said Kevin. "When I'm working outside on winter days, my fingers get so frozen that I can barely move them."

One evening when I was putting Tyler to sleep, I placed my hands on him and prayed. "Lord, help my son put You first in his life and never be rebellious."

A strong impression came into my mind that I should homeschool him.

At the time, home education was not popular and seemed archaic to me. I thought of the homeschooled children of my favorite dental patients, Sandy, Mary, and Misty. When they came into the dental office, their children were always respectful and well-behaved. I considered what it would take to educate Tyler and Amber at home. We would have to scale back on our housing and vehicle expenses greatly, and I'd have to cut my work hours down to two days per week at most. I realized, however, that there is no amount of money earned in my career that could be worth the value of my children's souls if our secular educational system destroyed their faith.

A word of caution is in order here. When we think God has spoken to us through an impression, dream, or vision, we should search the Scriptures to discover whether it contradicts the precepts of God, and we should carefully examine our hearts, not allowing our passions and personal biases to get in the way of deciding truth. God will never teach or instruct us to do anything which conflicts with His Word. I have chosen to include some of my own dreams, impressions, and thoughts which I believe God may have spoken to me. Keep in mind, though, that if anyone, including myself, purports to have had a vision or dream from God, it must be evaluated according to the Scriptures.

While there are excellent theologians who believe God still speaks to us through impressions, dreams, and visions, there are knowledgeable theologians who maintain that these subjective experiences are mystical, and possibly occultic. These encounters (when not subjected to Scriptural evaluation) can mislead people and have been the cause of many heretical teachings (like Mormonism and Islam), which have drawn people away from Orthodox Christianity. Many theologians say that we have the Word of God, and that is enough, Sola Scriptura-Scripture alone.

In this instance, I think that I heard from God. As a youth, Tyler was always courteous and respectful to me, never rebellious. I believe that was a result of his relationship with the Lord, which was heavily influenced by Christian home education.

If the service where church members would all testify about the miracles we harvested from sowing $56 seeds into Preacher Wisdom's ministry had occurred, then I missed it.

On our trip to Kentucky, I followed the U-Haul truck which Kevin was driving and felt relief that I would no longer have to watch my rear-view mirror to see if Mark was following me. Kevin found a decent job with an electrical contractor, and I was blessed to find a Christian dentist to work for, an answer to my prayers. We bought a new mobile home and placed it on a 10-acre piece of land, much smaller than the 80 acres we had in Wisconsin. This would allow me to work two days per week, rather than five.

"**I**'ve never heard of a dry county before. You mean alcohol isn't sold here?" I was pushing Amber in a stroller while Kevin's sister, Dana, pulled her two-year-old daughter in a wagon. Dana's two dogs trotted ahead of us, and at the front of the pack was Tyler, who was on his first bicycle with training wheels.

The smell of the freshly cut, wild onions—which grew like weeds in the lawns of the Bluegrass state—filled one's nose, and the hot, sticky air bore the pleasant sound of buzzing locusts.

"That's right. Alcohol isn't sold here." Having lived in Kentucky for five years, Dana's southern drawl was quite noticeable. Like Kevin, she had green eyes, and short, brown hair, along with a small nose.

"In our Wisconsin hometown, we had a bar on every corner."

Dana laughed. "Well, here in the Bible belt, there seems to be a church on every corner."

"Hey Dana. How ya'all doing?" A white pick-up truck with dual rear tires slowed down, and the driver stuck his arm out of the window, waving.

"Just fine. How are you?" Dana waved while Patches barked and chased the truck. The dog ran too close, and his right front paw got run over. We heard a sharp yipe as his body twisted and flipped next to the truck.

Jimmy stopped immediately but didn't get out because Patches, part pit-bull, was up and barking, fiercer than before. "I'm sorry, Dana. I didn't mean to hit your dog."

"Don't worry about Patches. Serves him right!" The army drill sergeant in Dana came through. "I've been trying to get him not to chase cars for years. Maybe this'll teach him." Though my sister-in-law had a tough exterior, she was a softie in her core. She sometimes skipped minor household chores to do things with her daughter, like drawing with chalk on the sidewalk, blowing soap bubbles, or wrestling on the floor. I admired her for that.

"Glad he's alright. See you later." Jimmy took off as Patches limped along the side of the road.

"One thing you're gonna miss from the Dairy State is the cheese curds." Dana resumed our conversation.

"Really? You can't get them here?"

"No. You can't buy bratwursts or kluski noodles either."

"When I asked my pastor's wife if they had a bubbler at church, she had no idea what I was talking about."

Dana laughed. "Yeah, water fountains are only called bubblers in Wisconsin! And maybe Minnesota."

"**I**'d like to try a different church," I said to Kevin. "Pastor Ricky's too negative, and I'm not learning anything." We had been attending the backyard church of our neighbor, a self-appointed preacher for about a year.

Kevin wasn't bothered that Pastor Ricky was a smoker, but I wanted a minister who would set a better example for Tyler and Amber. We decided to try a Pentecostal church 20 minutes from home.

"I don't allow people to call out prophetic words during my sermons," said Pastor John at Full Gospel Tabernacle. "If the Holy Spirit is giving a sermon through me, He isn't going to interrupt Himself."

Though Pastor John believed in being Spirit-filled, he wasn't Word of Faith. He never spoke about prosperity and rarely talked about money. Although his sermons were convicting and thought-provoking, I missed church services where prophetic words, healings, miracles, and spiritual power abounded. I was used to the uplifted feeling that came from hearing about being powerful, healthy, and wealthy and found myself feeling depressed because I wasn't getting my 'spiritual fix'.

It seemed strange that church members didn't command and demand spiritual forces or verbally bind evil spirits during prayer meetings. Sometimes they made negative statements like, 'I'm catching a cold', or 'My back is killing me', so I thought they were a little behind the times, not having the newest WoF revelation from God.

Though Kevin and I tithed, there was never pressuring to give extra money at Full Gospel Tabernacle. Pastor John didn't have televangelists come in to do fundraisers, and we never had to stand up in front of the church to announce how much we were pledging to a new building project. As a result, Kevin and I rarely fought about money and were finally able to start saving for retirement.

"**J**ob did nothing wrong. He didn't deserve the troubles which came upon him," said Pastor John during his Sunday sermon.

He's wrong, I thought. According to WoF revelation, Job's *fear* caused troubles to be drawn toward him.

While Pastor John commended everything Job had done right, I recalled my WoF teachings. 'Fear is the opposite of faith. Just as faith attracts what we pray for, fear attracts what we are afraid of, which is why Job suffered.'

Between the beautiful worship songs and the sermons which inspired me toward holiness, I began finding myself drawn to know the Bible more and more. My attraction to the Scriptures was beginning to change. I still enjoyed coming across promises and trying to figure out how the words of a passage might confirm my WoF beliefs, but I was discovering a depth and richness that led me toward something even better than material wealth, divine health, and feelings of spiritual empowerment. As a deer pants for the water brooks, I thirsted for more of the Word of God.

Pastor John began teaching a sermon series about being intimate with God, and the profound messages were agonizing to endure as I learned what it meant to be crucified with Christ. We were learning about dying to our selfish ambitions and surrendering our will to God, and we were becoming versed in the value of sacrifice and suffering. It was such a contrast to WoF Church, but I became used to being convicted of my sin. Strangely, part of me liked it, for each time an area of my carnal nature was reduced to ashes, I felt relieved. Liberated.

After 10 years of trying to get pregnant naturally, Amanda and Jerry decided to try In Vitro Fertilization.

"You wouldn't believe how painful the shots are!" exclaimed Amanda. "I look at baby pictures of my nieces and nephews as Jerry gives my shots."

While Amanda and Jerry were trying to make their dreams come true, I tried to convince my husband to get help for alcoholism. "Please Kevin, will you try a treatment center?"

"No. I'll never do that." The whites of Kevin's eyes had a yellow tint, and the skin on his face was jaundiced.

"What about AA. You could go to meetings."

"I don't need help. I can quit anytime."

There were times when Kevin would hit the shoulder of the road while driving our family to an evening church service. Once, our driver side mirror hit the mirror of an oncoming vehicle. Whenever I would ask him to pull over so I could drive, a fight would ensue. If he ran out of alcohol, he'd head to the neighboring county forty minutes away, no matter how drunk he was.

The longer one drinks, the more brain damage occurs. Eventually, the habit becomes a disease. I continued to pray that Kevin would tear down his altar to alcohol and choose to surrender his life to the Lord before it was too late.

"**I**t's finally happened after ten years of trying to get pregnant." Amanda's words tumbled over one another in a higher pitch than normal as we spoke over the phone. "We're going to have a baby before Thanksgiving!"

"Then you and Annie are due around the same time!"

"Yes, I'm so happy!"

Tears of joy filled my eyes. "It looks like your prophecy from Prophetess Deb is coming to pass. She said you would have two of your own children. Remember?"

After briefly skimming the book *Christianity in Crisis*, by Hank Hanegraaff, which criticized my favorite Christian ministers, I quickly assumed that my teachers had more truth than Hank. In my opinion, too many Christians were hyper-critical and overly judgmental, and I thought the author might have been jealous because he lacked the power and anointing of my 'Spirit-filled' televangelists.

To be honest, my idolized ministers and their teachings were a golden calf to me, and I doubt anyone could have convinced me they were wrong at that time. Though my heart appeared to be in the right place because I was doing my best to live a God-pleasing life, I strongly desired the health, wealth, and success message to be true.

A short while later, I came across the following citations on http://www.againstallheresy.com/. I assumed my esteemed preachers didn't really mean what they had said. The statements below reduce Jesus and elevate man, exactly as cults do. I didn't know the heretical ideas below are *foundational* to the movement.

"I was shocked when I found out who the biggest failure in the Bible actually is. The biggest one in the whole Bible is God."[13] (Kenneth Copeland)

"Adam committed high treason; and at that point, all the dominion and authority God had given to him was handed over to Satan. Suddenly, God was on the outside looking in. After Adam's fall, God found Himself in a peculiar position. God needed an avenue back into the earth. God laid out his proposition, and Abram accepted it. It gave God access to the earth and gave man access to God. Technically, if God ever broke the covenant, He would have to destroy Himself."[14] (Kenneth Copeland)

"God's on the outside looking in. He doesn't have any legal entree into the earth. The thing don't (sic) belong to Him. You see how sassy the Devil was in the presence of God in the book of Job? God said, 'Where have you been?' Wasn't any of God's business. He [Satan] didn't even have to answer if he didn't want to. God didn't argue with him a bit! You see, this is the position that God's been in. Might say, 'Well, if God's running things, he's doing a lousy job of it.'"[15] (Kenneth Copeland)

"God came from heaven, became a man, made man into little gods, went back to heaven as a man. He faces the Father as a man. I face devils as the son of God. Quit your nonsense! What else are you? If you say, 'I am', you're saying I'm a part of Him, right? Is he God? Are you his offspring? Are you His children? You can't be human! You can't! You can't! God didn't give birth to flesh. You said, "Well, that's heresy." No, that's your crazy brain saying that."[16] (Benny Hinn)

"When you say, 'I am a Christian, you are saying, 'I am mashiach' in the Hebrew. I am a little messiah walking on earth, in other words. That is a shocking revelation. May I say it like this? You are a little god on earth running around."[17] (Benny Hinn)

"Christians are little messiahs and little gods on the earth. Thus [encouraging the audience]...say 'I am a God-man. This spirit-man within me is a God-man.' Say 'I'm born of heaven — a God-man. I'm a God man. I am a sample of Jesus. I'm a super being.' Say it! Say it! Who's a super being? 'I walk in the realm of the supernatural.' Say it! You want to prosper? Money will be falling on you from left, right, and center. God will begin to prosper you, for money always follows righteousness. Say after me, 'everything I ever want is in me already.'"[18] (Benny Hinn)

"Man was created on terms of equality with God, and he could stand in God's presence without any consciousness of inferiority. God has made us as much like Himself as possible. He made us the same class of being that He is Himself. Man lived in the realm of God. He lived on terms equal with God. The believer is called Christ. That's who we are; we're Christ!"[19] (Kenneth Hagin)

I found the following quote on http://www.rapidnet.com/~jbeard/bdm/exposes/copeland/general.htm:

"God's reason for creating Adam was His desire to reproduce Himself. I mean a reproduction of Himself, and in the Garden of Eden He did just that. He was not a little like God. He was not almost like God. He was not subordinate to God even. ... Adam is as much like God as you could get, just the same as Jesus. ... Adam, in the Garden of Eden, was God manifested in the flesh."[20] (Kenneth Copeland)

I was able to detect the serious error in the above statements, but the human mind has a self-defeating tendency to rationalize away disturbing information. My yearning for the power and promises in Spirit-filled, WoF churches skewed my ability to reason objectively. The excitement of experiencing supernatural power pumped me up as much as my former drinking addiction did. Not only that, but the *healing energy* which I had received from Pastor Bill continued to move my body in yoga-like positions whenever I availed myself to it, cementing my prosperity beliefs. Denial—the tendency of the heart to hide truth from one's conscience—had a strong hold on me.

10 Shattered Dreams

You who have shown me many troubles and distresses will revive me again, and will bring me up again from the depths of the earth. Psalm 71:20 NASB

A television news program 'exposed' my favorite televangelist. Pictures of his extravagant, multi-million-dollar home, luxurious vacation house, and fancy vehicles were shown. Reporters suggested that my esteemed preacher shouldn't live in such opulence and luxury, but I was convinced of nothing. It was my belief that the news media didn't understand that God wants His anointed vessels to be rich and successful.

Fatigue, anxiety, and sadness were taking their toll on me. The searing nerve pain in my neck—worsened by exhaustion and tension—had been causing my shoulder muscles to spasm whenever I was awake. Sometimes the torment shrieked so loudly that I could think of nothing else. If not for God and my family members, whom I would never intentionally hurt, I might have considered taking my life. The torture was that unbearable.

When Amanda was almost three months along in her pregnancy, I was back in Wisconsin for a church conference. I'd arrived at WoF Church first and was watching the foyer doors when she arrived. With swollen eyes and a red puffy nose, my sister entered the loud, pulsating sanctuary full of energized, singing women and threaded her way toward me. Smiling through her tears, she set her leather purse on the chair next to mine, lifted her hands in worship, and struggled to sing.

When the music was finished, we took our seats, and I leaned over to whisper, "What's the matter?"

"I started bleeding today." Amanda pulled several tissues from her purse and dabbed her eyes.

"After the service, be sure to stop by the tables in the foyer and have a look. You won't want to miss out on these." Miss Televangelist, wearing a shimmering blue dress, was walking across the stage advertising various books and CDs.

After a moment, Amanda said. "I went to the doctor today. They did an ultrasound and told me that the baby is disintegrating."

"Maybe you can get a healing," I suggested.

After the teaching, Amanda and I stood in line, waiting for Miss Televangelist to pray for her. After praying for a multitude of others, she came to Amanda and pronounced, "You should NOT be crying. Your mind is too focused on yourself! You need to get your eyes off your problems and onto God."

Was this 'Spirit-filled' woman sharing the heart of God with a woman who was in the middle of a miscarriage? I silently wondered why our faith and superior prayer methods had not delivered faster, easier results regarding a baby for Amanda. *We must need more faith...*

"Ariel, how did your kitchen wall get that hole in it?" asked Allen. It was a Sunday evening in December, and I'd been babysitting Allen and Dana's children for the weekend while they were on National Guard duty. We were just getting ready to sit down for supper.

"Kevin threw a chair into it when he was drunk the other night," I replied.

"You'd better be careful," my brother-in-law warned. "In my continuing education class, we learned that physical damage to property is one step away from domestic abuse. When people no longer get satisfaction from breaking things, they begin to hurt their family members."

Between the verbal attacks on me, the physical damage to our home when Kevin smashed things, and the harsh way he treated our children, I began to feel like something needed to be done before the situation worsened.

"Dana, does Logan have a cold in his eyes?" I asked. "They were almost crusted shut this morning."

My sister-in-law looked at her infant's eyes. "They've been getting worse lately. I'll call the doctor tomorrow morning."

"Why don't you all come to church with us tonight? Tyler and Amber are performing in a skit."

After the church service, Dana and I took Logan up so Pastor John could pray on him. The following morning, Logan's eyes were clear for the first time since he'd been born two months earlier, and the infection did not return.

"Come on in." Amanda opened the living room door at our parents' house, and a cold gust of wind blew inside as Annie and Jeff entered with their newborn, Lilly.

Annie was beaming as she and Jeff took off their thick, winter parkas. "Hi Amanda. Hello everyone." Annie's sweet, gentle voice sounded timorous, as she toned down her joy, not wanting to rub salt in Amanda's open wound.

Later that evening, Amanda explained why she and Jerry needed to put pregnancy on hold. "Jerry hasn't been feeling well, and his liver enzymes are up."

"My doctors are planning to do a transplant as soon as a matching liver is available." The whites of Jerry's eyes were yellow, and his face had a jaundiced tint.

Christmas Day, evening—

"We could call a locksmith tomorrow." Dad said, trying to diffuse the situation. It was cold and dark outside as we stood next to our locked van.

Kevin swore in frustration at my father. My heart sank as my hero—the sacrificial dad who raised me, the generous one who paid for our wedding, the mechanic who had recently overhauled our van engine—was treated with disrespect.

"I doubt if anyone will come out tonight." Dad replied.

If only I hadn't left my purse and both sets of keys in the van when I locked it. I looked in the rear window, wondering why Kevin was so upset. One corner of an inaccessible case of beer peeked out at me from its hiding place beneath the back seat.

11 Immediate Gratification

Dear friends, I warn you as "temporary residents and foreigners" to keep away from worldly desires that wage war against your very souls. 1 Peter 2:11 NLT

"Why were you crying last night?" I asked. Our family sat at the breakfast table.

"My arm hurts," Amber replied.

"It does look a little swollen," I said, looking at her forearm. "I wonder if it's broken."

The day before, Tyler, Amber, and I had been at a park with several other home school families, whom we met with every week. My four-year-old had been trying to climb into the swing when she went over the seat and fell head first to the ground. After a few minutes of crying, she'd gone back to playing with the other children and had seemed fine.

"Can you move your hand?" asked Kevin.

Amber made a fist and opened her palm.

Tyler took a hold of her forearm and gave it a hard squeeze. "Does that hurt?"

"Ouch." Amber winced.

"I think I'd better take her in and have it looked at," I said. "I'll get the car seat out of the van so you can go to work."

In the front passenger seat of Kevin's vehicle, a cold six-pack of beer was beneath an ice pack. *No wonder Kevin hasn't been complaining about daytime tremors or hallucinations anymore,* I thought.

I considered our conversation from the prior week.

"I don't want you drinking when you drive the kids home from the babysitter," I had said.

"I'm not." Kevin looked me straight in the eye without flinching.

"Tyler said you drank a can of beer in the car yesterday."

"I drive better when I have a drink or two."

"Can't you wait until you come home?"

"Alright, alright. Get off my case, will you?!"

"**I** wonder what your daddy will say when he sees your cast. Does your arm feel better now?"

"Yes," Amber replied.

"I thought you landed on your head yesterday."

"I did." Then, in a most serious voice, my daughter said, "It's a good thing I didn't break my head off!"

The next day, when I went to a community ladies' prayer meeting, I brought my vial of anointing oil and Kevin's favorite jacket so everyone could pray on it. That way, I thought God's Spirit would convict Kevin about his drinking and would repel the 'spirit of alcohol' whenever he wore the coat.

"When you get home, walk the perimeter of your land seven times," instructed Prophetess Janet. "Take authority over your land, bind the demons, and release the Holy Spirit."

Several weeks later, at a church meeting, the women gathered around me as I explained, "Kevin's been swearing at me and breaking things around the house when he gets drunk."

Karen laid her hands on my back and began to prophesy. "God is bringing change to your home and is working to set things right in your marriage. He has heard your prayers, and He's about to deliver Kevin."

I hoped the prophecies about Kevin would come to pass quickly so we could go forward with baby number three and build our new home. A few weeks later, Mom called. "Ariel, God is showing me that Kevin will be delivered soon."

"That's the third prophecy I've had about his deliverance this month. I don't know what to do. Things are getting really bad here."

Mom was quiet.

"How's everything in Wisconsin?" I asked.

"Well, that's the reason I called. A donor liver has been found for Jerry, and his transplant surgery is scheduled for tomorrow."

"Really? That's great news!"

After the surgery, it took a few days for Jerry's new liver to begin functioning, but once it did, he recovered well. Unfortunately, the immunosuppressant drugs carried serious risks. Within a few years, Jerry's life would be on the line.

"People decide in their hearts what they want to believe," began Pastor John, "and then they look for evidence to confirm those beliefs, even though their hearts might be wrong. Studies have shown that even trained psychologists can't see through the deception in their own hearts. We cannot trust our hearts to lead us to truth, especially when the facts require us to sacrifice something we desire.

"Just as our appetites pull us toward those things which aren't healthy for our body, our hearts tend to pull us in directions which aren't beneficial for our souls. When searching for truth, try to take your heart out of the matter. You can always ask yourself, 'What is the worst that can happen if this is true,' or 'what is the worst that can happen if this proves false?' Turn in your Bibles to Jeremiah 17:9."

I opened my Amplified Bible.

> *The heart is deceitful above all things, and it is exceedingly perverse and corrupt and severely, mortally sick! Who can know it [perceive, understand, be acquainted with his own heart and mind]? Jeremiah 17:9 Amplified Bible*

"Truth doesn't become less true if we don't like it," continued Pastor John. "It just becomes harder to see."

(When Pastor John referred to our heart, he spoke about the emotional part of our being. He was not advocating that we shouldn't follow our conscience, which convicts us regarding morality).

A few days later, I was watching for Prophetess Janet at the community ladies' prayer meeting, anticipating the stimulation and excitement that surrounded her when she was operating in the anointing. After 45 minutes of worship, it became apparent that she wasn't going to show up. I was greatly disappointed and regretted coming to the meeting.

Hungering for spiritual excitement and knowledge of the future, my natural susceptibility to addictive experiences drew me more to Janet than to Jesus. Unfortunately, the unregenerate man has selfish tendencies and is inclined to make everything out for his own benefit. Though I was saved, there were parts of my human nature that still gravitated toward self-centered gratification, and this was one of those areas where I needed to become more like Jesus. Would

Jesus go to the synagogue so He could acquire a healing for Himself or receive a personal word from God the Father?

Like many in Charismatic circles, I sought the gifts of the Spirit so others would be built up, blessed, and brought to the Lord. However, I also wanted a prophetic word for myself and an experience with spiritual power. Once I tasted the excitement of supernatural phenomenon, I was hooked, like an addict.

12 Furnace of Affliction

Fire tests the purity of silver and gold, but the LORD tests the heart. Proverbs 17:3 NLT

Pink lightning peeled across the threatening sky as booming thunder rumbled continuously, and the clouds overhead veered in different directions. The greenish-yellow hue that had preceded the storm gave way to darkness. Gusting winds caused the trees to bend in prostration as the advancing storm violently assaulted the sanctuary of our home. Pea-sized hail clattered on our metal roof. As I looked out of the southwest window of our living room, I could see the black, cumulonimbus thunderhead with several tornadoes snaking viciously in our direction.

Rushing into the basement, Tyler, Amber, and I heard an ear-splitting crash as lightning hit our home. Our fuse box exploded. As fire engulfed the wooden joists of our basement ceiling, the kids and I ran toward the steps at the opposite end of the basement. Just as we started up the stairway, a large supporting beam, covered in flames, fell across the steps. There was a window on the other end of the basement, but we would have to go back...through the fire.

There are times in life when one stands before God's furnace of affliction and the only option is to enter it. Nightmares of heavy winds, tornadoes, and fire filled my nights as the children and I searched for a way through our valley of trials, fending our way together—yet alone. The spiritual leader of our home was AWOL, present in body, but absent in person. Our home was no longer a place of refuge, but one of anxiety, tension, and strain. The man who used to hum and sing when inebriated was becoming angry and unpredictable.

It looked as if a dark, spiritual storm seemed to be gathering force on the horizon of our family's future. Our marriage was being tested with fire. Like the home in my nightmare, would God allow it to be reduced to ashes?

Numerous Bible verses speak of God refining His children through fiery trials, like gold is purified in a furnace. When the dross (impurity) rises to the surface, it is skimmed away, and the gold is placed back into the furnace. The procedure is repeated several times until the refiner can look into the shining, melted metal and see his clear image reflected. In God's refining furnace, our iniquities flare up to be seen, repented of, and cleansed away. We are made in God's image, and the more we are purified, the more we look like Him.

> *"And I will bring the third part through the fire, refine them as silver is refined, and test them as gold is tested. They will call on My name, and I will answer them; I will say, 'They are My people,' and they will say, 'The LORD is my God.'" Zechariah 13:9 NASB*

"Sit on your butt at the table!" ordered Kevin.

Amber had been sitting on her feet so she'd be taller, and her wiggling had irritated her father. It seemed that he was harsh with her every evening. Our sensitive, obedient girl would've been happy to oblige without voices being raised. My heart broke to see her eyes fill with tears once again.

My closest friend, Louise, confronted me one evening. "Ariel, Ron saw Kevin do something to you that didn't look right at the church social."

I knew right away what she was talking about. Kevin had been plastered when he angrily whacked me between the shoulder blades, pushing me into the table where I had been seated. (While he had been in the bathroom, someone cleared his empty paper plate from the table, and that had frustrated him).

I've had a few influential friends in my life, and Louise rated at the very top. Some close friends led me toward drinking and away from the Lord, but not Louise. She encouraged me to be intimate with God and helped me see the benefits of being a loving, relational parent, rather than a strict authoritarian.

It would have been difficult to admit the instability in my home if Louise hadn't been open about trials of her own. A few days earlier, while we were sitting at her kitchen table, she had confided one of her deepest sorrows. "My baby would have been 16 this year, if not for the abortion." Her chin-length, brown hair fell in soft waves around her face as her hazel-colored eyes filled with tears. "Every September, around my baby's due date, I feel such sadness."

Taking the phone into my walk-in closet for privacy, I said, "Kevin's been getting so angry that I feel like I'm walking on eggshells every night."

"Have you thought about leaving him?"

"I have, but God hates divorce." My chest tightened.

"You wouldn't have to get a divorce, though…maybe just a separation."

After our conversation, I got on my knees and bowed my face to the closet floor, allowing a few quiet tears to slip out. It grieved my heart that Kevin was choosing alcohol over the children and me. Sometimes my emotions came flooding up, trying to erupt through my exterior facade. When I held everything inside, the tension headaches increased in frequency and severity.

During our counseling session, Linda and I digressed to the topic of the 'movement of holy laughter', which was taking place in an Assembly of God church in Toronto, Canada. Unbeknownst to her, I had been waiting for a similar revival in Kentucky.

"I don't believe the movement is godly," Linda stated. "I think an occult power is at work within the church."

Though I was certain she was wrong, I couldn't find a way to tell her that I believed in the Holy Spirit's gifts, that I spoke in tongues, and that I liked to feel the supernatural power in church services.

While reading the Bible to his four-year-old stepson, one of the young fathers from Full Gospel Tabernacle suffered a brain aneurysm. Within minutes, Luke was in a comatose state. A group of us stood around his hospital bed, singing worship songs and praying.

As I was preparing to leave, I overheard another church member tell Luke's parents, "The Lord says that Luke will live. He will stand in the pulpit and give his testimony before the congregation."

Several days later, flower arrangements surrounded Luke's casket, which was in the front of our church sanctuary. A long line of mourners extended down the center aisle, behind the back row of seats, and out the side door. Though his death felt like defeat, Luke's life had been a victorious testimony of our Heavenly Father's love toward His adopted children.

After they lost their son, Luke's parents, Adam and Denise, continued to serve the Lord in church, usually raising their hands during worship. As their ship was tossed on the stormy sea of life, they appeared unwavering, solid, and true. Like other elders in Pastor John's church, their mature devotion to the Lord was apparent.

Kevin and I were visiting our neighbor's church one evening. Pastor Ricky had his hand on my forehead as I staggered backwards, my rubbery legs unable to keep me upright. I caught my balance, then stumbled farther back, closer to the front row of folding chairs.

Suddenly, I fell backwards, along with Pastor Ricky's wife, who was supposed to catch me. I felt nothing as the crashing sound of metal chairs and a toddler's crying came to my ears. The two-year-old must have been behind us. I'm not certain what happened, but it seemed as if Pastor Ricky's wife fell into the child. The crying hushed quickly, and most of the congregation went outside to fellowship after the service.

Those of us who were *slain in the spirit* remained on the floor. When I tried to get up, my body felt like lead, as though an invisible force was holding me down. As I looked across the room full of people lying on their backs, a teenage boy was attempting to rise. Each time he got halfway up, he collapsed. After a few tries, he got into a crawling position and made his way across the floor. I burst out laughing because I knew just how he felt. Suddenly, all of us were laughing like hyenas, unable to stop.

The following day, I felt amazing, as though the laughter had released all my pent-up stress. I was certain Pastor Ricky was filled with the Holy Spirit and that those who spoke against Pentecostals and Charismatics lacked knowledge.

New Year's Eve—

As I evaluate the previous year, I realize that God has taught me how to say 'No' to commitments that take too much time from Him and from my family. He's been teaching me the value of simplicity and of freeing my schedule from being overly busy. Furthermore, as He refines my heart in the furnace of affliction, I'm discovering more darkness within my soul.

13 Wisdom of Counselors

Where there is no guidance the people fall,
But in abundance of counselors there is victory. Proverbs 11:14 NASB

"I'm afraid Kevin might commit suicide," I explained to Counselor Steve as we talked on the phone. "He can't stand to be alone and says he won't have a reason to eat when we're gone."

"By using alcohol, he's committing slow suicide while you stay," said Counselor Steve. "You need to protect your children, and the best way you can do that is to remove them from the situation."

"Are you sure?"

"The best thing you can do for your children is to leave him. The best thing you can do for yourself is to leave him, and the best thing you can do for Kevin…is to leave him."

"How can it be better for children to live without a father?"

"Living in a house where one parent is verbally abusive to the other parent is distressing to kids," said Counselor Steve. "Drunken tirades and breaking things can disturb their well-being. Children who remain in the home of an addict suffer more emotional damage, do less well in school, and handle life more poorly than those who are removed from the situation. Those who continue living with a dependent parent are more likely to become alcoholics."

"How will separation affect Tyler and Amber?"

"It won't be easy on them, but stability and love will go a long way."

I didn't want to be an accomplice to my children's downfall. For their sakes, I felt the need to take Steve's counsel. Yesterday's choices had become today's consequences.

I had always believed that God would have us stick with our marriage partner, no matter what we suffered. If the children and I were to leave, I didn't know where we would live or how we would pay our bills. *Lord,* I prayed. *I've followed Your advice and cut my work hours so I could homeschool Tyler and Amber. How can I afford to move out of our house?*

My answer came the following day when Mom phoned.

"Ariel, when Amanda and Jerry visited you last fall, they noticed Kevin wasn't treating you right, so I've been reading a book called *Loving Solutions* by Gary Chapman. I think you need to move away from Kevin so he'll be able to face the consequences of his drinking. That's one of the only things that can motivate him to change."

"I wish I didn't have to take that step."

"Your dad and I want you to come live with us. It often takes a year or two before a spouse can return home."

"Maybe it takes that long for regular people, but we know how to do spiritual warfare and make positive confessions. Kevin will quit drinking as soon as we leave. I just received a prophecy that his deliverance is right around the corner."

"We can hope and pray," Mom replied.

Dear Lord, this is so humbling. Yet, if my parents' house is the way You choose to provide, I must swallow my pride—the hideous thing that it is.

"**A**riel? This is Amanda." There was a quiver in my sister's voice.

"Hi Amanda. What's up?"

"We got some bad news from Jerry's doctor. You know the medicine he takes to keep his body from rejecting his new liver?"

"The immunosuppressants?" Standing in our master bedroom and looking out the window, I noticed Kevin's reflection in a garage window. He stood in our detached garage with his head tipped all the way back, chugging a can of beer.

"Well, the medications made Jerry's body susceptible to cancer. He has Burkitt's Lymphoma, and it's gotten into his bone marrow and liver. His doctor says…" I could hear muffled crying. "He says…"

Amanda didn't have to tell me. As far as I knew, once cancer metastasized to the liver, the prognosis was death. Staring out the window through tear-filled eyes, I wished Kevin could have been near me. Instead, I saw him tip his head back and chug another can of beer.

"**T**he longer the problem continues, the more ingrained the addiction," said Pastor John as I sat in his office.

"That's what concerns me." I opened my notebook and prepared to take notes. "One of my counselors explained that the chance of recovery gets lower as the brain damage continues. Kevin's been slowly poisoning his brain for 20 years. He speaks very slowly, as if he has trouble thinking, and he can't keep up with normal conversations."

"If you stay with Kevin, there's a very low likelihood of recovery, while leaving him can be a powerful incentive to change." Pastor John leaned back in his chair. "Not all addicts recover. The more destruction to their brain, the less likely recovery is."

"Perhaps I should've left him sooner when his chance of recovery was better. All the prophecies encouraged me to stay, though, proclaiming that his deliverance was about to take place."

Pastor John's eyebrows knitted together briefly. "Like I always say, 'if a prophecy is from God, it will come to pass. You don't have to *make* it happen.'"

I breathed a sigh of relief, realizing he wasn't telling me to put up with Kevin a little longer.

"Ariel, God doesn't require you to be a doormat, and He doesn't want you to be an enabler."

New Year's Eve reflections —

Though I usually read the entire Bible every year, I only made it one-third of the way through this past year. I've been delving deeper into the meanings of the verses. I need the Lord more than ever...

"Jerry's spinal tap revealed an increase in cancer cells, but we're determined to beat back the enemy," said Amanda. "We've been quoting Bible verses about healing and listening to Christian radio programs as we travel to Madison. We don't understand why the doctor's reports aren't better."

"Keep confessing the Word and be careful not to make negative confessions." The nerve in my neck began burning as I held the phone to my ear, so I switched it to the other side.

"We are."

It was a good thing I was moving back to Wisconsin. My sister would soon be facing one of the most formidable struggles of her life.

14 The Father's Love

Father to the fatherless, defender of widows— this is God, whose dwelling is holy. God places the lonely in families; he sets the prisoners free and gives them joy. But he makes the rebellious live in a sun-scorched land.
Psalm 68:5–6 NLT

"In light of biblical submission in marriage, I'm not certain how I can justify a tough love approach to Kevin's drinking." As we sat across from one another in McDonalds Play place, I bounced my concern off Louise. "Kevin doesn't want us to leave, and I'm not surrendering to the pressure he's putting on me to stay."

"Husbands and wives are supposed to submit their lives to God and mutually to one another," said Louise. "In choosing alcohol, Kevin isn't yielding his life to God, nor to you."

"True."

"And if he fails to surrender to God's authority, can he require your submission?"

"It wouldn't seem right," I replied.

"I don't think God wants women and their children to submit to destruction, Ariel. If you think God is advising you to take the tough love approach, it would be better to obey Him, than to submit to Kevin."

My husband's drinking kept him from turning to God, and I believed God wanted me to stop enabling his addiction. While Louise took her toddler to the bathroom, I turned to face the play area. There must have been at least 20 children laughing, screaming, playing, and fighting as they slid down the slide, buried themselves in colored plastic balls, and crawled through the tubular gym.

I watched Tyler and Amber. They needed a father who would sacrificially love them, demonstrating affection and affirmation, giving them a small taste of our Heavenly Father's love. How would their desires for a dad be met?

When Louise returned, she said, "Women are at most risk of being harmed when they are leaving their spouse. Do you think you might be in any danger?"

"No. I'm pretty sure Kevin would never hurt us."

The boisterous noises of children were echoing off the walls and reverberating through my frazzled brain as I recalled a recent news story. The night before his wife planned to leave him, a husband had fatally shot each family member before taking his own life.

"Here is a key to my house, just in case you ever need a place to stay." Louise reached across the table and pressed the key into my hand.

"Thank you," I replied. My heart began pounding the instant my fingers closed around her key.

"You can come over anytime, even in the middle of the night."

My father had always done a lot for me, but we didn't have the type of intimate relationship where we opened our hearts and shared our feelings with one another. Now that my marriage was in trouble, I felt embarrassed to need Dad's help, as though I'd failed in one of the most important areas of my life. I grappled with feelings of humiliation, thinking that Dad might look down on me. That would never have been the case, and I knew that Dad wouldn't have been thinking such thoughts, but the heart doesn't always feel what the mind knows.

Dad came the evening before my intended moving day in early March, and we began to prepare for the following morning. He took apart the kid's bunk beds, and we loaded a few items into his trailer. Kevin was very quiet after supper and stole away to our detached garage, as if he could drink his problems away.

The next morning, Dad and I finished packing up. "Look how low to the ground the Dodge and trailer are squatting," Dad remarked.

"Do you think we've loaded it down too much?" I asked. Bunk beds, mattresses, dressers, bikes, and toys filled the trailer, and the steel-blue caravan was packed to the roof with clothing, jackets, and more toys.

With about 220,000 miles, the van looked remarkably good for its age, especially considering it had been driven on the salted, winter roads of Wisconsin for ten years. Dad had bought it used and rebuilt the motor himself. (He and Mom preferred to save money for their future and to be generous with others, rather than spending it on vehicles).

"The van can handle it." Dad turned toward Kevin and offered, "Would you like to come out for breakfast with us? My treat."

"No thanks. Probably couldn't eat anyway." With his hands stuffed in his pockets, Kevin hung his head toward the ground, just as he had done when he'd walked the halls of our high school so many years ago.

I stepped up to my husband of twelve years and gave him a hug. "We need you and will be waiting to come home. When you can turn away from alcohol, we can be a family again."

He wiped away a tear. While I felt bad that he was hurting, I'd wept many times over the years. Hopefully, his tears for himself would eventually turn into tears of sorrow for displeasing God and for allowing his family to suffer because of his choices. Kevin had appointments set up with Counselor Steve and with Pastor John, and he was talking about things he planned to do in the upcoming days, so I wasn't worried that he might commit suicide anymore.

An hour later, Dad, the kids, and I waved good-bye to the yellow daffodils, the green grass, and the budding dogwood trees of Kentucky as we crossed the Ohio River. We then said 'hello' to the Land of Lincoln, where there was an abundance of white-tailed deer, cardinals, and state troopers.

At a rest area halfway through the trip, the van decided it didn't want to go back to Wisconsin and refused to start. Having made the trip without a coat, Dad spent some time under the hood trying to troubleshoot the problem in the cold wind and driving rain. The temperature was already significantly colder than Kentucky, and I felt sorry that my life's decisions were causing discomfort to him. Unable to solve the problem, he called a tow truck and had the van taken to a Dodge dealership in Bloomington. By nightfall, we were back on the freeway, fighting the wind and watching for police cars.

Tyler tucked his pillow next to the window and leaned against it. Amber rested her head against his shoulder and drifted off. Looking at the sweet sight of my innocent, sleeping children—both of their mouths slightly open—I regretted that my selfish, youthful decisions were dragging them through troubles. If only I had sought the Lord's will earlier in life...

At 2:00 AM, the moonlight glimmered on the snow in my parent's large front yard as we pulled into their driveway. Stepping out of the van, I felt the crisp, cold air, which carried the comforting scent of wood smoke that was rising from the chimney of their tri-level home. After tucking the kids in for the night, I entered my childhood bedroom. The twin bed was freshly made with fragrant bedsheets, and a soft, velour nightgown was lying on top. Mom had thought of everything. I knew that I might miss the warmer climate of Kentucky, but a supportive family beats the weather anytime. Hands down.

Kevin was slurring his words every evening on the phone, and would ask the same questions over and over, unable to hold a coherent conversation. If I let the phone ring, he'd call again and again, up to 50 times.

I began pouring myself into God's Word with a new fervency, reading for at least an hour after the kids were in bed each night. There was a hunger and thirst in my soul that could not get enough of knowing God.

I had heard that music can make the burden of work seem lighter, and the Bible says that a joyful heart is good medicine. With the support of my family, songs began to well up in my heart, and as I went about my daily work, the melody often came out of my mouth.

While I didn't have a supportive husband to lean upon, I was beginning to learn that the Lord is close to the broken-hearted, our ever-present help in times of trouble.

"Grandpa, Grandpa, you're home!" Tyler and Amber rushed down the steps to greet Dad as he entered through the garage door.

After his week-long trips, Dad usually preferred to go straight to bed, without having to interact with people. He always pushed himself hard and was bone-tired by the time he came home. He gave each of the kids a hug and a pat on the back as they bounced around him, talking excitedly and asking questions.

I almost told them to leave him alone, afraid that our presence in the house would become a nuisance. It seemed as if God wanted me to allow the kids to bask in my father's attention. They needed him, and it was Dad's opportunity to be used by God.

A week later, Dad told Mom, "I used to like being left alone when I came home from my trips, but I think this is a good change for me."

Because he was a truck driver, Dad's vehicle was available most of the time, so he shared it with me. Mom was working two jobs, so I took care of the house cleaning, cooking, and laundry, and she insisted on paying me $20 per week. Kevin allowed me to keep a debit card, which I used for groceries, and I started working in a dental office one day per week.

We went to our first service at WoF Church on Sunday, and I enjoyed socializing with several relatives and friends. There were many new faces filling the seats of those who no longer attended. Almost half of the leadership was gone, replaced by younger members.

At our midweek prayer meeting, Pastor Bill laid his hands on Jerry's head. "'The devil will not win this battle,' says the Lord. 'Cancer will be defeated, and you will live.'"

15 Prophecies

You may say to yourselves, "How can we know when a message has not been spoken by the LORD?" If what a prophet proclaims in the name of the LORD does not take place or come true, that is a message the LORD has not spoken. That prophet has spoken ***presumptuously****, so do not be alarmed. Deuteronomy 18:21-23 NIV (Emphasis mine)*

"Your marriage is being restored, even at this moment," declared Prophetess Deb, after giving the sermon at WoF Church. "The Lord says, 'as frosting is spread on a cake, I'm putting the finishing touches on your marriage.'"

Prophetess Deb seemed to have a deep relationship with God. She encouraged us to walk sincerely in our devotion to the Lord and to be broken for Him. Many church members surrounded the stage after the service, waiting for a prophetic word from her.

One woman was told that large amounts of money were coming to her, and a young man with colon cancer received a proclamation stating that he would live.

Within a few weeks, Kevin started an outpatient treatment program in Kentucky. He was able to go to his job during the day and stay at the rehab center the rest of the time.

"Denise was telling others that you should be working a full-time job and shouldn't be homeschooling Tyler and Amber," said Amanda. "She says you're freeloading off of Dad and Mom."

It's one thing to be criticized by those outside the church, but it's worse when a sister in Christ gossips about you. Although I understood that God's opinion was more important than the ideas of others, my brooding mind continued to stew. I found myself judging Denise in return. *Who is she to determine how I should raise my children?* When I looked at the results of her parenting, it was easy to condemn her.

The Refiner had turned up the heat, and my dross (being easily offended and judgmental) began to surface.

"I haven't been smoking either," said Kevin. "Cigarettes are a trigger for me. They make me want a drink."

"That's good, Kevin. Are you going to Full Gospel Tabernacle for the midweek service?"

"No, I think I'll go to Pastor Ricky's church this evening."

"Won't it be hard to be around smokers?" I asked.

"I can handle it."

The following evening, when Kevin called, he was slurring his words.

"Are you drinking tonight?" I asked.

"I can have a...[hiccup]...beer once in a while."

"We should be glad God has blessed our pastor with abundance. If any of you feel opposed to what Pastor Bill is driving, you need to get your heart right with the Lord." One of the church elders stood at the podium addressing the issue of our pastor's new Cadillac Escalade.

"Preach it brother!"

"Amen!" Many of us, on-board, shouted our agreement. We wanted the best for our pastor.

It had been several months since Kevin had resumed drinking, and I called both of his counselors to see what they thought.

"I told Kevin that he needed to get sober for one week if he wanted to continue with therapy," said Counselor Steve. "He told me, 'That's impossible,' and walked out the door without making another appointment."

Pastor John related, "Kevin is still coming for appointments, and claims he isn't drinking, but there's always alcohol on his breath. I don't think counseling will help him if he can't be honest with me."

Hope deferred was making my heart sick. When I saw a woman on TV, dancing to the song *I'm Walking on Sunshine,* by Katrina and the Waves, it seemed hard to believe anyone could be as happy as she appeared. *"She's faking it,*" I thought, as my mind darkened with cynicism. I felt like I was drowning in sorrow.

During the worship music at a Ladies' conference in Minnesota, I felt the Lord letting me know that I could lean on Him since I didn't have a husband to rely upon. The emotional pain that I'd been stuffing beneath the surface pressed upward. It seemed as if God wanted me to release my pent-up sorrow.

Everyone else was worshiping in various ways. Some were dancing, others were lying prostrate on the carpet, and many were raising their hands. Most of the women had their eyes closed, focusing on the Lord. I surrendered my outer facade to Jesus, allowing my grief to be released in full abandonment. I must have lain on the sanctuary floor nearly an hour, sobbing and weeping, allowing myself to feel the pain harbored within. In my brokenness, God reached down and loved me, accepted me, and affirmed me. He began to bring healing to my addiction-prone personality.

The tension headaches, which had bothered me daily, subsided after I allowed myself to feel the pain, to cry, and to understand God's love toward me. When we can know the Father's unconditional love, acceptance, and affirmation toward us, we can become parents who are able to share these things with our children. As we forge a deeper relationship with God, He helps us begin to build more intimate relationships with our children. Then, rather than pass the scourge of addiction to them, we can pass a torch of love, acceptance, and affirmation.

"**A**riel, there's an anointed prophetess coming to the Assembly of God tonight," said my friend, Kathy. "You should come."

It was a Friday evening, so the kids and I went.

"'Divine order is coming to your home,' says the Lord. 'Within six months, there's going to be so much order in your home that you won't recognize it,'" proclaimed Prophetess Julie.

By this time, so many prophecies had lagged that I wondered if I could trust this 'Word from the Lord'.

In my prayer time, I would go through the ritual of 'putting my spiritual armor on,' followed by thanking and praising the Lord. Then I would attend to my list of prayer requests, such as Kevin's deliverance, Jerry's healing, my need for patience, etc. Next, I addressed the evil spirits, calling them by names (such as

Alcohol, Cancer, Poverty, Lust, and Sickness), verbally binding them powerless over our lives. After that, I released the Holy Spirit to operate in all areas of our lives. Lastly, I visualized the answers to my prayers, claimed that the victory belonged to us, and confidently thanked God that we would triumph.

Sometimes it felt as though I was following rituals and formulas for the first hour of my prayer-time, and by then, duties would be calling. Housework, meal preparation, and home education waited.

One time, as I was praying, I inserted my name into the verse, "The wealth of the wicked is stored up for the righteous (Ariel)." Suddenly, a feeling of strong displeasure seemed to surround me, as if I had done something treacherous against God.

What's wrong, Lord? Don't You want me to pray like that? God did not immediately answer me, as is often the case. He would wait a few years for me to develop the humility to accept the truth. I'll reveal His answer, which came from the mouth of a former witch, in an upcoming chapter.

In the prophetic books of the Bible, there are many accounts where prophets forewarned others that troubles were coming. They admonished kings, priests, and common people to change their wicked ways, predicting calamities before they occurred.

None of the prophecies I received prepared me for the struggles I would be facing. In hindsight, it might have been better to have had ten prophetic warnings telling me that suffering was on the way rather than one fortune-telling prophecy that encouraged false hope.

Unfortunately, I didn't realize the disparity between biblical prophets and those in the modern church. Though I saw prophecies failing for other people, I thought they might not have met some conditions. Since we live in a time of New Testament grace, I was taught that it was OK for prophets to miss the mark of accuracy occasionally. Did the Holy Spirit become less accurate from the Old Testament to the New? And if we couldn't discern whether we were speaking His Words or not, did we have the right to make such proclamations?

"**H**i Peggy, I miss seeing you and your family at church." I had just arrived at Aldi and had parked in the spot next to my friend's minivan.

"Yeah, well, we've been pretty busy. Our kids are all in sports now, and Word of Faith Church is too far away." Peggy opened the back of her van and began unloading the bags from her full cart.

"Oh, are you going to a different church?" I took my glove off and fumbled through my wallet, searching for a quarter in exchange for her cart.

"No. We aren't. I take it you still go to Word of Faith Church?"

"Yes," I replied. "There are a lot of others, though, who aren't coming anymore. Why did you leave?"

"It's just that..." Peggy hesitated and placed the last couple gallons of milk into her van. "You know, our 'Spirit-filled' church was said to have more of God than other churches, yet there was so much manipulation and ungodliness. We heard too many false prophecies and...well, if that's the best of Christianity, we don't want it."

"Really?" I couldn't think of anything to say, so I handed her my quarter.

"Yeah," she accepted the coin, and I took her cart. "I can't even read God's Word anymore because He doesn't keep His promises."

In the WoF movement, we took general principles of God's Word and claimed them as absolute promises. For instance, we presumed the commandment about honoring one's parents guaranteed a long life 100% of the time, especially if we quoted it to God and demanded that He 'keep His Word'.

> *Children, obey your parents in the Lord, for this is right. "Honor your father and mother" (which is the first commandment with a promise), "in order that it may be well with you, and you may live a long time on the earth." Ephesians 6:1–3 LEB*

God is sovereign over His Word, and while those who honor their father and mother are more *likely* to live a long life (because they discipline themselves and follow rules), God is not obligated to give *each* and *every* person who honors his parents a long life.

The precept that God blesses righteous people is not meant to be claimed as a promise in every case. For instance, because of Israel's sin, impending national disaster was imminent. Josiah, the most righteous king of Judah, died young to spare him from living through the tragedy, a blessing in disguise (2 Kings 23).

Most of the apostles' lives were cut short in martyrdom, not because they dishonored their parents, but because they were faithful to God. They demonstrated that truth is worth dying for.

There are times when God allows our suffering for higher purposes. Imagine if the righteous martyrs had declared the protection verses in Psalm 91 while they awaited their death sentences. At their stonings, Paul and Steven could have claimed the protection of angels so they would not hurt their feet upon the rocks—as if that would have stopped them from being stoned. Their testimony would have been weakened, though, and those who witnessed their deaths might not have come to saving faith.

"**A**ll he talks about is money. My parents were right," said my cousin, June, as we sat side by side in my grandparents' living room. "Churches only care about one thing."

"Actually, speaking about money has been one of the hardest areas for Pastor Bill to teach on," I defended.

"I've given up on trying new churches," she replied.

"**T**he cancer has progressed, and it's too late for medical treatment," said Jim's doctor. It had been a few months after Prophetess Deb predicted that he would live. Rather than accepting chemotherapy when the cancer was treatable, Jim had decided to walk in faith and stick to natural remedies. From this point forward, we would verbally cancel the doctor's words and make positive confessions. The physical symptoms were to be denied, and healing was to be claimed.

16 Jerry's Dance

Yes, remember your Creator now while you are young, before the silver cord of life snaps and the golden bowl is broken. Don't wait until the water jar is smashed at the spring and the pulley is broken at the well. For then the dust will return to the earth, and the spirit will return to God who gave it. Ecclesiastes 12:5-7 NLT

"The doctor found an increased number of cancer cells during Jerry's spinal tap," said Amanda when she called from Madison. "They're starting a new round of chemotherapy, and we'll be staying here for another week."

"I'm praying for him," I replied.

"Thanks. When he gets his healing, he's going to have an awesome testimony."

Though the cancer alternately waned, then surged stronger, we believed our faith-filled prayers would accomplish what the Scriptures said. I wondered how often Jerry's doctor at the University of Wisconsin Hospital and Clinics had seen this type of behavior with Christians. Perhaps his physician thought we were in denial, but we were determined to show him what real Christianity could do.

"I got an anointed healing cloth for Jerry," Amanda said. "A minister on the radio was giving them away, so I ordered one."

"Did you have to send money for it?"

"No, but they wanted a donation."

The idea of consecrated or anointed cloths, which are given away at the time of a donation, comes from a New Testament passage.

God gave Paul the power to perform unusual miracles. When handkerchiefs or aprons that had merely touched his skin were placed on sick people, they were healed of their diseases, and evil spirits were expelled. Acts 19:11–12 NLT

Did Paul ask for donations for the cloths that touched his body? No. Neither did Jesus and His disciples accept compensation for miracles. I found one instance in the Bible where payment was taken for a healing, but it ended poorly for the recipient.

A Syrian army commander, Naaman, suffered from a skin disease called leprosy (2 Kings 5:1-27). He was healed when he followed the instructions of the Israelite prophet, Elisha. Even though Naaman urged him to take payment, Elisha refused. (My own heart could have made wonderful sounding justifications, like suggesting that the profit could be used to further the gospel).

Elisha's servant, Gehazi, ran after Naaman to accept gifts for the miracle and received two talents of silver and some garments. For his sin, the leprosy of Naaman clung to Gehazi for the rest of his life.

According to the gospel of Matthew, Jesus told His disciples,

> *"Heal the sick, raise the dead, cleanse the lepers, cast out demons.* ***Freely you received, freely give****." Matthew 10:8 NASB*

A special cloth can become like a magical charm or amulet in which a person puts his faith. Not only is this a form of witchcraft, but it can cause a person to put the 'anointed leader' or the item on a pedestal, rather than looking to God.

Prophetess Julie was back at the Assembly of God and gave me another 'Word from the Lord'. "You will be rising up to a ministry like mine."

Could it be possible that our mortal enemy was trying to seduce me into the sin of pride? A recent word from Prophetess Deb declared, "In the next move of God, you will rise up to prominence and a new position. Everyone will be amazed." Lastly, there was the word from a speaker at the Minnesota women's conference, "You will be up on a stage in Sweden with lights shining down on you."

I considered how God had been refining me in the furnace of affliction and supposed that if people could see me in the spiritual realm, they'd be impressed. The next afternoon, during my time of prayer and meditation on the Scriptures, I began to drift off to sleep. When I awoke, this thought was in my mind.

When one has been refined to the nth degree, the tendency is to say, 'I'm so fine.'

*My meditation included memorizing Scripture and thinking about God's intended meaning. According to Psalm 1, we are to meditate on God's Word day and night, filling our minds with His instructions. I was not practicing—and do not advocate—contemplative/centering prayer, or lectio Divina, which closely resemble eastern, occult practices.

As to the thought regarding the tendency to say, 'I'm so fine', pride doesn't leave us alone as we grow in God. Rather, it lurks about in the shadows of our heart like the serpent in the Garden of Eden. It waits for an opportune moment to beguile us and impair our walk with Jesus. You may find this strange, but when this idea about becoming proud came to me, I didn't realize that my own prideful ideas about becoming a great prophetess had anything to do with the tendency to say, 'I'm so fine.'

Through the mouths of the 'prophetesses', our adversary had placed a tempting fruit before me, and in blindness, I took the bait. I couldn't wait for the next move of the Lord, assuming I'd be a greatly anointed prophetess or healer in the upcoming revival.

"**I**'d love to see Pastor Jamie get hit with laughter," I said, waving my hands in her direction as though I could fan the power toward Pastor Bill's wife.

"So would I," said my cousin, Laura. "Lord, send some of the anointing to her." Both of us giggled.

WoF Church had invited a Pentecostal radio talk show host to do our mid-week evening service, and a fire was burning in our church, consuming us.

One of the church elders, normally a serious and composed older gentleman, let out a huge guffaw and then snorted loudly. Tears streamed down his bright red face as he took off his glasses and pulled out a handkerchief.

The music leader acted like he was picking fruit from an invisible tree, and several people were rolling on the floor, practically splitting their sides open. Laura and I couldn't stop laughing.

"**Y**ou must be outside," I said. "I can hear the whippoorwill in the background." Kevin and I were talking on the phone.

"Yeah, I'm sitting in the backyard," he replied. "The phone doesn't have service inside the house."

"I miss hearing the whippoorwill every night."

"Why don't you come for a visit?" Kevin asked. "I promise I'll stay sober."

I began making plans for a two week stay so Kevin could have visitation with the kids and so I could be in my own home.

When the children and I arrived in Kentucky, our dog was visibly thinner, and we couldn't find any dog food to feed him. Empty beer cases were strewn about the yard, and there were four new cases of beer in the bedroom closet. Counselor Steve had been right when he said, "After you leave him, Kevin will begin drinking more for a while."

On the second evening of our stay, Kevin came into the guest bedroom where I was reading my Bible. Swaying from side to side, he slurred, "Please don't go back to Wisconsin. I need you to stay here."

"We can't move back while you are drinking, but we could live with you all the time if you would get sober."

Suddenly, he grabbed a rifle off the gun rack. Haphazardly pointing the barrel toward the next room, he said, "Might as well shoot myself right now." A thin, mobile home wall separated the barrel of the gun from our children as they played in their room.

Was the rifle loaded? Dare I try to wrestle it away from him? I breathed a silent prayer and paused a moment before speaking the next thought that entered my mind. "I should have you committed. You're crazy." (This wasn't a good thing to say. Please do *not* follow my example. Kevin had been bluffing, but many are serious when they threaten suicide).

Kevin began trying to put the gun in the rack as he pleaded, "Please don't have me committed. I won't do it again."

The following evening, Kevin was drunk again when he said, "Copper isn't coming when I call!" Having been out in the garage for 15 minutes, Kevin had burst in the kitchen door while I was scraping the rest of his unfinished supper into the garbage.

"What's unusual about that?"

"You don't even care about our dog!" Before he stormed out the door, he shouted, "I'm going to Ricky's church. You *better* show up by the time service starts!"

Within a moment, the receding sound of Kevin's 4-wheeler assured me that we could prepare to leave. "Hurry, kids. Let's load our suitcases into the van and go visit Louise and her family. We'll spend the night with them and leave for Wisconsin in the morning."

Two days later, when the kids and I were back in my parents' home, Mom and I stood in her kitchen as I poured myself a cup of coffee. "Jerry and Amanda are on their way home from Madison," said Mom. "Dr. Roth says Jerry has up to six weeks to live. A hospice nurse is going to visit with them tomorrow morning."

"How are they taking it?" I asked.

"Jerry's expecting his miracle and is talking about getting back into shape."

"I heard that Jim [the man with colon cancer] passed away," I said. "How is his wife doing?"

"I don't know, Ariel. Since their baby is only a few months old, it must be difficult."

That evening, most of our immediate family went to visit Amanda and Jerry. As we sang worship songs around his bed, he attempted to raise his arms in surrender. He didn't have the strength, and Amanda, from behind him, began supporting his uplifted arms.

The next morning, I drove to Jerry and Amanda's house to meet the hospice nurse. My sister was going to need help caring for her husband until his healing was manifested. When I arrived, Amanda met me at the door. "Jerry's sleeping soundly this morning."

With the anointed cloth in his hand and a death rattle in his chest, my brother-in-law's mouth was hanging open. Moments later, the hospice nurse, Amanda, Jerry's mother, and I stood at his bedside as he began to thrash about. Suddenly, he tensed his muscles and opened his eyes wide. The anxiety on his face turned into peace as he looked at the bedroom ceiling. It seemed as if he was a lost child who suddenly found his loving parent. In acquiescence, he closed his eyes and relaxed, relinquishing his soul. The silver cord of life had snapped. The golden bowl was broken.

In desperation, Amanda climbed on top of him. "No! You cannot die! The cancer will be defeated!" She quoted Pastor Bill's prophecy and began reciting Scripture verses, one after another. "You are the God who heals all our diseases. My husband will live, and not die. He shall declare the works of the Lord." Tears streamed down her face.

What do we do now? I wondered. *Do we try to resurrect him?* Other members of our church had made such attempts when their loved ones died.

Jerry's mother placed a gentle hand on Amanda's shoulder. "Let him go, Amanda. Let him go."

Privy to one of the most agonizing moments of my sister's life, her heartrending anguish tore at my heart as tears cascaded down my cheeks.

The following day, Amanda said, "I feel numb. I never imagined I'd be planning Jerry's funeral on my birthday." Our family members sat with Amanda around the kitchen table, helping with funeral arrangements. "How could God let this happen? Did we do something wrong?"

Like a football receiver who gets thrown to the ground by an unseen opponent, Jerry's death had completely blindsided Amanda.

"Was our faith too weak?" I wondered aloud.

If divine health is an absolute promise in God's Word, there were two other possibilities that I dared not mention. Either Jerry's faith was lacking, or…

The conversation of a former WoF Church member haunted me. "God doesn't keep His Word, and I can't bear to read my Bible anymore," Margaret had concluded…before she turned from Christianity.

My mind returned to the conversation as Amanda quoted James 5:14-15. *"Are any of you sick? You should call for the elders of the church to come and pray over you, anointing you with oil in the name of the Lord. Such a prayer offered in faith will heal the sick, and the Lord will make you well. And if you have committed any sins, you will be forgiven." [NLT]* Then she asked, "Our pastor and elders anointed Jerry. What about their faith? Why didn't their prayers heal him?"

"I don't know." I changed the subject without considering that we might have misunderstood the Scriptures. "Do you have any special music or songs to play at Jerry's ceremony?"

While we were planning the funeral, Kevin's employer talked to him about going for inpatient treatment. I found a Christian rehab center in Phoenix, Arizona, with the hopes that they would teach Kevin how to put Jesus first in his life.

The words of their wedding song, *The Dance* (composed by Tony Arata and sung by Garth Brooks) were playing.

> *And now, I'm glad I didn't know, the way it all would end, the way it all would go. Our lives are better left to chance, I could have missed the pain, but I'd have had to miss…the dance.*

If Amanda and Jerry had known the future, they might have made different choices…and missed the dance. Interestingly, there aren't any Bible passages where God encourages people to seek to know the future. Maybe it's better that way.

17 In the Midst of the Storm

You will keep in perfect peace all who trust in you, all whose thoughts are fixed on you! Isaiah 26:3 NLT

"It looks like your life is coming together, and mine has just fallen apart," said Amanda as we walked on the nature trail near our parent's house. "At least you have hope for your marriage. How's Kevin doing?"

"Well, now that he's through with detox, he's not swearing at me on the phone," I replied. "It was rough for a few days."

"Do you think he'll stay sober after treatment?"

"The six-month mark on the 'divine order prophecy' just passed," I said. "This should be the time when Kevin takes his place as the head of our family."

"It looks like storm clouds are gathering." Amanda pointed to the west.

"Yeah, we'd better turn around."

A few days later, the kids and I were taking care of the house in Kentucky while Kevin was in Arizona. At the Sunday service before Thanksgiving, Pastor John taught, "Many televangelists are teaching a false Gospel. Their self-centered lives and deceptive teachings are infiltrating Christianity and drawing people away from Jesus. Books, videos, and audio tapes fill the shelves in many Christian bookstores, enticing the naive to a different Jesus and a false gospel. They are wolves in sheep's clothing, who condemn stealing while they fleece their sheep."

Honestly, I never considered that he might have been speaking about any of my favorite teachers. When the sermon was over, Pastor John led me to the church kitchen, where the food for an entire Thanksgiving dinner was gifted to me. The prior year, when I had purchased Thanksgiving dinners for several other families, I never imagined I would be the recipient a year later.

When Kevin's treatment was over, I was concerned because he hadn't filled the empty place in his heart with Jesus. He smoked like a chimney, as though he had replaced alcohol with cigarettes, and he didn't say he was sorry or act repentant for the pain his drinking had caused our family.

By the third night after he came home, Kevin was drunk. I don't recall what set him off, but he grabbed a wooden chair from the kitchen and threw it into the living room. Rushing into my bedroom, I closed and locked the door, hoping the commotion wouldn't wake the kids. For several minutes, I heard smashing sounds.

After it became quiet, I tiptoed past the table set that Grandma had received on her wedding day more than fifty years earlier. Her ornately carved chair was lying on the floor, in pieces, and Kevin was passed out on the sofa.

Sobriety, which depleted our savings account, lasted three days. As I was crying, I realized there are other families in our society suffering because of the insanity of addiction. My heart felt sorrow for those marriages which are being torn to pieces and for those children who do not receive sacrificial love from one or both of their parents.

It would be easy to become angry with God for life's difficulties, but one benefit of enduring trials is that we develop an understanding of the problems which other people face. Our experiences help us empathize and come alongside of them as they trudge through similar situations.

The following day, while Kevin made a trip to the neighboring county for alcohol, the kids and I headed back to Wisconsin.

December 31 journal entry—

A few thoughts as the year ends: When times are troublesome, we can learn patience and endurance, and though we may not be walking on sunshine, there are many joys to be found. As we follow God and wait on Him, He carries us through our storms and trials. His Word can bring a measure of peace and contentment, even amid the storm.

18 Rose Among Thorns

Charm is deceptive, and beauty does not last;
but a woman who fears the LORD will be greatly praised.
Proverbs 31:30 NLT

The six-month 'divine order' prophecy held back, as did all the other 'Words from the Lord' that I had received. Days dragged into weeks, and then into months. One year had gone by, and then two. I couldn't believe Kevin was still drinking. Even so, I remained optimistic that God would deliver him soon. Tyler and Amber were hopeful too, as I instilled the same expectation in them.

In the meantime, Pastor Bill and his family upgraded another vehicle. Some of our church members were also prospering, though not any more than people in other congregations. It was as if we were in a two-tiered pyramid scheme, where Pastor Bill profited from those beneath him. Those of us on the lower rung didn't have hundreds of people under us giving into our pockets.

"I've been so tired and worn out." Annie had dark circles under her eyes.

"Her doctor wants to run some tests," Jeff added, as their toddler, Lilly, squirmed on his lap.

"What kind of tests?" I asked.

"Blood work."

A few months earlier, Annie and Jeff had run a marathon together. She had been strong, muscular, and lean, but now, her pale face contrasted with my parent's burgundy sofa, which she was leaning into. We would soon learn the serious nature of her illness.

A new book in our church bookstore caught my eye. It was called *Breaking Generational Curses*, by Marilyn Hickey. As I read through it, I felt inspired and better equipped to defeat the enemy that had brought the curse of alcoholism upon my husband. I came to believe that anger problems, mental illness, alcoholism, physical abuse, and adultery could be caused by generational curses that were handed down from one generation to the next. It felt empowering to learn how to defeat the enemy's strongholds, and my confidence for Kevin's deliverance grew stronger.

"Ariel, there's been a terrible news release," Mom called from the top of the steps. "A school shooting in Columbine, Colorado."

My irritable mood dissipated. Tyler and Amber had been getting on my nerves that morning, but it was my own fault. I was in a tizzy like Jesus' friend, Martha, when Mary was sitting at His feet. I had so much to do, and every time I walked through the kitchen, one of the kids would ask a question.

With the catastrophic news, I suddenly wanted to take my children in my arms and hold them. As other parents were mourning the massacre of their precious children, I had allowed myself to feel resentful of my two treasures. It always helps to see our situation from another perspective, which is why we should be in the Scriptures as often as possible, seeking to understand God's view, for His ways are higher than our ways, and His thoughts are higher than ours.

"The good news is that I'm pregnant." Annie smiled.

"The bad news is that Annie has Hodgkin's Lymphoma." Jeff's words hovered ominously in the air. "The doctor recommended we terminate the pregnancy."

"But that isn't us," said Annie.

As I looked at my aunt, I remembered how she'd helped me get into my locker that first day of high school. I thought of all the hours we'd spent picking cucumbers together and swimming in Mission lake afterwards, of picking choke cherries on my great grandparent's farm, and of nights spent at one another's houses. I could not bear the thought of losing her.

Annie reminded me of Queen Esther in the Old Testament. There were many women who went to King Xerxes (whose former wife had made herself beautiful outwardly) ahead of Esther. These candidates chose to decorate their outer person with jewels and gold. Esther, however, chose to be simple in her outward apparel, while beautiful on the inside.

Our Heavenly King is not impressed by worldly adornments which fade with time, but He cares about the inner life of a woman who reflects His image back to Him.

WoF Church promoted a Ladies' Conference at a church in Saint Paul, MN. During the weekend, there were many prophetic words spoken. At one session, the female reverend prophesied, "Israel is coming into her darkest hour, and five hurricanes will hit the state of Florida before the summer is over."

How nice to have the inside scoop on the news before it happens, I thought.

However, by the end of the summer, Florida wasn't hit by five hurricanes, and Israel's darkest hour didn't occur.

Annie called to let us know that her second flower had been born. When Rose's lungs were mature enough, labor was induced so Annie could be given a more aggressive type of chemotherapy. Even though my aunt took a chance with her own survival, the Hodgkin's Lymphoma went into remission shortly after Rose's birth.

In *Foxe's Book of Martyrs,* I read about a 22-year old woman named Mrs. Cicely Ormes. She was brought to the chancellor, who would have allowed her to live if she would have promised to go to church and to keep her beliefs to herself. Convinced the church was idolatrous, she wouldn't consent.

The chancellor said he didn't want to condemn her because 'she was an ignorant, foolish woman'. She replied that 'however great his desire might be to spare her sinful flesh, it could not equal her inclination to surrender it up in so great a quarrel.'

On September 23, 1557, she was brought to the stake. After declaring her faith to the people, she laid her hand on the stake, and said, *"Welcome thou cross of Christ."* When the fire was lit, she said, "My soul doth magnify the Lord, and my spirit doth rejoice in God my Saviour."[21] (Emphasis mine).

Throughout history, many Christians have lived righteously for the Lord, even when they faced destitution, persecution, and/or death. These martyrs had the type of faith that saw past this tiny realm of time into a magnificent eternity with their Creator. Our family would need the martyr type of faith for Annie's next battle.

My aunt had been pushing herself physically, exhausting her body through hard work. She'd become very tired again, and her doctor wanted to run some lab work. We hoped the fatigue was not caused by a new malignancy.

"Obedience brings us to a place where God can bless us," said Pastor Bill. "Amen?"

"Amen," we parroted.

We learned about living in integrity in order to position ourselves to receive from God. Pastor Bill then took us through many Bible passages and entreated us to be honest, forgiving, kind, and loving. Although purity of heart was taught, our focus seemed to be about attaining prosperity, success, health, power, and happiness in this life.

A few months later, we had another guest speaker. "Jesus would probably own a private jet if He lived in these days. That way, He could travel faster and reach more people with the Gospel." Televangelist J.D. kept us laughing the entire evening. In the church offering that night, he brought in as much money as Kevin made in six months.

While Annie was resting at home, Amanda and I sat across the table from Jeff in McDonalds as Tyler, Amber, and Lilly enjoyed the Play place. "If we can get the Hodgkin's to go back into remission, we can do a bone marrow transplant," explained Jeff. "The doctor said that Hodgkin's comes back with a vengeance. Most people lose the battle in this stage."

In the following church service, our health and wealth type of faith was given a boost.

"Believe that you are the body of the living Christ, who came to destroy the works of the devil," said Guest Speaker Alex. "Really believe for supernatural, spectacular things. This church is strategically located in Wisconsin. God is pouring out His Spirit between the Midwest cities. God is getting ready to explode in Wisconsin."

Loud cheering erupted from our congregation.

"**T**he cancer seems to be slowing down," said the doctor as he palpated the lymph nodes under Annie's arms and in her groin area. "How have you been feeling?"

"Very tired," Annie replied.

"You've dropped a few pounds."

"I've lost my appetite, but not my hair." Annie gave a weak smile.

My aunt was given a different chemo-cocktail that wouldn't cause her blood levels to drop as severely as the prior formulation. Even so, recovery periods were taking longer, and her blood levels needed to come up before another treatment. If only the cancer would be poisoned before Annie's body succumbed to death.

"When we pray in tongues, it's supposed to edify and strengthen us, but I'm perplexed," I said. "I spent an hour using my prayer language, and yet, as soon as Tyler and Amber were up and asking questions, I got frustrated and angry." Aunt Mae and I were walking on the road in front of her neighbor's house, and Tyler and Amber followed closely behind, having a conversation of their own. "Does it matter to you that the gift of tongues isn't accepted at your church?" I asked.

"I've thought about it," she replied, "and I'm OK with that. My Christian walk involves much more than speaking in tongues."

Truer words could not have been said. Time and again, Aunt Mae had gone out of her way to visit people and tell them the Gospel, whether they were in prison, in the hospital, or down the road. She and Uncle Pat invited friends and neighbors to Bible studies in their living room, brought relatives to church, and had been on multiple missionary trips.

"We've been living with Dad and Mom for three years," I said. "I'm so tired of waiting. I almost wish God would take over Kevin's will and force him to stop drinking."

"Having a free will means there's pain, suffering, and heartache in life," Aunt Mae replied. "But it's good that God gives us the chance to choose for ourselves."

"These have been the hardest two years of my life," said Amanda. "I've missed Jerry's affection on his birthday, during each holiday, and on our anniversary."

"There aren't many like him." I replied. We visited in Mom's kitchen as I prepared supper.

"No, there aren't," Amanda smiled. "Have you heard any news about Annie?"

"No, but I'll be taking her to the doctor tomorrow."

The next day, as her physician palpated Annie's lymph nodes, he said, "There are quite a few more lumps. By the time your body is ready for another round of chemotherapy, I'm afraid the cancer will have advanced too far."

No! This cannot be! Life can't go on without my sweet aunt.

The exam room, with its clean, white walls and hard tile floor, suddenly seemed sanitary and cold. Annie didn't reply. With my thoughts, I cancelled the words her doctor had spoken, silently confessed several healing verses, and tried to believe she would overcome. *By Jesus' stripes, Annie is healed. You are the God who heals all our diseases. Annie will live and not die, and she will declare the glory of God.*

"It's time to put your home in order," said the doctor.

Again, Annie was silent. It felt as though the air had been sucked from the room.

Lord, help her to live and be able to raise her girls, in Jesus' name. I looked out of the window and watched people walking in the sunny parking lot. How could they continue as if everything was alright while my gentle-natured aunt was lying on a white, papered exam table being given a death sentence?

After the doctor left the room, Annie began to get dressed. Without a word regarding herself, she said, "I'm concerned about Jeff. This is going to be hard for him."

A month later, when I was visiting Annie, she said, "My body feels heavy, like a burden to hold up." Wearily, she leaned her gaunt form against the wall just inside the entrance to her home, out of breath after the short walk to her mailbox and back. After a moment, she gathered her strength and walked to the recliner in her living room. Looking out of her window, she said, "I love watching the sun set over the bay."

"It looks so beautiful," I replied.

"A few years ago, I was outside with the chainsaw, clearing away the trees that hid the water from my view, and now I can barely stand." Annie paused a moment. "Has anything changed with Kevin?"

"Nothing that shows, but I believe he'll quit drinking soon." I would not make a negative confession. I began to wonder if I had done the wrong thing in moving out of our Kentucky home. Maybe if Kevin was the one who had to give up our house, as well as the sounds of the whippoorwill and tree frogs at night, he'd be more motivated to change.

A few days later while talking on the phone, I suggested to Kevin, "If you would find somewhere else to live, the kids and I could move back home."

"What if I move in with Bubba?"

"Can you work that out?" I asked.

Annie was in the hospital, and her siblings came from out of town to visit while she was still conscious. Though she was very weak, she insisted on spending some time alone with each sister and brother. She also asked to speak with Amanda.

"Will you help Jeff through this? You'll understand what he'll be going through."

"I'm not sure if I'd know how to help, but I could try." Amanda bit her lip.

Tyler came down with the influenza and got a painful ear infection. Hesitant to use antibiotics, I bought homeopathic ear drops from a local health food co-op. In my view, going to the doctor would have been an expression of doubt, which would have kept my son from receiving a miracle. I put my trust in the WoF version of spiritual warfare, positive confession, and the divine health doctrine.

After several weeks, Tyler couldn't hear out of his ear. On the Internet, I read that it could take six weeks for hearing to return to normal after an eardrum ruptures, which can happen in untreated infections. I recalled the astonishing third-hand account about the baby who grew limbs in church, as well as many other miraculous stories from ministers over the years. I decided to give Tyler's ear a little time...and a lot of faith.

Like myself, many parents place the health of their children in the WoF teachings, rather than in the hands of trained medical professionals, often with detrimental consequences. Unbeknownst to us at the time, a hidden disease had entered Tyler's head, destroying the bone behind his ear and making its way toward his brain.

The head of Annie's hospital bed was at a 45-degree angle, and the heart monitor was steadily beeping. Jeff gently combed the few hairs on her head as family members filled the room, singing, praying, and applying lotion to Annie's mottled feet. Her mouth hung half open, reminding me of Jerry's last hour of life.

"Annie's teeth look perfectly white and straight," I admired aloud.

"Yeah," said Jeff. "She insisted on brushing them last night. When I tucked her in bed, she said, 'Don't worry. Everything will be alright. See you later.'"

My eyes filled with tears.

"We didn't say goodbye," Jeff faltered, "because that's too final. Two hospital volunteers told us about Jesus, and we know that if we don't see one another again in this life, we'll meet in Heaven."

When Mom and I left Bellin hospital for the night, Annie's oxygen levels had dropped to 90 percent, and her heart was racing over 100 beats per minute...unable to keep up with her body's needs.

As we walked to the car, Mom said, "I wish Annie could've walked across the platform at the crusade we took her to."

"I don't understand why Benny didn't go near the wheelchair section," I replied.

"You know," Mom paused. "I can't imagine Jesus doing miracles with such flamboyance on a stage."

"I know. Jesus didn't try to bring attention to Himself."

"Ariel, is there any chance we've been wrong about Benny Hinn?"

"I don't think so. He seems so sincere for the Lord."

"But what about all his money?"

"Well, Mom, we know that Jesus was rich. He wants us to be wealthy, doesn't He?"

"I've been wondering about that. If I hadn't heard the Word of Faith teachings, I don't think I would've come to that conclusion."

"**A**nd now, I'm glad I didn't know, the way it all would end, the way it all would go. Our lives are better left to chance. I could have missed the pain, but I'd have had to miss...the dance." The same song Amanda had used at Jerry's funeral was playing as Amanda and I sat down on the hard, wooden pew. My sister's thin shoulders quivered as she wept.

Brilliant rays of the sunshine radiated through the colorful, stained-glass church windows, reaching eagerly for Annie's elegant maple casket. Roman Chamomile, Frankincense, and Patchouli scented the air as the middle-aged priest walked around the pall swinging a silver censer. The wisps of swirling, dancing incense—illuminated by the shafts of sunlight—rose above the coffin.

"Annie and I were visiting the other day," said Father Lewandowski, "and she told me about a dream she had a few days ago. In that dream, she saw her casket...but she was not in the casket." He paused. "Annie saw herself *above* the casket...and she was dancing."

Perhaps I was not the only person who looked above Annie's coffin—now closed over the still, lifeless form of her earthly abode—and imagined her there, twirling amid the glimmering rays of sunshine. Energetic, spunky, and free.

The bitterly cold, north wind pushed a polar vortex into Wisconsin, blowing furiously as Amanda and I hurried through the church parking lot toward my 10-year-old Mercury Sable. Once inside the car, I started the engine and turned the heater on low, knowing that the air wouldn't heat up for at least 10 minutes, *if* such frigid air could be made warm at all.

"Annie asked if I would help Jeff get through this." Amanda's teeth were chattering.

"She mentioned that she was considering who might make a good mom for her girls," I replied.

"Yeah, it's too bad I don't have feelings for Jeff. I really do love those girls."

The somber-looking, black hearse, with its headlights on, pulled toward the exit drive of the parking lot. Though Annie's body was on its way to the mortuary, she left the world a better place, with two flowers among the thorns. Lilly and Rose.

From the WoF perspective, death looked like defeat to me. Our prayers and faith didn't bring my aunt to health. Had we failed Annie and Jeff and their children?

As I lay in bed, stung by Annie's death, I realized that Jesus' crucifixion initially seemed like defeat, even though it was a victory. Likewise, as the disciples were martyred one after another, they were not overcome. These believers triumphantly and gloriously stood in their faith during persecution, torture, and death.

I thought of Luke, the young man at Full Gospel Tabernacle, whose last cognitive moments were spent reading the Bible to his stepson. I considered Jerry, who raised his weary arms in worship to the Lord the last time he was conscious. I recalled how Annie had given her heart to the Lord amid her illness. She knew she was on her way to heaven, which is why she would never say goodbye, but always said 'see you later'. Christian deaths, which might look like defeat from our earthly vantagepoint, are victorious from a heavenly perspective.

Then, when our dying bodies have been transformed into bodies that will never die, this Scripture will be fulfilled: "Death is swallowed up in victory. O death, where is your victory? O death, where is your sting?" 1 Corinthians 15:54–55 NLT

19 Invisible Illusions

"The infiltration of the occult into the Church today has been cleverly planned and well-executed, not only by its visible proponents ***but by its invisible ones****."[22] (Emphasis mine)*
—Walter Martin, Jill Martin Rische, and Kurt Van Gorden

"What is the occult?" I asked, as Mom and I cleaned the kitchen after dinner.

Mom looked up from the dishwasher. "Occult means hidden, mystical, or secret. The occult is Satan's source of magic and his forbidden knowledge, such as fortune telling, psychic abilities, and divination."

"So, the occult is composed of two aspects?"

"Yes," Mom clarified. "Satan's power, which makes man feel like gods, and the mystical knowledge of the spirits."

"That reminds me of the temptation in the Garden of Eden, where Satan told Eve that she could be like God [having supernatural power] and could have special knowledge. Do you think the Tree of the Knowledge of Good and Evil might have been an introduction to the occult?"

"We cannot know for certain, but Gnostics believe the fruit had psychedelic properties to induce trances," Mom replied. "These altered states of consciousness connect one's mind to evil spirits, and demons mingle truth with their deception. They provide evil knowledge which is designed to lead people astray. The Bible doesn't say this, but mysticism may have its roots in the Garden of Eden."

"I've heard that Satan can use his power to remove disease so a person will believe false doctrine."

"Yes, Ariel. When evil spirits give supernatural experiences, like visions or healings, people become convinced that they've found truth."

"That's shrewd," I replied.

"I've read that demons pose as deceased relatives, Bible characters, and angels. Some even claim to be God, or Jesus," said Mom.

"They do?"

"Yes. There are people who claim their books were dictated by spirits that pretended to be Jesus, or God."

"Demons co-author books?"

"Yes," Mom replied. "Some spirits take control of a person's hands and write or type. Others put words into a person's mind or speak through their mouth."

"That's almost hard to believe. Do you think people could be making these experiences up?"

"Some might be, but well-known occult experts, like Walter Martin, tell us about automatic writing and channeling. God warns us not to dabble in the occult because the spirits give false information."

Crossing over to her desk, Mom picked up her Bible and found a passage.

When you enter the land the LORD your God is giving you, do not learn to imitate the detestable ways of the nations there. Let no one be found among you who sacrifices their son or daughter in the fire, who practices divination or sorcery, interprets omens, engages in witchcraft, or casts spells, or who is a medium or spiritist or who consults the dead. Anyone who does these things is detestable to the LORD; because of these same detestable practices the LORD your God will drive out those nations before you. Deuteronomy 18:9–12 NIV

After I read the passage, Mom took her Bible back to the desk and said, "A woman named Alice Bailey co-authored 19 books with the help of a spirit guide, which taught that Lucifer is the light bringer and that the God of the Bible is an evil tyrant."

"Really?" I resumed cleaning the counters.

"Yes, and many consider Alice to be the mother of the New Age Movement."

"So, new age spirituality is of the occult?" I asked.

"Yes. Though new agers don't realize it, they tap into the same power source as witches and Satanists."

I stopped wiping the counter next to the stove and turned to face Mom again. "Are all cults part of the occult?"

"No. The Jehovah's Witnesses, for instance, are a cult because they claim to be Christian while they diminish Jesus' position, but they don't dabble with spirits or use occult power." Mom returned to loading the dishwasher.

After a few minutes, she asked, "Did you hear that Angie [from church] had a serious car accident and is in intensive care?"

"What happened?"

"She had a head-on collision on the icy roads last weekend."

"Oh, my goodness! Is she okay?"

"She can't walk," Mom replied. "Doctors expect her to be in a rehab center for several months."

"Didn't another one of your friends from church have a crippling accident recently?"

"Yes, Laura is still recuperating." Mom closed the dishwasher and began washing the pots and pans in the sink.

"Shouldn't our church members have less accidents than others?" I asked. "I mean, we put on the armor of God, do spiritual warfare, and quote Bible verses about protection."

"Yes, we shouldn't be sick as often either."

"Sometimes it seems as though we have more diseases and accidents than other people, as if we're opening a door to the enemy."

Just then, Tyler walked into the kitchen for a snack. "Mom, the bone behind my ear hurts really bad, and the ibuprofen doesn't seem to be working."

"Would you like something more for the pain?"

"Yeah, maybe that would help." Tyler set a bowl on the kitchen table, filled it with cereal, and headed to the refrigerator for milk.

"We need to bind up the spirits of sickness, disease, and pain," I said.

As he stood by the refrigerator, I placed my hand over Tyler's ear and began to rebuke the devil and all his cohorts.

Mom joined us, laying her hands on his shoulders. "You are the God who heals Tyler," she prayed. "You sent Your Word and healed his disease. We thank You that Tyler is healed and made whole, in Jesus' name."

"Amen," we said together.

As Mom went into the living room to watch TBN, I handed two acetaminophen tablets to Tyler.

"Do you think it's a good idea to move back home while Dad's still drinking?" Tyler popped the tablets into his mouth and took a swallow of water.

"It'll be quieter there, and we won't have people stopping in to visit so often. That'll make it easier to get our school work done."

"But what if Dad comes over drunk?" Tyler started eating.

"He promised to stay away when he's drinking."

Tyler swallowed. "Yeah, but can we trust him?"

"I hope so." As I left the kitchen, I said, "Maybe if I put a Benny Hinn CD in your stereo, the anointing will heal your ear while you sleep."

Just as I wasn't aware of the hidden disease, which was creeping toward my son's brain, many Christians are incognizant of the fact that the occult is at work within churches around the world.

Because the doctrines of New Age Spirituality (NAS) are seeping into Christianity through books and music, I feel it is important to make some distinctions between God's power and the occult force of our mortal enemy.

> *For we are not fighting against flesh-and-blood enemies, but against evil rulers and authorities of the unseen world, against mighty powers in this dark world, and against evil spirits in the heavenly places. Ephesians 6:12 NLT*

Various people groups attempt to explain, interact with, and manipulate the power of the occult. This force has many names, including Prana, Chi, Ki, life force, life energy, Ka, Pneuma, the Presence, and the 'I am', to name a few.

Several of the most common techniques used to interact with this spiritual energy include yoga, positive confession, visualization, tarot card reading, fortune-telling, guided imagery, automatic writing, Reiki, acupuncture, and eastern meditation. (In biblical meditation, one fills the mind, thinking about the Scriptures. Eastern meditation does the opposite, emptying the mind of all thoughts—entering the silence—making one susceptible to the influence of evil spirits).

While most of these practices are generally known to be anti-Christian, some of the techniques (which connect a person to satanic communication and experiences) have been making inroads into mainstream Christianity for several decades. A basic knowledge of the occult can keep us from inadvertently taking part in these dangerous activities. Because spirits of the occult usually claim to have humanity's best interests at heart and pretend to be loving, they appear trustable. We must consider what the entities of various religions teach to determine whether they are good or evil so we know whether to believe what they purport. What do the ethereal beings of satanism, witchcraft, and NAS say?

Satanists recommend we do what we desire. 'Do what thou wilt' is their motto. It's OK to cheat on one's spouse, to lie, to smash the cheek of those who slap you, and to step on the weak.

Wiccans and witches use incantations to manipulate the free will of others. For instance, a love spell will be used to turn a partner back to the one they have chosen to leave.

The spirit guides behind NAS align themselves with those of witchcraft, satanism, and luciferianism (the belief that the fallen supernatural entity, Lucifer/Sophia, is the giver of light and wisdom who helps mankind attain divinity) in speaking against the Bible. They may attempt to foretell events, but they do not have a record of accurate and precise prophecy.

These entities initially portray themselves as lovely, mingling good advice and Bible verses with their pleasant-sounding ideas, such as 'all paths lead to God', but their goal is to alienate us from God. Eventually, spirit guides present their evil nature, becoming oppressive to their host, especially if he or she considers turning to the real Jesus.

In contrast to the spirits of the occult, the God of the Bible tells us to be honest, to keep our promises even when it hurts, to turn the other cheek when someone slaps us, to be faithful to our spouse, to be generous to the poor, to be humble, and so forth. He sets an example of love in that Jesus was willing to suffer the shame and humiliation of the tortuous crucifixion and to sacrifice His life for those who would choose Him. There is no shapeshifting with God.

Jesus Christ is the same yesterday and today and forever. Hebrews 13:8 NASB

Now that we've contrasted the morality of Christianity with occult religions, let us compare the knowledge of the Lord Most High with the gnosis of demons. Regarding their myth about Sophia, Gnostics admit that she didn't know what her dreaming would produce when she fell. Neither is Sophia able to foretell the future. In Genesis 41:1-37, the evil spirits who gave esoteric (private, secret) information to Pharaoh's diviners were not privy to Pharaoh's disturbing dreams. Therefore, the demons could not provide an interpretation to Pharaoh's seers.

At the same time, the Hebrew slave named Joseph sought the Lord's wisdom on the matter and learned the dreams from the all-knowing God. Joseph gave an explanation which warned of a severe, seven-year famine and then provided wise advice that prevented the starvation of many nations when the prediction came to pass.

In Daniel 2:1-49, the evil spirits of King Nebuchadnezzar's astrologers could not tell him what his dream was, and therefore, couldn't explain its meaning. Daniel, a devout servant of God, was supernaturally given the dream and its interpretation from the Lord.

Not only are demons inferior when it comes to advice and knowledge, but their strength is no match for that of the Most High. Pharaoh's magicians were unable to perform signs as powerful as those God did through Moses. Neither could they reverse the demonstrations of the Lord. (Exodus 7:1-12:32)

In 1 Kings 18:18-40, we read of a showdown to establish whether King Ahab and Queen Jezebel's god was greater or lesser than the God of Elijah. The 450 prophets of Baal cried out with loud voices all day, trying to convince Baal to magically light their sacrifice on fire. They cut themselves until their blood flowed, but Baal failed. Yet, with Elijah's first prayer, the God of Israel lit His sacrifice on fire, even after it had been doused with water repeatedly.

We might also examine how differently the Holy Spirit operates in comparison to the spirits of the occult. When God gave prophetic words to His prophets, they had complete faculty of their mind, and He never expected them to go into an empty-headed trance so He could take over. While some occultists become so attuned to their spirit guides that they retain their own thoughts while channeling entities, most need to disengage from their mind/soul so the demon can completely take over.

New Year's Day—

As I prayerfully reviewed the past year of my life and looked toward 2003, I understood that there were more corrupt tendencies in my soul than I was aware of. I continued to be hopeful that a move of God would set Kevin free from alcohol, and I listened to tapes from 'Spirit-filled' deliverance ministries that specialized in exorcisms. These claimed that their warlike prayer techniques were the answer to breaking the demonic strongholds and generational curses that held people captive to sinful behaviors like lust, greed, and drunkenness. (While demons can cause their victims to be lustful, greedy, and drunk, most people who practice these sins are probably not possessed by evil spirits).

"Ariel, come see this program on my computer!" Mom was excited. "Watch how I can go from one Bible version to another and compare the verses." She made a few clicks with her mouse to demonstrate. "I can even look up words in the Hebrew and Greek Lexicons."

"You can look words up in their original languages?" I watched over her shoulder as Mom sat at her desk.

"Yes, and I have access to Matthew Henry and Albert Barnes." Mom pointed to the long list of commentaries on her computer screen. "The men who wrote these were experts in Jewish history, their culture, and the religious beliefs during Bible times."

"Interesting." The left side of my neck burned, and I rubbed the corresponding trapezius muscle.

Mom was setting an example of good biblical exegesis for me. Having read through the Bible about 13 times, it was time for me to begin studying the Scriptures on a deeper level.

Day after day, I prayed and waited, my life on hold as the ruts in Kevin's brain became more firmly entrenched. Week after week, I felt as though I was in a limbo of Kevin's making. Month after month, the kids and I remained on stand-by. Eleven long years had passed since Church Leader Judy prophesied that Kevin and I would teach marriage classes together. The kids and I had been with Dad and Mom for three years, and I was anxious to be in my own home.

In Kentucky, our little pond at the bottom of the hill rippled its welcome, and tall cedars waved a greeting as we drove up our long, gravel driveway. Barren oak trees had blanketed the ground with a thick covering of brown leaves, making it feel as if we were driving into a campground.

Earlier that morning, we had driven past a frozen Wisconsin lake where four-wheel-drive trucks were solidly parked alongside ice shanties. How thankful I was that Kevin had moved in with his friend, Bubba, for I had missed our land, the warmer weather, and our secluded country home.

Now that Kevin was the one who was displaced from our house, I hoped he would feel the consequences of his drinking and work harder to be reunited with us.

"But I don't...wanna leave. Can't I stay here tonight?" Kevin was slurring his words.

"No, Kevin."

"C'mon. I just wanna...be a...family again," Kevin pleaded, wiping a tear from his eye. He hiccupped, buried his face in his hands, and started sobbing.

I felt no sympathy, only annoyance that he was breaking his promises. Again. "I'm calling Bubba to come get you. You're drunk."

"Dammit! You don't care a thing about me! I should just end it all!"

My chest tightened, and my breath caught in my throat. Blinking back tears, I turned my back to him and headed to the bathroom, determined not to let him see me cry.

"Mom!" Amber called to me through the bathroom door.

"Can't it wait until I'm out?" I blew my nose, wishing I had more patience, yet needing a few moments alone. The pleasant melody of tree frogs drifted through my open bathroom window, filling the country air with song as I leaned against the wall, trying to find peace. I took a deep breath in and slowly exhaled...

"But Dad just walked through the house with a shotgun!" Amber's voice was shrill, and her words frantic. "And he cocked it on the way out the door!"

When the bullet exploded from the barrel of Kevin's rifle, a burst of heat surged through my entire body, starting at my feet and exiting through my head. *What was that?! Did I literally feel Kevin's spirit leaving our world?*

The tree frogs became silent. Amber screamed! Rushing to the kitchen door, I grabbed the doorknob. I halted. *What might I find?*

Terrified, I opened the door and looked toward the garage.

Jauntily walking alongside the boat, as if he hadn't a care in the world, Kevin was holding the gun in one hand and straightening the canvas boat cover with the other.

The heat surge which I'd experienced when I heard the gunshot was not Kevin's spirit leaving our world, but rather, it was my body's alarmed physiological reaction. "Why did you fire the gun off?" I attempted to conceal my distress.

"I thought you might let me stay here," came the nonchalant reply. Kevin continued walking around the boat, not bothering to look in my direction. His pursuit of alcohol seemed to have destroyed his ability to care, to empathize, to be honest, and to love.

Backing into the house, I turned toward Amber. She was talking to me, but I couldn't concentrate on what she was saying. My brain seemed to be going numb.

As I struggled to fall asleep that night, I wondered, *What should a woman do when her drunk husband haphazardly carries a loaded shotgun through the house, cocks it in front of the children, and then shoots it off outside?* The following morning, I headed to the police station.

"When did the gunshot occur?" asked the middle-aged, female police officer. The shiny badge on her uniform caught my eye as it mirrored the light from above, briefly reflecting it onto a clipboard she was preparing for me.

"About 7:00 PM last night." My voice caught in my throat, and I felt my right eyelid twitching. The small, windowless room—devoid of pictures and decorations—felt suffocating. I could barely focus as Officer Smith slid a clipboard and pen across the table to me.

"I need you to fill this out."

My hands trembled as I wrote down the events that had transpired the previous evening. After filling out the forms, Officer Smith explained how a Domestic Violence Order could help.

Kevin hadn't been physically violent but using a gun in such a manner worked against him. The judge granted the order, stating that Kevin was not to be within 2500 feet of me when drinking.

"**F**ire!" shouted Benny Hinn from the stage, as he violently waved his suit coat toward the crowd.

"Did you see that, Mom?" asked Tyler. "A whole group of people fell backwards at the same time."

"Yeah, and their eyes were closed. There's a powerful force in that auditorium."

Benny always led beautiful worship songs and spoke in soothing, hypnotic tones. His words seemed to drip sincere love and adoration unto the Lord. After a time of mesmerizing worship, people testified about their miracles on stage. Tyler, Amber, and I were glued to the TV whenever *This is Your Day* was on.

"**Y**ou're it!" Breathlessly, Tyler tagged Louise's son, Elijah, and dodged off. Chasing one another across the small, wooded park, the youthful exuberance of our boys filled the air. Our daughters, Amber and Hannah, quietly played in the sandbox.

"Have you read any good books lately?" I asked.

"I'm just finishing *Christianity in Crisis* by Hank Hanegraaff." Louise began taking food out of her cooler. "Have you read that one?"

"I skimmed it once at my Mom's house," I replied. "Hank criticized my favorite ministers. Christians shouldn't be so judgmental, should we?"

Louise pressed her lips together momentarily as a playful breeze toyed with the pile of napkins on the table. She quickly set an apple on top of them. "Paul warned the Corinthians and the Ephesians about false apostles, didn't he?"

"I guess he did," I replied. After a moment of silence, I asked, "What do you think of the book?"

"I think Mr. Hanegraaff raises some good points." Louise sat down across from me. "The Word of Faith movement paints a picture of God as though He is impotent. Do you believe God can't do anything on earth without our permission?"

"Well, that was a challenge when I first heard it, but Pastor Bill did a good job teaching it." My mouth suddenly went dry, and I took a long drink from my water bottle. "You see, God gave dominion over the earth to Adam, but he sinned, turning jurisdiction over to Satan. Then, the devil lost the authority to Jesus at the crucifixion." My neck felt hot, so I pulled my hair into a ponytail as I spoke. "Jesus gave the authority to His followers, so we're the ones in charge. Now, God needs our permission to do anything here on earth."

"Well, that's a mouthful," Louise laughed, though not in an unkind way. Then she probed, "Do you believe everything Pastor Bill teaches?"

"Yes. I've never had reason to question his teachings. He's honest, sincere, and very knowledgeable about the Bible." Then I added, "And he graduated from Rhema Bible College."

"Rhema?" Louise's eyebrows went up.

"Yeah. Kenneth Hagin, the founder of Rhema, got visions directly from God. That's why the Word of Faith message has more truth than other Christian denominations."

"What if Kenneth Hagin is wrong?" asked Louise. "Mohammad [the founder of Islam] had visions and conversations with a spirit that pretended to be Gabriel."

"I suppose Christian leaders would be standing up against his teachings, wouldn't they?"

"Many of them are," Louise replied.

"No one on TBN refutes the Word of Faith message."

"Hmm. I suppose it wouldn't make sense for a Word of Faith network to feature Kenneth Copeland one hour and have someone dispute his teachings the next."

I looked over Louise's shoulder to the entrance of the park as Julie's station wagon and Teresa's van were pulling in. "Looks like we'll have enough kids for a ball game."

I could understand that Jehovah's Witnesses—who won't consider evidence against their organization—have closed minds, but I was blinded to my own heart's deception.

"**A** time is coming and may already be here," stated Pastor John, "when people *will let their hearts deceive them* into believing evil doctrines. There are many Christians who would rather hear messages that do not convict them than hear a word from the Lord. Open your Bibles with me to the book of Second Timothy, chapter four, starting at verse three."

As I unzipped my Thomas Kinkade Bible cover and looked for the gold-edged Timothy tab, I thought, *Goodness, it's unfortunate that [other] people aren't more serious about God.* Isn't it amazing how we don't usually consider that the great end-times deception within Christianity might include ourselves?

"I'm reading from the New Living Translation today," continued Pastor John. "For a time is coming when people will no longer listen to sound and wholesome teaching. They will follow their own desires and will look for teachers who will tell them whatever their itching ears want to hear." Pastor John looked up from his Bible.

My mind began to wander when Pastor John said, 'itching ears,' and I thought about Tyler's earache. We'd been steadfastly praying, yet there seemed to be no change in the physical realm. I dared not speak those words aloud, nor think about the illness, for I was afraid my thoughts might attract disease.

I considered Dana's husband, Allen, when he'd been diagnosed with a lymphoma. I recalled the sensation of power as it flowed through my hands into Allen's body while several of us Word of Faith believers prayed for him. Allen said he felt it, too.

A few days later, Allen stated, "I no longer see death when I look in the mirror."

The following week, when his doctor took a sample from Allen's hip bone, he had said, "We must have made a mistake. There are no cancer cells."

My mind returned to the sermon.

"It's exciting to hear a guest speaker give a prophetic word," said Pastor John. "But we also ought to desire to be convicted of our sin so we can turn from it and be changed."

After the sermon, one of the eldest women in our congregation approached me. Virginia's love for the Lord was apparent to all, and I had deep respect and admiration for her. "Ariel, I had a dream about you and Kevin last night," she said. "You were in a white, wedding gown at the front of the church, and Pastor John was performing a marriage rededication ceremony. Kevin is going to get delivered."

Depression is usually the root cause of our desire for those things we use to temporarily lift ourselves out of our emotional suffering. Things that invigorate us, emotionally charge us, or dull our pain can develop a strong hold on our lives. Unfortunately, these temporary distractions, like the prophecies I received, will never be enough, and may leave us in worse shape.

We need to replace the pain, hunger, and emptiness inside our hearts with the truth that comes from knowing our Creator and finding our intrinsic value in Him. Then we can begin to experience emotional health in the deepest recesses of our souls, which sets us free to turn our minds more fully to our Savior.

While I do not have all the answers, there were a few things that helped me make it through my valley. The Scriptures change the way we view God, ourselves, and our world. Renewed thinking can modify our brain's neurochemistry, which results in neurotransmitters that make us feel better. I began to see God's goodness in everything and thought more about things that are noble, true, praiseworthy, and lovely.

Creating new thought patterns, however, is not a complete solution to all cases of depression, which has many contributing factors. Our genetics, environment, health, and habits all play a role in how we feel. While I faced my struggles, I found several key areas helped to uplift me over the years. These included: taking walks with my children and relatives, serving others by making meals for them, counseling with a therapist, visiting friends, leading Sunday school classes for women, writing skits, teaching kids' church on Sunday nights, getting enough sleep, and eating healthy food. Yet, even all those things were not enough to fully lift my spirits.

I'd been having painful esophageal spasms since Tyler had been born, and my doctor put me on a medication to help the smooth muscles of my esophagus relax. The medicine happened to be a tricyclic antidepressant. Not only did it help reduce the spasms, but it made a world of difference in my anxiety levels. This, in turn, helped me relax and become gentler and kinder with my children.

My desire for power, prestige, and the purse began to diminish, and I commenced to love the Lord so deeply that the Word of Faith portion of the Gospel meant less to me. This would eventually free my heart to see through the deceptions I had been defending for years. First, however, I would sink further into falsehood.

I poured myself into reading books by several questionable authors, such as these by Neil T. Anderson: *The Bondage Breaker, Victory Over Darkness*, and *The Steps to Freedom in Christ.* (I am not recommending any of these books, only including them so others can understand the beliefs that I clung to). After that, I studied a few works by Derek Prince: *They Shall Expel Demons: What You Need to Know about Demons—Your Invisible Enemies, Blessing or Curse: You can Choose*, and *Spiritual Warfare*. Then, Mom sent me a set of CDs by Pastor Jack Hayford—an expert (as far as I knew at the time) on spiritual deliverance and cleansing. He was the pastor of Paul and Jan Crouch, the founders of TBN (Trinity Broadcasting Network), which is the largest 'Christian' television network in the world. I listened to his sermons whenever I was driving.

The books and CDs which I gravitated toward convinced me that Kevin was the victim of a demonic stronghold of alcoholism which had been passed through generational curses in his family. One Sunday after Pastor John's sermon, my gracious friend, Cecelia, approached me to let me know how her husband attained freedom from alcohol.

"Matt went to a deliverance counselor named Susan at the Assembly of God and got delivered from alcohol."

"He did?"

"Yes, and he hasn't had a drink for two years."

"**M**y ear really hurts," Tyler complained, rubbing the bony area behind his ear again. "And I can't hear anything out of it, except for a whooshing sound, like the blood flowing."

"We're going to try a course of antibiotics and some steroid ear drops." Dr. Jones removed his otoscope from Tyler's ear. "Hopefully, things will be better in a week or two. For now, discontinue the echinacea, which could be making things worse. It's an herb from the ragweed family, and a lot of people are allergic to it."

When Kevin showed up on our doorstep smelling like alcohol, I complained. "You're not supposed to be coming around when you're drunk."

Kevin took a bite of the large dill pickle in his hand. "You worry too much. Everything's gonna be fine."

"That's what you've always said, but there have already been a few incidents, like the other day when you almost ran me over with the four-wheeler."

"I had it all under control."

"You really scared the kids, you know. I don't want Tyler and Amber to have a lot of bad memories with you. Would you please come back when you're sober?"

Kevin's lower lip came out, but he wasn't drunk enough to insist on staying.

The WoF movement was finally making headway into Pastor John's church, as it had in many other Spirit-filled congregations. In our large church van, a group of twelve women went to an Oral Roberts University conference, and I was excited to be among them.

We felt blessed to be able to listen to Marilyn Hickey, Lindsey Roberts, and a former celebrity.

"Doctors give us facts, but the truth in God's Word over-rides facts," said Miss Celebrity. "We need to continue believing the truth, in spite of the facts."

We then listened to a story of a pregnant woman whose doctor explained that her baby was deformed, suggesting an abortion. The mother chose to believe the truth—that her baby was fine, despite the facts her physician had spoken. According to Miss Celebrity, a perfectly healthy infant was born months later.

Stories like these caused me to distrust the medical community and to disregard their information. I mentally applied the sermon to Tyler's situation. It was a fact that my son had ear pain and could only hear a whooshing sound. According to the homily, however, Tyler was already healed in the spiritual realm, soon to be manifested in the physical dimension.

WoF televangelists teach that sickness and disease don't exist in the physical realm, unless we ***admit*** we are sick or diseased. We are to ignore rational information—like doctor reports and physical symptoms—and put our faith force toward divine health. Signs of illness are considered to be illusions of the devil, designed to destroy our belief in divine health and to cause us to make negative confessions.

In prosperity teachings, denial of the physical realm runs a close parallel to the Christian Science and New Thought cults, which teach that one must refuse to agree with physical symptoms in order to be healed. Hinduism, a religion developed and taught by demonic entities, teaches a similar concept called Maya, alleging that this physical world is only an illusion of the mind. In various occult religions, evil spirits allege that we should not make negative confessions, nor should we admit that we have a problem. They propose that we should use thought power (sorcery) to refute the 'illusion' so we can overcome sickness, poverty, and other maladies. This main theme in New Age Spirituality has been promoted by many books and DVDs, such as *The Secret*, by Rhonda Byrn.

Cloaked in Christian terminology, have demonic doctrines crept into the church? By changing the words 'thought power' into 'faith force', do church goers unwittingly use sorcery to be free from disease and pain?

"The MRI and CT scan have both confirmed the presence of a Glomus tumor," said Dr. Evans, an ENT surgeon in Nashville, TN. "Glomus tumors can go into the mastoid bone and may even invade the brain."

"I see. What can be done?"

"There is the potential for profuse hemorrhage with these tumors, so we'll need to do an angiogram. We'll thread a small plastic tube into the femoral artery at the top of Tyler's leg, then take a series of X-Ray pictures as we thread the tube up to the artery near the tumor. Next, we'll plug the artery to control the bleeding so we can remove the tumor..."

At Tyler's age, his rapidly growing cells would be more susceptible to the damage done by radiation, so I was quite concerned about having an angiogram done. One afternoon, as I rested and prayed, I fell asleep.

Skip the angiogram, and I'll control the bleeding.

I woke up. *Was that thought from You, Lord?*

When I asked the doctor if the angiogram could be omitted, he said, "There's too much risk of hemorrhaging with these tumors."

Within a few days, however, his nurse called with a change of plans. "The hospital refused to allow an angiogram on such a young patient," she said, "so Dr. Evans agreed to do the surgery without it."

When I hung up the phone, I felt as though God would control Tyler's bleeding during the surgery. It seemed as if the Lord had been holding Tyler in His arms since the ordeal began, and there was much peace in my heart. I had done the best I knew, considering my beliefs.

As we stood at the altar, the Pentecostal guest speaker at Full Gospel Tabernacle laid his hand on Tyler's ear and prayed that the tumor would disintegrate. "God healed me of a tumor when I was young," he stated, "and He can heal you also."

We continued confessing that Tyler was healed and whole, and we did not talk as if the tumor existed, except on one occasion.

"Have there been any changes in Tyler's medical history?" asked the dental hygienist as she prepared to take him back for a routine cleaning. She caught me off guard, and I didn't know what to say about the tumor.

"Yes, there have," I replied. "He has a glomus tumor in his left ear, but everything else is the same."

On the way home from the dental office, Tyler said to me, "Mom, I don't want you to say that I have a tumor because I believe that the tumor has disintegrated."

"That's a good idea, Tyler. Next time, I'll just say that you've been *diagnosed* with a tumor, not that you *have* one."

Luke's parents, Adam and Denise, who reminded me of my own parents, made the two-hour drive to Nashville to be with Tyler and me at 7:00 AM. They filled a special place in my heart because I missed Dad and Mom during such times. After the three hour surgery, the doctor came out to talk with me.

"There was no glomus tumor," said Dr. Evans. "The bone in Tyler's mastoid and beneath his brain was destroyed, and granulation tissue had filled in the space. When I removed the granulation tissue, I could see the covering of his brain.

"Because Tyler is still growing, his bone will fill back in, and in a few years, it will look like this never happened. His three hearing bones weren't damaged, so time will tell how much of his hearing returns. Remarkably, he lost no more than a teaspoon of blood during surgery."

I do not know how the tumor disappeared, or whether there ever was one. At the time, I believed God had removed it, and that was the testimony I shared in church. But would God have left granulation tissue instead of healthy bone? It's possible that the diagnosis of a tumor was erroneous and that the damage in Tyler's head was the result of a runaway ear infection.

If not for my aversion to antibiotics, my affinity for homeopathic remedies, and my confidence in the Word of Faith teachings, one thing is certain: Tyler's treatment in the doctor's office would have begun four months earlier than it did, sparing him *much* suffering. If I had continued to stand on my faith teachings and hadn't taken Tyler to the doctor, his brain would have been affected. He could have become disabled...or worse. He might have died, like Jim, the young man with colon cancer who chose to put off treatment while believing for a miracle.

"**H**ey Ariel. It's Dana." There was a catch in my sister-in-law's voice.

"Oh, hi Dana. What's up?"

"Monica's in the hospital and might not make it through the weekend."

"Oh no!" I hadn't seen Kevin's sister, my high school best friend, in a long time. (Most of my former drinking companions didn't seem to want my friendship once I gave up alcohol and started living for Jesus).

When the pain in her abdomen had become excruciating, Monica had awakened her husband in the middle of the night to take her to the hospital.

The ER physician was blunt. "The amount of alcohol in your system has caused your pancreas to begin digesting itself. You have a 20% chance of living through the weekend."

"What have I done to myself?" Monica lamented.

There was no turning back for Kevin's sister. When I called the hospital, she was heavily medicated, on a respirator, and couldn't talk. A few hours later, her heart stopped beating. I would never hear her bubbly laughter again. I hoped Monica's death would help Kevin turn his life around before something serious happened to him.

20 Blindsided by Faith

Then we will no longer be immature like children. We won't be tossed and blown about by every wind of new teaching. We will not be influenced when people try to trick us with lies so clever they sound like the truth.
Ephesians 4:14 NLT

"What is the make and model of his vehicle?" asked the police dispatcher.

"It's a blue Chevy Astro."

"Do you know where he's headed?"

"He took off toward County Road 208 and will probably turn west toward town."

Kevin, with glassy eyes and dilated pupils, had shown up on our doorstep the night after we returned from Monica's funeral in Wisconsin. "I want to spend some time with my kids," he demanded, swaying back and forth.

"You're not supposed to be here when you're drinking."

"I'm not drinking."

As Kevin heard me on the phone with the police dispatcher, he took off. When the officers stopped him, his blood alcohol was 0.033%, over four times the legal limit in Kentucky.

"**W**hooo hoooo!" With hands raised over his head, running up and down the church aisle, the balding, maniacal man seemed overcome by what he was feeling. Several others began jumping and shouting, as though they were plugged into a powerful, electrical source.

"Thank you, Jesus." I tried to join in. Perhaps my mood was too low. "I need you, Lord. I need you." I started to cry, deeply desiring the Lord, trying to be as close to the anointing as possible.

Healer Drew, a distinguished, 60-year-old preacher, was holding the service in a small Pentecostal chapel 45 minutes southwest of my home. He often ministered at the healing crusades of my favorite televangelist, and the supernatural power around him was usually palpable.

"Praise you Jesus. We love you Lord." Wearing gray suit pants, a white shirt, and a gray and black striped tie, Healer Drew stood in front of the podium. Like President Trump, his white hair and eyebrows stood out against his tan/orange complexion. With his head bowed and eyes closed, he prayed in an adoring—almost hypnotic voice.

The bizarre manifestations that were occurring in the sanctuary concerned me. *Could this power be coming from demons?* I wondered.

My fears were laid to rest as Healer Drew lovingly crooned the name of Jesus over and over throughout the evening. *The power must be from the Holy Spirit,* I thought. *If only Kevin could partake of this anointing, maybe God would deliver him from alcohol.*

"**A**lright, alright, I'll agree to see my doctor." Kevin sounded cross as we spoke over the phone. "Just bring the bail money and get me out of jail. It's cold in here."

"First, I'm going to call and see when the doctor can get you in."

"Yeah, sure."

"By the way, Hazel [our neighbor] chewed me out on the phone for calling the police on you."

"That's nice."

Surprised by his apparent lack of empathy, I thought maybe Kevin hadn't been listening. "What do you mean 'that's nice?'"

"Well, I'm glad *somebody* is sticking up for me!"

Kevin felt vindicated when he heard that our alcoholic neighbor had cussed me out, which should have been a warning sign to me. I wish I'd spoken to a counselor about my plans, but I was bent on trying an antidepressant and Antabuse (a medicine that makes a person violently sick when they drink alcohol) in hopes that these medications would give me a happy, sober husband.

"**T**he anointing of God feels like electricity on me," said Healer Drew, "and it's all over me right now. It can be transferred to you. Hurry up. Get close to me." The man who was standing next to Healer Drew let loose with a long shout and started jumping up and down. It seemed crazy, but I let go of my inhibitions and did the same thing. If I could just enter the power, letting go of my reasoning inhibitions, maybe I'd get a life-changing miracle. After all, God occasionally asked the Old Testament prophets to do very strange things.

As Healer Drew was praying over one woman, she stated, "Every time I get healed here, the pain comes back once I return home."

I approached her when Healer Drew moved on the next person in line. "You have to keep claiming your healing and don't let the devil take it away from you."

"People didn't lose their healings in the Bible," she returned. "Something doesn't seem right here."

Though the pain in my neck didn't go away when Healer Drew prayed for me, a perceptible prickliness came upon me and remained during my drive home. Once at my house, I headed to the bathroom and was praying in tongues with the door slightly ajar when Amber tried to push in. My temper flared, and I roughly shut the door. Her pinky got caught, and she began crying.

"Oh, I'm so sorry, Amber," I felt terrible and couldn't understand why the Holy Spirit anointing didn't make me like Jesus—patient, loving, and kind. Does God give out the charismata—like tongues, healing, and prophecy—apart from the fruit of the Spirit?

I gave Amber a hug and looked at her finger. There appeared to be a thin, red cut about 3 mm long. I began praying in tongues and felt the power surge. Within seconds, the cut turned to a red line, and then the red line faded to white. Suddenly, there was no mark. Right before our eyes, it vanished! *Did I just see that happen?* Had we witnessed a supernatural miracle of God, or did we experience an occult manifestation of Satan? Naturally, I didn't consider the latter.

"Tyler, come quick," I called out. "Let me pray for the warts on your foot!"

Kevin was in jail attire and handcuffs when the two police officers brought him to the front desk.

"That will be $1500," said the officer as I signed the bail paperwork. "And if he has any traffic violations before his arraignment, the entire amount is forfeited."

Upon hearing that piece of information, I should have turned around and left Kevin there. However, the doctor appointment was set, and I desperately wanted Kevin to try the medications.

After Dr. Jones saw Kevin, we were on the way to the pharmacy, and I said, "You know, we lose our bail money if you have any traffic violations. If you'll let me take you to work and pick you up after, and if you'll take the Antabuse and promise not to drink, you can stay with the kids and me."

"Okay," he replied.

After some convincing, Kevin came with me to one of Healer Drew's services. When the offering was over, the usher whispered into Healer Drew's ear.

A scowl came over the minister's face. "We need to take another offering then," he huffed. Turning to the people, he said, "You can do better than this. The money that you sow into the offering tonight will help fund my trip to a healing crusade. It will return to you pressed down, shaken together, and running over."

The basket was passed a second time. The usher counted it and whispered into Healer Drew's ear again.

"Well then, we'll just have to take a third offering!"

Kevin was not impressed, nor did he get delivered.

"Being superstitious causes people to walk in fear, which is the opposite of faith." Pastor John opened his sermon. "There are many types of superstitions in the world, ranging from the benign—such as believing that breaking a mirror dooms oneself to seven years of bad luck—to the occult practices of astrology, black magic, divination, and sorcery.

"When we're afraid to speak the truth of our situation because we think a negative confession will draw those circumstances upon us, we are walking in superstition. The truth of Christianity overcomes superstition. We need not be afraid to admit we have cancer, a backache, a cold, or whatever affliction is upon us."

He's right. I realized that my WoF teaching on negative confession was unbiblical, but I had no idea how closely my beliefs resembled the doctrines of demons in spiritistic religions. (More on this in a later chapter).

"God doesn't tell us to walk in denial," Pastor John continued. "In fact, we should admit and be honest about our problems."

"That witch on the phone had the nerve to criticize Benny, who carries the healing anointing of God." Healer Drew's countenance darkened in a sinister way as he spoke. "Heresy hunters cause dissention in the body of Christ!" Healer Drew went from beautiful displays of worship to venomous hostility, and the discordance made me wonder again if his anointing might have come from the demonic realm.

A guest speaker took the pulpit, and spiritual power began to flow freely. People were laughing, dancing, hooting, and hollering. Suddenly, evil shrieking pierced the atmosphere, followed by maniacal laughter. If I've ever heard a demon, that was the time. I wondered why an evil spirit would be enjoying itself during church.

After the service, the guest speaker prophesied, "The next big revival is coming to this area of the country. Sinners from the north, south, east, and west will begin to pour into this church."

"Are there any instances in the Bible where people were slain in the Spirit?" asked my good friend, Darcey, one evening.

I considered the time when the soldiers told Jesus that they were looking for Him.

As Jesus said, "I Am he," they all drew back and fell to the ground! John 18:6 NLT

"Well," I replied. "when the soldiers were looking for Jesus, He said, 'I am', and they fell backwards."

"Yes, but these men weren't saved. Do we find unbelievers being filled with the Holy Spirit in the New Testament?"

I wasn't ready to be convinced, so I thought, *Who is to say that God wouldn't do something outside of the Scriptures?*

Kevin put the Antabuse tablet in his mouth, took a swig of water, and made a quick exit through the kitchen door. An hour later, he was off visiting Hazel. When he returned, it seemed like he might have been drinking, but I wasn't certain.

The following day, rather than giving Kevin the Antabuse outright, I crushed it and blended it into a shake. Though I felt bad about the deception, I watched with satisfaction as he drank it down.

"Mom, the warts are gone." Tyler walked into the living room and held the bottom of his foot up. "Look."

"They are! Amazing!" The disappearance of Tyler's warts seemed to confirm that Healer Drew's power was from God and strengthened my hope that Kevin would be delivered by the same type of anointing.

A short while later, my husband's face was bright red, and he was sick. Both symptoms were a result of drinking while the Antabuse was in his system. We couldn't afford to lose the bail money if he were to be stopped for a traffic violation, so I decided to let him stay with us until his arraignment, which was several days away.

During my mid-afternoon prayer and meditation on God's Word, I considered the biblical account of Moses, who was in the desert for 40 years as the Lord prepared him to be used. This insight came into my thoughts: *'The longer the trial, the more the fruit.'*

When difficult seasons last a long time, we can rejoice because our iniquities are being purged. As our inner sin is exposed, confessed, and cleansed, we become more like Jesus and can produce more fruit.

Kevin had his arraignment day in court, and the judge put him on probation. We received half of our bail money back because the rest went toward court costs. After we returned home, Kevin stated, "I'm going for a walk."

"Please don't go to Hazel's."

When he returned that evening, I needed to make a phone call. "Bubba, can you please come and pick Kevin up? He's really drunk."

The next two Bible characters I studied would help me face one of the hardest trials of my life. While Job was a man of great faith, who walked in as much righteousness as he knew, carnality still lurked within his heart. For instance, while defending himself to his friends, he spoke presumptuously of his innocence and accused our Creator of injustice in his suffering.

The adversity of poverty, the death of his children, the onset of severe disease, and the criticism of men brought the darkness within his heart to the forefront, making it visible for him to recognize. In God's furnace of intense heat and pressure, the dross in Job's heart rose to the surface. Pride was exposed and uprooted, the fruit of humility was planted in its place, and he was godlier after his troubles than he had been before them.

My suffering was good for me, for it taught me to pay attention to your decrees. Psalm 119:71 NLT

After studying about Job, I looked intently into Moses' life. In faith, Moses chose to be led away from the temporary pleasures and riches of Egypt as God drew him toward greater riches than this world could ever offer. He could have continued living in the palace. Perhaps he was positioned to become the next pharaoh (king).

Instead, he found himself in a desert, like the valley which many of us face when our lives seem to be falling apart. In the desolate land, Moses could have complained that life was unfair, but instead his heart was humbled. He saw past the burdensome times and focused on those things which would make an eternal difference in his own life. In doing so, he was able to be used by God to change the course of an entire nation—the children of Israel.

If we can choose to look beyond the pleasures that this world values, and if we can become intimately acquainted with the Scriptures while we travel through our personal deserts, consider what the Lord can do to change the course of our lives and to impact the eternal destiny of the people we influence.

Tyler and Amber had spent the night with Dana and Allen, so they were not with me at church when Kevin showed up, sober and crying. He had run out of alcohol Saturday night, and the nearest liquor store was hours away. (On Sundays, even the neighboring counties in Kentucky didn't sell booze).

After the service, Adam and Denise invited us over for pizza and fellowship with another couple from church, Matt and Cecelia. It seemed odd that Matt—a sober man with an apparent testimony to the delivering power of God—barely spoke.

While Cecelia, Denise, and I were in the kitchen preparing beverages, Cecelia explained how Matt was delivered from alcohol. "Susan bound the spirits of alcohol and cast them out of Matt. Would you like me to call her and set up an appointment for your husband?"

"Let me check with Kevin first."

Kevin agreed, and an appointment was set up for the following evening.

Alcoholics Anonymous, inpatient and outpatient treatment, counselors, Antabuse, and antidepressants hadn't worked for Kevin. *Surely God's way will work,* I thought.

As we ate pizza in Adam and Denise's living room, Matt did not attest to having a better life, nor did he talk about the Lord. Instead, he remained quiet and somber, as though he was hiding something.

Monday evening—

As Susan—a Pentecostal, WoF Christian who seemed to have great understanding about evil spirits—led us down the hall to one of the Sunday School classrooms in her church, Kevin was noticeably tense and uptight. He hadn't had a drink since Saturday night.

After we sat down, Susan began. "We plead the blood of Jesus to surround every person in this room, each person in this church, and every person within the vicinity of this building." Susan bound up and commanded a multitude of evil spirits with names like Alcohol, Lust, Licentiousness, and Greed.

It seemed to me as though the Holy Spirit had gifted her a with special anointing to deliver people from addictions, like the healing anointing which Healer Drew possessed. As with Amber's finger, Tyler's warts, and the time Pastor Bill prayed on my neck, the spiritual power seemed tangible. By the time the deliverance was finished, Kevin's demeanor had become entirely relaxed.

On Thursday, as Tyler, Amber, and I bustled off to a playdate with our homeschool friends, my feet didn't seem to touch the ground. My miracle had finally come, and I felt as though I was walking on sunshine.

When we arrived at Louise's house, she had just announced to our friends, "I'm pregnant!"

After everyone congratulated her, I said, "You must be so happy! I hope to be the next one pregnant. Kevin went to a deliverance counselor a few days ago and got set free from alcohol."

You could have heard a pin drop.

Wouldn't it be great to arrive in old age with perfect teeth—no cavities or periodontal disease—without flossing, brushing, eating the right foods, and visiting one's dental office several times each year? It would be exciting and wonderful to expect a miraculous crop at harvest-time without the blood, sweat, and tears of hard work. How easy it had been, although unrealistic, to expect a miraculous recovery from alcoholism and to latch on to the fortune-telling prophecies. How inspirational it felt to be told that I could verbally bind the demons, cancel the curses, and speak positive confessions using the words of Bible verses. Abracadabra, like magic, the spiritual force brings about what I claim.

While God miraculously delivers people from alcohol, drugs, and other addictions when they willingly turn from these idolatries to follow His promptings, it is not always easy. Usually a painful, character-building process of obedience is part of the journey toward righteousness and emotional health. The road which appears more difficult will bring better results than the solution that seems quick and easy.

Addiction-prone personalities are susceptible to searching out immediate gratification, seeking effortless satisfaction and pleasure, rather than working hard to reach long-term solutions. One can recognize this phenomenon in those who are enticed by alcohol, pornography, sex, and drugs, using these as an easy way out of their pain and/or a quick way into pleasure. However, it was almost impossible to perceive that I had an addiction which propelled me toward seeking the immediate gratification of spiritual power, as well as the uplifting expectation of forthcoming prosperity, perfect health, and success. Just as Kevin had come out of the treatment center smoking excessively, having replaced his drinking with cigarettes, I had given up alcohol in my early years at WoF Church and replaced it with a religious addiction to the supernatural.

My idolatry may not have been as physically consuming or brain altering as alcoholism, opiate addictions, or pornography, but it had the potential of weakening my walk with the Lord. The delusion was eating away at my soul, subtly filling the place in my heart where Jesus belonged and affecting my witness for the Lord.

Like the law of gravity, which governs the physical world, occultists believe that there are spiritual laws which allegedly govern all spiritual power, whether good or evil. Through the WoF teachings, I had come to believe that spiritual laws rule over both God and the dark powers, which is not a biblical precept. If spiritual laws rule over God, then He isn't sovereign. Yet, the Bible says,

The LORD has established His throne in the heavens, and His sovereignty rules over all. Psalm 103:19 NASB

In New Age Spirituality, demonic spirit guides allege that God is an impersonal force, controlled by spiritual laws, rather than being sovereign. I thought my positive confessions, through the supposed *law of attraction*, would draw what I spoke toward us. Picturing Kevin free (*visualization*) and using my faith-force (*thought power*) would bring about success. These sorcerous practices were supposed to manipulate the spiritual realm (since my words held god-like power), and then manifest in the physical realm.

For an alcoholic, the easy road of immediate gratification leads to further bondage. Is it any different for the believer who counts on occult formulas to magically turn suffering into joy? Eventually, like wine that sparkles in a glass, it stings like a poisonous snake and bites like a viper.

"Lord, how could you let this happen?" Collapsing to my knees, I bent forward until my face pressed into the blue shag carpet near the foot of my bed.

Kevin had come home drunk. My dream-family plunged into the jagged rocks at the bottom of the lowest valley. I had placed all my eggs in one basket and handed it to the Jesus of my Pentecostal, WoF belief system, to the Jesus who had given me prophesy after prophesy.

Anger rose up in my heart against God because of the expectations I had been developing. A portion of my beliefs lay shattered at the feet of my Lord. The stormy tempest came upon me with violence, and my ship tossed to and fro. To throw me off course, the enemy had hit me with a magnitude of force from an unexpected position—from inside the church. Like my sister Amanda when Jerry died, I had been thoroughly blindsided.

Lord, did I not have enough faith? Weren't my prayers powerful enough?

I quieted my mind and listened. In that moment, I realized God would not violate Kevin's free will. It didn't matter how hard I prayed, how great my faith was, or what I named, claimed, and positively confessed. The Lord wasn't saying He would answer my prayers the way I desired. He wasn't telling me to hang onto my dream for a strong, Christ-centered marriage with Kevin. My world—this small speck of dust in time—appeared to be collapsing.

Then, I remembered Pastor John's words during a recent sermon. "If all God ever did for me was provide a way to heaven, and if He never answered any of my prayers the way I wanted, I'd still serve Him."

I thought about the time in the Gospel of John, when many disciples deserted Jesus because they didn't like His hard sayings. After they left, He asked His twelve hand-picked disciples, "Are you also going to leave?"

> *Simon Peter replied, "Lord, to whom would we go? You have the words that give eternal life. We believe, and we know You are the Holy One of God. John 6:68–69 NLT*

Where could I turn when denied my dreams by the free will of man? Could I desert the One who gave His life for me? No. I could only throw myself at Jesus' feet, next to my broken dreams, and cling to Him, no matter what tomorrow would bring...

Though the fig tree does not bud and there are no grapes on the vines, though the olive crop fails and the fields produce no food, though there are no sheep in the pen and no cattle in the stalls, yet I will rejoice in the LORD, I will be joyful in God my Savior. The Sovereign LORD is my strength; he makes my feet like the feet of a deer, he enables me to tread on the heights. Habakkuk 3:17–19 NIV

"Putting God's armor on isn't about speaking words; it's about who you are in Christ and what you do," said Pastor John. "We don't need to keep reapplying the helmet of salvation every day because our salvation isn't lost when we go to bed."

I considered Mrs. Cicely Ormes, the young martyr who thrust her hand into the scorching flames that would reduce her mortal body to ashes. Her shield of faith showed brightly for all to see. Her breastplate of righteousness was glaringly apparent when she refused to silence her faith to save her life. Her feet, which stood upon the pile of wood may have been covered with grime, but they were shod with the Gospel shoes of Peace—for perceiving that she had been reconciled to God and therefore would be spending eternity with Him; she exuded serenity during her severe trial. Her belt of truth—the comprehension of the truth in God's Word—covered her better than the clothing she might have worn. The sword of the Spirit—the Word of God—came from her mouth as, before her accusers, she uttered the words recorded in Luke 1:46-47. *"Oh, how my soul praises the Lord. How my spirit rejoices in God my Savior!" (NLT)* Without question, the helmet of salvation covered her head as her spirit rejoiced in her Savior. And yet, for all her spiritual armor, she wasn't expecting to be saved from her physical enemies.

Regarding the teachings on the armor of God, I realized that I had previously accepted a shallow interpretation because I hadn't understood the Scriptures well enough.

Louise moved to Indiana, and there weren't many home schoolers at our church, so we were lonely. I wasn't working, and the children and I had an abundance of time. Every week we were at Full Gospel Tabernacle for Sunday

School, which was followed by the morning service. Then we returned for the Sunday evening service, the Monday prayer meeting, Bible classes on Tuesday, and the mid-week service on Wednesday. On weekdays, I was often in my room until noon, reading my Bible and praying while the kids did school work at the kitchen table.

"I love you, Mom." Tyler hugged me as my back was against the countertop, and the familiar feeling of being trapped assaulted my senses. I struggled not to pull away and asked God to heal me from the traumas I'd experienced with my first boyfriend, Mark.

As I drew nearer to the Lord, He began mending the wounds in my soul, and I began to realize my intrinsic value, which started to change my addiction-prone personality. The rejection which I'd faced from peers in grade school no longer troubled me because I felt accepted by the most important One of all, my Creator.

The Lord is near to the broken-hearted, and some of my dreams, impressions, and thoughts seemed to be coming from God, though it may not be possible to discern whether these come from one's own mind.

While resting and praying, a scene floated through my mind of the devil shooting arrows at a Christian. Each arrow was an idea to be planted in the mind of the believer, intended to frustrate and distract him. One such thought might have been, "This person doesn't like you."

With every suggestion that the demon shot, the Christian remained unmoved, seemingly unaffected. This pietist was on his knees with his Bible in hand, praying and keeping his focus on God, rather than on the thought arrows. The evil spirit eventually became vexed and infuriated. Finally, it fled in fear.

Was my idea of spiritual warfare mistaken? I wondered if we WoF believers gave too much credence to verbal commands, trusting in our forceful words as a means of resisting the devil. Rather than focusing on word battles with the enemy, perhaps we should have been concentrating on walking in the peace which comes from our Gospel shoes. Offensively, it might have been better to sharpen our swords by studying the Word of God and to strengthen our breastplate of righteousness by searching our hearts for sin.

Submit yourselves, then, to God. Resist the devil, and he will flee from you. James 4:7 NIV

I dreamt I was binding spirits named Alcohol, Pain, Sickness, Disease, and Lust when I heard a thought.

"The greatest thing my children need deliverance from...is self."

Really? I wondered if we had given the devil more credit than he is due, blaming him for our own inclinations toward sin. While the Bible shows Jesus and the apostles setting demon-possessed people free, they never attributed the names of mankind's sinful behaviors—like lust, greed, or licentiousness—to evil spirits, nor to generational curses.

Some of the signs of demonic possession that we find in the Bible include having superhuman strength, talking in a different voice, being unable to speak or see, speaking in a foreign language, exhibiting another personality, and experiencing seizure-like symptoms. (This is not to say that a person with multiple personality disorder or someone with epilepsy is possessed by an evil spirit, because these disorders almost always have physical causes).

Exorcisms have their legitimate place in this world, especially in cases where one has opened oneself to occult practices. Just as Jesus and His disciples freed people from demons, evil spirits are being cast out of people today by Christ followers in many denominations. Kevin, however, had none of the above symptoms of demonic possession, and his deliverance didn't resemble the evil spirit expulsions we find in the Bible.

"To find the true meaning of 'binding' and 'loosing,'" said Pastor John, "one must look to the Jewish customs at the time of Jesus. When our Lord taught about authority, the keys to the kingdom of heaven, and binding and loosing, His disciples understood exactly what He meant.

"He wanted His disciples to make good rulings regarding the New Covenant that God was instituting with mankind. The disciples could make godly statutes by basing their rulings on the Scriptures and listening to the Holy Spirit.

"We see an example of this when Peter and the disciples decided what the Gentiles must do once they were saved." Pastor John glanced at his notes. "For instance, they determined that Gentiles should not be required to be circumcised, as the Old Covenant had required, but they were to abstain from drinking blood."

Pastor John then read a Bible passage written to Gentile converts regarding what the New Covenant would *bind* them to and what it would *loose* them from.

For it seemed good to the Holy Spirit and to us to lay no greater burden on you than these few requirements: You must abstain from eating food offered to idols, from consuming blood or the meat of strangled animals, and from sexual immorality. If you do this, you will do well. Farewell. Acts 15:28-29 NIV

"Binding and loosing, as the Scriptures indicate," continued Pastor John, "refers to the authority Jesus gave to the disciples to make binding rulings *based on* Scripture with the direction of the Holy Spirit. This may have included binding (forbidding or excommunicating) from fellowship those disobedient church members who refused to repent of their sin, as well as loosing (restoring/releasing) to fellowship those church members who obediently repented of their sin."

I recalled leaders in WoF Church commanding, 'We loose wealth to come upon our congregation,' and 'Satan, release the tithes that have been kept back by church members.' I tried to think of instances where the disciples verbally loosed the Holy Spirit, rebuked Satan, or bound demons. I couldn't remember one biblical example of these types of 'prayers'.

Pastor John continued his sermon, reading passages from Christian commentaries and *The Jewish Encyclopedia*, expounding upon the meanings of the New Testament words from the Greek language.

Though I had been taught (at WoF church) that God needs us to loose (release) Him because He is unable to do anything apart from our permission, the Holy Spirit chose to come upon the disciples on the day of Pentecost *of His own volition*, not needing to be liberated. He also fell on the Gentile converts when the disciples laid hands on them, astonishing everyone. Would they have been surprised if they had been verbally releasing the Holy Spirit?

In the book of Job, we find that God does what He wants to do.

*But once he has made his decision, who can change his mind? **Whatever he wants to do, he does**. Job 23:13 NLT (Emphasis mine)*

21 The Hardened Heart vs. the Surrendered Heart

So I let them follow their own stubborn desires,
living according to their own ideas. Psalm 81:12 NLT

"It's your fault I can't live with you and the kids," Kevin argued. "You should just accept me the way that I am." Kevin was staying with Bubba and continued to be drunk every evening. He expressed no sorrow for the choices he had made throughout our marriage and wasn't willing to get sober so he could go to counseling. Thankfully, I'd saved up money while living in Wisconsin because he stopped giving me money to support our children.

The first step toward sobriety is to get past one's denial. A person who points his finger at his spouse is not walking in humility or repentance (feeling sorrowful over one's sin and turning away from it), which are both required for true change. God's Word tells us:

> *If we say that we have no sin, we are deceiving ourselves and the truth is not in us. If we confess our sins, He is faithful and righteous to forgive us our sins and to cleanse us from all unrighteousness. 1 John 1:8-9 NASB*

I've known many people, including my dad, uncles, aunts, and church members who gave up alcohol when they turned their lives over to the Lord. For 20 years, I had watched Kevin make one decision after another where he gave in to his body, rather than make his body give in to the will of God. While I had been looking for signs of repentance, Kevin hardened his heart, blamed me, and justified himself.

Similarly, I wasn't ready to hear the other case in the courtroom, having hardened my heart against those who warned against the prosperity message. I wouldn't consider that my favorite preachers might have been introducing heresy.

"When Job lost all that was precious and dear in this life," Pastor John began, "including his children, his wealth, and his health, and when his heart ached with the loss, and his body suffered immense physical pain and disease, he stood firmly in faith, saying, 'I know my Redeemer lives', and 'Though He slay me, yet will I trust Him', and 'The Lord gives, and the Lord takes away'. Job's heart was faithful to God, and his aim in life reached beyond earthly treasures, comforts, and pleasures. His purpose helped him look beyond the excitement of fleshly desires—such as building houses, growing vineyards, and filling barns.

"When disasters came upon her household, Job's wife, however, had a different heart toward God. She suggested that her husband should 'curse God and die'."

Pastor John had us turn in our Bibles to the following passages, which I'd never heard preached by any WoF preachers.

But Job replied, "You talk like a foolish woman. Should we accept only good things from the hand of God and never anything bad?" So in all this, Job said nothing wrong. Job 2:9 NLT

We give great honor to those who endure under suffering. For instance, you know about Job, a man of great endurance. You can see how the Lord was kind to him at the end, for the Lord is full of tenderness and mercy. James 5:11 NLT

Dear brothers and sisters, when troubles come your way, consider it an opportunity for great joy. For you know that when your faith is tested, your endurance has a chance to grow. James 1:2–3 NLT

We can rejoice, too, when we run into problems and trials, for we know that they help us develop endurance. Romans 5:3 NLT

"Did you notice that Job, James, and Paul didn't recommend that we rebuke our sufferings with warlike words?" asked Pastor John. "Did they tell us to make positive confessions? No, rather, they help us understand that we are to embrace God during our hardships. Can we develop enduring faith like that of Job, who stood by the Lord amid his tragic calamities? His actions were based upon the substance of those things he hoped for in eternity and the evidence of things he had not yet seen. Turn in your Bibles to the book of Hebrews, chapter 11."

I opened my Bible.

Faith is the confidence that what we hope for will actually happen; it gives us assurance about things we cannot see. Hebrews 11:1 NLT

"Our present difficulties can develop a deeper faith in us, a faith that is willing to go through any amount of anguish for our Savior, a faith that is willing to look beyond what this world offers, a faith that reaches toward eternity." I forced myself to listen to Pastor John's words. "By their faith in action, Abel, Noah, Enoch, Abraham, and many others demonstrated that they were strangers and pilgrims upon the earth."

After the teaching, I thought back to one of the first sermons I'd heard Pastor John preach. He had said, 'Job did nothing wrong to bring the destruction that came upon him'. At that time, I'd thought that Pastor John was wrong. After all, my WoF teachers said things like, 'Job was not walking in faith', 'Job walked in fear that his children would sin against God', and 'his lack of faith brought his fears upon him'.

In the Bible, God says that Satan incited Him against Job **without cause**.

And he [Job] still maintains his integrity, though you incited me against him to ruin him ***without any reason****. Job 2:3b NIV*

Contrary to my WoF teachings where faith helps us achieve our worldly desires, I began to realize that our faith is to be the sustenance that helps take our focus off the temporary things of this world. As with Job and Moses, it should reinforce our beliefs, deepen our commitment to God, and strengthen us to forego worldly ambitions. Then, we can let go of the enticements of this transitory life as we look toward the joy that lies ahead in Heaven.

Like the steadfast faithfulness of Luke's parents during their anguishing ordeal, our faith should proclaim the inner transformation which is brought about by the power of the living God. Adam and Denise reminded me of Habakkuk, who chose to rejoice in the Lord when the fig trees did not blossom, when the crops failed, when the flocks died, and when the barns were empty.

Our faith should sustain us when we face life's tragedies and when our desires are smashed at the bottom of the valley.

It was enthusing to receive prophecies and promises that I would have those things I proclaimed or that I would be greatly anointed one day. Could the Lord illumine the Scriptures to me so I understood that He would allow Kevin to have the free will to go in the wrong direction? Could I be the believer—with faith like that of Job—who was able to say, 'The Lord gives, *and the Lord takes away*. Blessed be the name of the Lord.' Could I speak those words—free of the fearful superstition that voicing them would *take away* my desires?

Though I understood the above truths, I didn't recognize that faith has been redefined by WoF teachers, making it diametrically opposed to the type of faith we see in the biblical characters of Hebrews 11. WoF leaders have made it sound as if faith is intended to be an avenue to refute and escape suffering, as well as to attain worldly desires.

The misleading concept that our faith is meant to be a conduit to perfect health, prosperity, and success—keeping our eyes on this side of eternity—hadn't caught my attention as being wrong. I was still on fire for the new revelations of 'anointed men of God', but I would soon make a discovery which would help me understand that their teachings come straight from the pit of hell.

In all the time of our separation, though others seemed to be hearing from God on my behalf, the Lord had not told me personally that Kevin was going to quit drinking. I was reading a portion of my diary about a dream which I'd had three and a half years earlier. At that time, I hadn't given much thought to the message because most dreams are a result of our own thought processes, and we can easily be led astray if we follow them. Besides that, this dream contradicted all the prophecies which people were giving me.

In my dream, Kevin and I were walking along a straight stretch of road while Tyler and Amber wandered ahead. We couldn't see the Lord, who spoke from behind us, instructing Kevin about raising Tyler and Amber.

"Demonstrate my fatherly love to your children. Take your son around the block. Teach your daughter her value."

Tyler and Amber came to a side road and turned to the left to go around the block. There would be many days ahead when they would need a dad, special moments when Kevin could shape their hearts and demonstrate his love, plenty of opportunities for him to be their spiritual leader and teach them about God.

With his eyes upon our children, Kevin nodded his agreement and acted like he was going to obey God's counsel. When the Lord finished speaking and left us, Kevin turned to me and said, "See to it that it gets done." His eyes were devoid of compassion, his voice hard. My husband turned his back on us and headed off on a road to the right, never looking back. With a crushed heart, I watched as he abandoned us, putting his arm around the buddy he was with, whose name was Alcohol. It was time to stop clinging to Kevin's broken marriage vows to love, honor, cherish, and be faithful.

Yet if the unbelieving one leaves, let him leave; the brother or the sister is not under bondage in such cases, but God has called us to peace. 1 Corinthians 7:15 NASB

"**K**evin is drinking at work and driving under the influence every day," I said. "He's taking unconscionable risks with the lives of other people. If he kills or maims someone in an accident, we could lose everything."

"Your separation didn't cause him to hit bottom," said Counselor Steve. "Losing his family wasn't a severe enough consequence to help him turn his life around. For some addicts, bottom is hit when they lose their job and can't provide for their family. Many hit bottom when they end up in jail or prison. For others, death is their bottom."

"What can I do?" I twisted my wedding ring around my finger. "God hates divorce."

"In cases of abuse, addiction, adultery, and abandonment, which demonstrate that a spouse has hardened his heart against the marriage, the innocent party is free to divorce. You have biblical reasons to end the marriage."

On my way home from the counseling session, I felt as though my chest was being ripped wide open and half of my heart was being carved away. I couldn't believe that I needed to begin the process of legally ending on paper what Kevin had tossed aside in action. Life seemed unfair, but words spoken by my previous employer came to mind.

Dr. Barry had said, 'I'm glad God isn't fair. Otherwise, He wouldn't have allowed Jesus to pay a penalty He didn't deserve, and we wouldn't be able to get to heaven.'

While I didn't have a husband, who was willing to die to his bodily desires for Tyler, Amber, and me, there was a Man who endured an excruciatingly painful death for us 2000 years ago. Living for Him mattered more to me than anything else. After this world has passed away, and I am in eternity, perhaps I'll look back on my present sufferings, and they'll appear like a small speck in time.

New Year's Eve journal entry—

I've discovered a few tiny cracks in my Word of Faith beliefs and learned that people's prophetic 'words from the Lord' are not always from God.

Kenneth Hagin—the father of the faith movement (who had long ago proclaimed that God healed him of heart problems) died this year...of heart problems.

I close the year with a Bible verse and quote from a favorite author.

My old self has been crucified with Christ. It is no longer I who live, but Christ lives in me. So I live in this earthly body by trusting in the Son of God, who loved me and gave himself for me. Galatians 2:20 NLT

When Christ calls a man, he bids him come and die.[23] —Dietrich Bonhoeffer

I've given up my dream for two more children. In my prayer time, these words were impressed upon my mind. ***Live to die.*** My focus this year will be to live for Jesus and to die to my carnal nature.

"I won't have to worry about any problems soon. I have the day picked out." Kevin began saying that he planned to shoot himself before our day in court. Whether or not a person seems to be serious when speaking of suicide, we should call a suicide hotline, alert friends and family members, and speak with a professional counselor for guidance.

I chose to talk to Pastor Ricky's wife.

"Kevin's been telling us that he plans to commit suicide, too," said Betsy. "We took him for a ride the other day, and he was so drunk that he could barely talk."

As I began to prepare my business cards and brochures with updated Wisconsin information, I wondered if I was making the right decision about where the kids and I should live. There wasn't room for us at my parents' house because Grandma and Grandpa had moved in with them, so I was planning to rent my grandparent's empty farmhouse.

I called the phone company, and the operator began to check for available phone numbers. While her computer was searching, she asked, "Is there a particular number you would like?"

I thought for a moment and asked for my grandparents' old number. "Is 454-6483 available?"

"You're never going to believe this. From our entire database, that is the exact number my computer just pulled up!"

Though I was elated that things seemed to be falling into place in Wisconsin, I was concerned Kevin might break the Domestic Violence Order, show up drunk, and follow through with his suicide threat.

Saturday evening—

"Let me in!" Kevin demanded, pushing against the door as I tried to keep him from entering our home. "I just want my gun. Then it will all be over!"

"Call the police!" I shouted to Amber, who stood in the kitchen. Inch by inch, Kevin was forcing the door open.

"I can't!" Amber fled to the back of the house as Tyler came running to help me.

"Tyler, quick. Call 911!"

When Kevin heard our son on the phone with the dispatcher, the battle was over. He left immediately and was apprehended within minutes.

Three days remained until the children and I would leave for Wisconsin. Since Kevin was incarcerated, there wouldn't be any dangerous incidents. I thought we would be safe… until the phone rang the next morning.

"You shouldn't have called the police on Kevin!" Bubba was clearly agitated.

"He said he wanted his gun so he could shoot himself." I looked at the clock. I needed to leave for church so I could teach the Sunday school class for women.

"He would never kill himself! I'm going to bail him out first thing tomorrow!"

When I hung up the phone, I prayed that Kevin wouldn't show up the following morning.

"**T**here were two types of prophets in the Old Testament," Pastor John taught. "False prophets spoke their own dreams and notions, gave messages of ease and prosperity, and were popular with the people. True prophets were the ones who wouldn't compromise, who told messages requiring repentance, and who didn't accept money or offerings. They were regularly persecuted, sometimes thrown in dungeons, and often murdered."

While Pastor John elaborated, I contemplated the type of prophetic words I had received, and those I had given to others.

"In the New Testament, Jesus prophesied the destruction of Jerusalem. Several prophetic warnings were given to the Apostle Paul about what he would endure if he went to Rome, and a man named Agabus prophesied a famine."

I couldn't remember one prophecy in the Bible where anyone was told they would become rich, as had been foretold regularly at WoF Church in Wisconsin. Neither could I recall any personal prophetic words in the New Testament that resembled those of fortune tellers—like those I'd heard, received, and spoken to others. Unfortunately, there are no biblical examples where the disciples had church services in which they planned to give prophecies, nor did they have people line up to receive prophetic words. Can we direct the Holy Spirit to give prophecies by our will?

"In the midst of a plethora of false prophets who promise health, prosperity, and power, God still has prophets like those in the Old Testament." Pastor John's voice interrupted my thoughts. "These prophets teach the principles in God's Word and entreat people to repent of sin and to turn wholeheartedly to God."

As the sermon concluded, I closed my notebook and put my pen away. I would miss the sincerity of Pastor John and the teachings at Full Gospel Tabernacle.

While the kids and I were packing our vehicle Monday morning, the paperwork for Kevin's bail was being filled out, and he was about to be released. Because he had been too long without a drink, he had a seizure. An ambulance was called, and he was taken straight to the hospital. What a relief! He would not be showing up on our doorstep after all. The tension in my chest dissipated, and I could breathe deeply again.

As we left the Bible Belt, I prayed that no one would be injured or killed in an accident with Kevin, once he was out of the hospital.

"**W**here did our worship leader go?" I asked. It felt wonderful to be back in my home church where many of my family members and relatives attended. I had made a lot of good friends over the years at Word of Faith Church, and Pastor Bill's mom and sister were some of the sweetest people I knew.

"He and his wife had some serious issues and left the church," replied my friend.

I will not repeat the horrible rumor that followed, as often was the case when people left WoF Church.

"Oh, that's too bad. I liked how he led worship. It seems like the new youth director is nice."

"Yes, he's been doing a wonderful job. My kids really like him."

"What happened to the Sunday School teacher who taught classes on spiritual authority?"

"He and his wife don't go to church anymore." My friend revealed a few details that do not need to be repeated, and then she asked, "How's Kevin doing?"

"Well, he's back in jail. Shortly after his friend bailed him out, he was caught for a hit and run. Bubba probably didn't get his bail money back."

Several months later—in his orange jail suit—Kevin stared me down from across the courtroom as the judge questioned us about our divorce. The dance that was supposed to last for the rest of our lives had come to an end. My finger felt bare when I returned to Wisconsin and placed my wedding ring in the jewelry box.

22 Spirit of Coercion, Armor Bearers, and Kings

The refining pot is for silver and the furnace for gold [to separate the impurities of the metal], And each is tested by the praise given to him [and his response to it, whether humble or proud].
Proverbs 27:21 Amplified Bible

"Did you hear that Prophetess Deb has breast cancer?" asked Mom. She stood on one side of Grandma's bed, and I leaned over the other as we changed the bedding.

"No, I didn't," I replied.

Turning to Grandma, Mom asked, "Can you roll toward me, Mum?"

"Can you roll toward me Mum?" Grandma's speech was slow, and her disease caused her to repeat everything back.

"Deb decided to stand on the WoF teachings and claim her healing rather than follow the doctor's recommendation," said Mom.

"Well, if anyone has enough faith to get healed, it will be Prophetess Deb. She's one of the godliest women I know."

After Grandma turned on her side, I pulled the used sheets from under her and straightened the fresh ones, tucking them under the mattress. Looking toward Grandma, I asked, "How does that feel?"

"How does that feel?" came the sluggish reply.

"I love you Grandma," I smiled and gave her a hug.

"I love you Grand..." She paused momentarily, thinking hard. Then, with a triumphant smile, she added, "child!"

Amanda and I sat together at our midweek service listening to Miss Televangelist. After the sermon, a lot of us lined up at the altar to be prayed for by her, including me. Since one of the discs in my neck had slipped, I had severe pain down my right arm. Nothing happened when Miss Televangelist prayed for me, and I couldn't figure out why the power in church didn't seem to touch me anymore. However, a little boy was able to remove his thick, coke-bottle glasses and read without them.

Miss Televangelist divined that the next large revival would be coming to our area. "Sinners will pour into this church from the north, the south, the east, and the west. Mighty miracles will be happening at WoF Church."

It was nearly 10:30 PM as Amanda and I walked out of the sanctuary and into the foyer. To our left, the door to the conference room was open, and church volunteers were preparing a fine dinner. Platters of roast beef, steaming baby red potatoes, large red strawberries, and several desserts were being set on a long table in preparation for Pastor's family and our guest minister.

Amanda and I stepped out of the glass entry doors into the cool, night air and walked past the black limousine, which waited to take Miss Televangelist to her hotel.

On the following Sunday, Pastor Bill took the pulpit and preached the basics of the prosperity message. Jesus was rich. God wants us to be healthy and wealthy. Our thoughts and words are powerful to accomplish what we believe and speak forth.

The recent influx of new members cheered enthusiastically upon hearing this 'good news'.

As he was speaking, Pastor's *armor bearer, Daniel, set a fresh glass of water on his podium.

*According to Terry Nance, a graduate of Kenneth Hagin's Rhema Bible Training Center, an armor bearer is one who waits on, serves, fully submits with unquestioning obedience, and lays down his life for his pastor, like armor bearers did for their kings in the Old Testament. He surrenders completely to his leader, trusting him implicitly and obeying without hesitation his every command. He exalts, respects, and always uplifts his leader , and sacrifices his own life and well-being for the betterment of his leader.[24]

While I was naïve enough to believe that an armor bearer was a biblical concept, I did begin to wonder if Daniel was being taken advantage of when I saw the sacrifices he was allowed to make, and commended for, at the expense of his own family. It seemed like leaders in our church were given rewards, such as flattery and status upgrades for their submissive obedience. These types of manipulation can create a flock of followers like those in social cults. Being instructed not to speak against 'anointed men of God' further solidified the idea of keeping our leaders on a pedestal where they were considered above questioning.

I wish I didn't have to bring this subject up because I don't want anyone to be hurt or offended. However, this type of spiritual elitism is widespread in the WoF movement and needs to be addressed. When a person—such as a king, televangelist, 'anointed' prophet, 'apostle', or WoF preacher—receives too much deference, the temptation to consider him or herself above others is heightened. One doesn't have to look far to confirm the fact that kings and queens get used to being served by their people and become accustomed to luxuries and power, often taking more than they should from their subjects. The human heart has selfish tendencies when it is given power and praise.

We see this in 1 Kings 21, when Queen Jezebel had an innocent man murdered. Rather than mourning Naboth's life, King Ahab was happy to steal the vineyard from the widow and children of the deceased. In 2 Samuel 11, King David selfishly took Uriah's wife to bed while her righteous husband was serving his country on the battlefield. David then had Uriah murdered and snatched Bathsheba for his own wife.

From what I've seen, many WoF preachers tend to expect preferential and exalted treatment. Their hearts may convince themselves that it is in their congregants' best interests to bestow honor upon them, to submit to their authority, and to give them royal treatment. Living in mansions, driving fancy cars, owning private jets, and expecting to be served become normal for these 'men of God' as they watch their sheep sacrifice financially into their coffers, often to the member's financial detriment.

WoF leaders may not murder others to get their way, but while they gain lucre from the message they preach, people in their congregations place their faith in the prosperity teachings. Many believe they have divine health instead of seeking appropriate medical attention. These church members and their children, (who are regularly denied medical treatment by parents like me), suffer detrimental consequences and sometimes die, as I've seen several times.

While Pastor Bill encourages people to go to the doctor *if they don't have enough faith to be healed*, he has had people in his congregation with serious conditions that could've been treated medically. These people have suffered the catastrophic effects of false teachings and prophecies, which run rampant in WoF churches.

The following week, the prophetic word by Miss Televangelist about revival starting with our church had been transcribed, put in a picture frame, and hung in the church foyer. I could never consider leaving a church where the next big revival, such as those which had been experienced in Toronto, Canada and Pensacola, Florida, was about to take place.

When the revival comes, maybe I'll be a prophetess, or a healer, I hoped.

With Kevin in jail, my income dipped below poverty level, and health insurance through his employer was not feasible. Helping take care of Grandma one to two times per week gave me some spending money and enabled Mom to get out of her house.

Though I had tithed and given in faith—above and beyond—to the churches where I'd attended over the years, the seed money concept hadn't begun working for me, and I needed to sign up for government insurance. Still, I steadfastly believed it was only a matter of time until my prosperity seeds would come to fruition. When a special offering was taken for a piece of property near WoF church, I gave $1000 from my nearly depleted retirement account.

"Tyler, if you can bring all the groceries in, Amber and I will put them away." It was a frigid Wisconsin evening with wind chills well below zero, and we had just returned from town.

"I'll turn the heat up," Amber said, as she walked through the living room.

"Set it at 65 degrees," I said.

Grandma and Grandpa's house was perfect for us, except that the kids didn't have a father figure in the home. Our closest neighbors had been supplying us with chicken eggs, my cousin across the cornfield had given us the meat from a good-sized buck, and whenever the house needed a repair, I could always count on two of my uncles.

As a single mom, I didn't have time to do everything that needed to be done. Tyler had to take on a manlier role in our home, and he told his counselor, "The anxiety makes me feel like an overstretched rubber-band." Not only did Amber need a dad to love her, but most of the girls attending the WoF church school had formed little cliques, and she was lonely for a friend. She could have been involved in sports, drama, and classes with the homeschool coop in the neighboring county, but I didn't have the energy to add anything to my plate, nor the money for gas costs.

After the groceries were put away, we grabbed blankets to make tents over the heater vents. As we trapped the toasty air next to our chilly bodies, I read from our Bible, a devotional, and a Christian historical fiction book. This was our favorite time of the day. Life was good, outside of being overstrained and lonely.

When special offerings weren't enough to purchase the property near our church, Pastor Bill took out a large loan. I couldn't imagine that he might not have been following God's Spirit, for I thought the next revival was coming to our church. However, 20 years earlier, Pastor Bill had stated, 'The Holy Spirit told me our church needs to pay off our loans and *never go into debt again*.'

Which spirit is leading Pastor Bill now? I wondered. *If he isn't following the Lord regarding church finances, might he be losing sight of the Lord in other areas?*

"The Lord has given me a plan on how to pay this loan off," said Pastor Bill. He put an outline on the overhead screen which showed how many people were supposed to give $10,000, how many needed to give $1,000, and how many of us should give $100.

With the new debt came an increase in sermons about money. Two positions at our school academy had to be eliminated. Some members succumbed to complaining about Pastor's new home and lavish lifestyle, which clashed with the economic level of most of our church workers. He seemed to be at the top level of a two-tier pyramid where the prosperity message didn't seem to be working for some of the most committed church members on the bottom rung.

I began to notice that the WoF message is man-centered. We were mostly concerned with whether we felt happy, whether we could experience our best life now, whether we were confident in our ability to achieve success, whether we could avoid suffering, and so on. Instead of bowing to God's will, we thought we could make Him bend to our desires through alleged spiritual laws. Rather than placing ourselves humbly at the foot of the cross and allowing Jesus to be on the throne of our hearts, we ascended to the center of the 'gospel' message and focused on our own 'exalted positions' of power.

We wanted to hear that our sick family member would recover from his illness and gain the ability to care for himself, rather than consider that his affliction could teach us to become better servants. It was easy to swallow honeyed words proclaiming that we would have great marriages, large amounts of money, success, and happiness, instead of accepting the fact that our trials could mold us into selfless Christ followers.

Our sorrows in this life can serve as reminders that we will have tribulation in this finite world. While we are pilgrims, foreigners, and outcasts on earth, we are cherished sons and daughters of the Lord Most High, and our gaze needs to be fixed upon Him, not on self.

The self does not like to hear about brokenness before God, surrender to His will, endurance under trials, perseverance during persecution, humility, or sacrifice. Rather, self quickly gravitates to the message of power, prosperity, superiority, success, and magnified status. We want to be the admired miracle workers on center stage and the prophets with insider information about the future. The self filters out the information it doesn't want to hear, creating reluctance to acknowledge the WoF message as heresy, which may be why it is so hard to comprehend and takes very long for many of us to give the false gospel up.

"I wonder why Pastor Bill didn't teach about repentance whenever he gave the salvation message," Mom remarked one day. "We didn't learn that we needed to turn away from our sin *in order to* turn to Jesus."

"I didn't know what repentance was until Pastor John taught about it."

"Well, Ariel, maybe that's why we see people who claim they are saved, but who never allow Jesus to turn their life around."

"Pastor Bill claimed that some people take Jesus as their Savior without taking Him as their Lord."

"You can't take Jesus as your Savior *without* making Him your Lord."

"Well," I replied. "Acts 16:31 tells us that we need to believe in the Lord Jesus to be saved, and I think people don't realize that demons believe that Jesus is God, yet they aren't saved."

"Believing faith produces loyal worship of God, which brings a person to love the Lord with all of one's heart, mind, and soul. This causes a person to surrender to His Lordship, giving Jesus first place in one's life."

Salvation includes repentance. In regard to whether some Galileans who died were worse sinners than others, Jesus explained,

*"I tell you, no, but **unless you repent**, you will all likewise perish. Luke 13:3 NASB, emphasis mine*

Regarding 18 people who died when the tower in Siloam fell on them, as to whether they were the worst sinners in Jerusalem, Jesus repeated,

*"I tell you, no, but **unless you repent**, you will all likewise perish." Luke 13:5 NASB, (emphasis mine)*

I considered the words of a close relative, a member of WoF Church for many years, who admitted, "I honestly don't know if I could choose Jesus over my wealth." Did she commit her life to the health and wealth portion of the message, but not to Jesus? As I prepare to publish this book, my cherished relative no longer goes to church anywhere, and this breaks my heart.

Many of us sincerely loved and searched for the Lord, though we were initially naïve and biblically illiterate, which led to temporary deception. It seemed like our church had revolving doors, and I couldn't understand the frequent cases of shipwrecked faith. A lot of us had built our church attendance on sand, on the shallow foundation of health and wealth teachings, and on the supernatural experiences and the social setting that offered temporary gratification.

Perhaps more of our 'conversions' would have been genuine if we heard the Gospel message as presented by John the Baptist and the apostles. Many people who have left the WoF movement believe they are saved because they've said a prayer, even though they've never turned from their carnal mindsets. This is one of the biggest tragedies of believing in the prosperity message. It isn't the genuine Gospel and, often, doesn't lead to salvation.

Many will say to me on that day, 'Lord, Lord, did we not prophesy in your name and in your name drive out demons and in your name perform many miracles?' Then I will tell them plainly, 'I never knew you. Away from me, you evildoers!' Matthew 7:22–23 NIV

"**I** want to become a doctor," said Tyler. "I'll never be satisfied being a physician's assistant."

I didn't know how we could ever afford to send Tyler to medical school but didn't want to squash his dream. "I think you'd make a fine doctor."

Tyler became a certified nursing assistant in a local nursing home and began saving every penny for college and med school. He worked hard in our home school to prepare for a double college major.

New Year's Eve—

Four things are bothering me as I close the year. First, I'm concerned that our pastor is taking advantage of our leadership. In addition to working full-time, these parents are required to attend all the mandatory staff meetings, prayer meetings, Sunday and mid-week services, as well as being encouraged to host small groups, volunteer, and take classes at our Bible Institute. Second, Prophetess Deb passed away. Third, I'm worried that I might be disappointing God by thinking negative thoughts about my pastor. I dare not 'touch God's anointed one'.

Lastly, several ministers who have a lot of supernatural power have fallen into serious sin this year. Wouldn't the Spirit of Holiness purify the vessels He inhabits? Why doesn't the anointing to heal or prophesy go away when these ministers pursue depravity?

It didn't occur to me that the spiritual power of worldly ministers might not have come from God. Neither did I have any idea that there is such a thing as an evil 'anointing' that masquerades as the Holy Spirit.

It is easy to understand how churches that brandish the 'Touch not my anointed ones' doctrine tend to have a high rate of spiritual abuse, coercion, and toxic relationships. Members are afraid to speak their concerns about those in positions of spiritual authority and are taught to obey without questioning.

One can comprehend the importance of learning to be respectful to those in positions of authority, such as a child behaving for his parent or a citizen obeying the laws of the land. However, submitting to authority figures without questioning them can open the door to being manipulated and coerced into doing things against one's better judgment.

These instructions conveniently attempt to squelch the critical thinking skills of followers. They are a form of mind control which can keep followers from evaluating whether the theology being taught is biblically accurate or not. Additionally, teachings like this establish a type of hierarchy where certain believers are set above others. It is not so in the kingdom of God. The Bible says that all Christians have the Holy Spirit's anointing.

*But you have an anointing from the Holy One, and you **all** know. 1 John 2:20 NASB (Emphasis mine)*

*Now He who establishes us with you in Christ and anointed **us** is God, who also sealed us and gave us the Spirit in our hearts as a pledge. 2 Corinthians 1:21-22 NASB (Emphasis mine)*

Or do you not know that your body is a temple of the Holy Spirit who is in you, whom you have from God... 1 Corinthians 6:19a NASB

Regarding the 'Touch not My anointed ones' teaching, Berean Research author, Marsha West, says, "Unfortunately, churches that wield this false teaching like a weapon usually do so because they are pastored by a false teacher who **needs** to be (or is being) biblically criticized, corrected, or rebuked."[25]

"We need to find creative ways to fund a youth recreation center on our new property," said Mr. Lay Church Member, who gave the tithes and offering mini-sermon, which always preceded the regular homily. "Is your employer offering extra hours or overtime? Can you work a second job or give a portion of your retirement?"

My mind drifted to our youth. Some of our teenagers had recently been caught dealing and using drugs, as well as engaging in premarital sex. I wondered if it was in the best interest of our church youth—those who needed more time and better relationships with their parents—for us to take on more hours at work? Perhaps it would've been better to work less hours, to lighten our stress loads, and to build intimate relationships with our children.

According to Josh McDowell, "Kids are looking for something to satisfy their deep God-instilled needs: love, acceptance, approval, affirmation and intimacy... and when those needs go unmet in home, church, and school, adolescents intensify the search in other less healthy areas."[26] Children raised in a family with close, loving relationships and who are given plenty of affirmation, affection, and acceptance are less likely to engage in premarital sex than those who feel incomplete, inadequate, and unappreciated.[27] Those with a low self-esteem are more likely to use drugs and alcohol.[28]

While it may be obvious that children of addicts don't get their emotional needs met, there are many children in church households that appear intact, yet the depth and quality of parent/child relationships is not enough. When Mom and Dad work long hours and then give an excessive amount of time toward work and church activities, children suffer. Perhaps we weren't being told to work less hours because our tithes would go down when our income decreased.

"You know, if you had enough faith, she would be healed," said Church Elder Jake, as we stood around Grandma's bed.

Several of our family and church members laid hands on Grandma as Aunt Mae began to reverently pray, asking God to bring about His will. Peace surrounded us, and it felt as though God's Presence was enveloping us. When she finished praying, another church member took over. With demanding and commanding tones, she began to rebuke the devil, bind the 'spirit of disease', and call forth Grandma's healing, much like I had done in the past.

Suddenly, it felt as if God's peace was wrenched away, and a strong sensation of displeasure pressed in on me. I include this with hesitation because we are too often led astray by feelings, sensations, and experiences. Consider a woman whose boyfriend makes her feel loved in the bedroom. While he is using her for his own immediate gratification, she interprets his self-centered lust to be love.

Because we can't be certain whether our impressions come from God, our imagination, or another spirit, feelings are not solid enough to base theological doctrine upon. We should always give deference to the Scriptures over sensations and experiences. I believe, however, that there may be times when God gives the gift of discernment, moments when He supernaturally steers us in His direction.

The sensation which I felt alerted me to the idea that something was very wrong. While the Bible tells us to resist the devil, it does not instruct us to rebuke Satan, nor to verbally bind demons. In fact, doing so might be dangerous. According to the Bible, the Lord is the One who rebukes the devil, and the archangel, Michael, didn't dare to do so.

> *The LORD said to Satan, "The LORD rebuke you, Satan! Indeed, the LORD who has chosen Jerusalem rebuke you! Is this not a brand plucked from the fire?" Zechariah 3:2 NASB*

> *Yet in the same way these men, also by dreaming, defile the flesh, and reject authority, and revile angelic majesties. But Michael the archangel, when he disputed with the devil and argued about the body of Moses, did not dare pronounce against him a railing judgment, but said, "The Lord rebuke you!" But these men revile the things which they do not understand; and the things which they know by instinct, like unreasoning animals, <u>by these things they are destroyed</u>. Jude 1:8-10 NASB (Emphasis mine)*

I had no idea of the diabolical nature of some of our spiritual warfare and positive confession techniques, but that discovery would soon be made.

"**I** don't understand why the little boy at church is back to wearing his thick glasses," I said.

"Me neither," replied Mom.

This phenomenon had happened to many others in the past. People would claim to be healed at a church service and be able to do without their canes, walkers, hearing aids, or glasses, and then they would eventually return to church with those devices.

Some of us may have had an emotional experience which caused us to feel healed temporarily, but when the placebo effect wore off, the disease was still there. Others, like myself, may have been touched by supernatural power, which helped initially and then failed. Any way a person looked at it, this situation with the little boy and his glasses was downright wrong. A god who rescinded a child's healing would not deserve to be followed.

I thought about several disabled children who had been to our church over the years and hadn't been healed. Their parents had been taught about divine health, which hadn't occurred. Did they go to church somewhere else? Were they angry with God? Did they leave the faith because of the inconsistencies? What is the true effect of the WoF movement on Christianity?

23 Spiritual Warfare, Anointing for Wealth, and Visualizing God

But I am afraid that, as the serpent deceived Eve by his craftiness, your minds will be led astray from the simplicity and purity of devotion to Christ. For if one comes and preaches another Jesus whom we have not preached, or you receive a different spirit which you have not received, or a different gospel which you have not accepted, you bear this beautifully.
2 Corinthians 11:3-4 NASB

Music with a heavy, voodoo-like drum beat intruded on my attempts to intercede during the prayer meeting at church. Congregation members walked in different directions throughout the sanctuary using various spiritual warfare techniques, such as cursing the spirit of poverty, binding demons, rebuking the devil, commanding spiritual forces to obey, and demanding that God keep His Word. Some were using angry sounding tongues, as I had done in the past when I thought I was rebuking demons in another language. A strong feeling of discord—as if two opposing spirits were repelling one another—made me want to leave.

Lord, are You repulsed by an evil presence in this sanctuary?

Spiritual warfare has different meanings within various Christian denominations, even among Charismatic and Pentecostal churches. Not all Spirit-filled and/or WoF churches use the same music, but most utilize similar warfare-like 'prayer' methods. Even though one doesn't find such techniques in the Bible, books and movies like *War Room* give these types of 'prayer' an aura of godliness, bringing them into mainstream evangelical churches.

I decided to go to Evangelical Free Church occasionally. The following Sunday, Tyler, Amber, and I went to Uncle Pat and Aunt Mae's church. Pastor Doug talked about the importance of reading our Bibles and the priority of relationships between parents and their children. He commended a life of simplicity, sacrifice, and intimacy with God. I experienced no confusion at the end of the sermon and didn't have to try to harmonize the teaching with the writings of the Bible, as had been the case with WoF doctrines.

"**I**'ve been reading about repentance, surrender, and humility, and I think these characteristics are vital to the Christian life," I said to Mom. We were seated in our usual row, talking before the Sunday morning service began. "We need to learn more about them."

The church leader behind us, a relative of ours named Roger, interrupted our conversation. "People don't want to hear about those things." His thick eyebrows pulled together, forming two vertical lines in between. "We need to be telling people how they can be successful. That's what they want to hear."

After we sang a few songs, Church Leader Daryl gave the sermon. (Pastor Bill was in Africa, spreading the WoF message).

"Jesus became poor so we could become rich. In fact, being poor is a sin because it is God's will that we prosper."

"That's right," said Leader Roger, from behind us.

"Amen, praise the Lord," Daryl's wife cheered from the front row.

"Because they don't practice the prosperity principles, the poor remain in poverty. We shouldn't give money to them because they aren't good ground. Instead, we should be investing money into ministries that promote kingdom principles.

"We need to be wealthy and powerful so we can promote the kingdom of God with our money. Our world is filled with broken people who are looking for success, and we have the answer to their problems!"

If the prosperity message is correct, then it would be true that poor people could become wealthy by applying the WoF principles. Therefore, those who remain in poverty could be blamed for their ignorance. However, the New Testament writers didn't instruct the poor to sow financial seeds into the ministries of rich preachers. The Bible says,

A person who gets ahead by oppressing the poor or by showering gifts on the rich will end in poverty. Proverbs 22:16 NLT

All they [the apostles] asked was that we should continue to remember the poor, the very thing I [Paul] had been eager to do all along. Galatians 2:10 NIV

The generous will themselves be blessed, for they share their food with the poor. Proverbs 22:9 NIV

Whoever is kind to the poor lends to the LORD, and he will reward them for what they have done. Proverbs 19:17 NIV

Whoever gives to the poor will lack nothing, but those who close their eyes to poverty will be cursed. Proverbs 28:27 NLT

Give generously to the poor, not grudgingly, for the LORD your God will bless you in everything you do. Deuteronomy 15:10 NLT

While many of us in the WoF camp truly loved the Lord, the idea of a poor Jesus was almost repulsive. Some of us would not have given our lives to a Savior who doesn't promise power, prestige, and purse in this life. Our hearts had appeared changed because we switched from bars and nightclubs to church fellowship, and we had given up well-known addictions for a subtle, religious one with the potential to be eternally fatal.

"**T**oday, I'll be giving my yearly sermon on money," said Pastor Doug.

I groaned inwardly, expecting to endure the same verses that I'd heard so frequently. Pastor Doug, however, taught about the importance of giving to the poor, the danger of seeking worldly wealth, the importance of simplifying our lives so we could have time for deeper family relationships, and the value of stay-at-home mothers. He shared Scriptures that had never been taught at WoF Church.

Sodom's sins were pride, gluttony, and laziness, while the poor and needy suffered outside her door. Ezekiel 16:49 NLT

"What sorrow awaits you who are rich, for you have your only happiness now." Luke 6:24 NLT

The seeds that fell among the thorns represent those who hear the message, but all too quickly the message is crowded out by the cares and riches and pleasures of this life. And so ***they never grow into maturity****.* *Luke 8:14 NLT (Emphasis mine)*

Now the Pharisees, ***who were lovers of money****, were listening to all these things and were scoffing at Him. And He said to them, "You are those who justify yourselves in the sight of men, but God knows your hearts; for* ***that which is highly esteemed among men is detestable in the sight of God****." Luke 16:14–15 NASB (Emphasis mine)*

He has brought down princes from their thrones and exalted the humble. He has filled the hungry with good things and ***sent the rich away with empty hands****.* *Luke 1:52–53 NLT (Mary—the Magnificat, emphasis mine)*

Pastor Doug's sermon about money stood in stark contrast to the message at WoF Church the following week.

"Jesus talked about money more than any other subject, so it is important to address finances in church." Our worship leader at WoF Church walked across the stage as he began his sermon. "Poor people are more preoccupied and obsessed with money than rich people because they don't have the finances to pay their bills. You see, money is always on their minds. Once a person becomes wealthy and doesn't have to worry about finances, their mind is free to think about other things."

In my devotional time after the service, I meditated on this Bible passage:

So, because you are lukewarm—neither hot nor cold—I am about to spit you out of my mouth. You say, ***'I am rich; I have acquired wealth and do not need a thing.'*** *But you do not realize that you are wretched, pitiful, poor, blind, and naked. I counsel you to buy from me gold refined in the fire, so you can become rich; and white clothes to wear, so you can cover your shameful nakedness; and salve to put on your eyes, so you can see.* *Revelation 3: 16-18 NIV (Emphasis mine).*

I wondered to myself, What if we are the ones who assume we are rich, proclaiming our wealth, when we are spiritually poor, blind, and destitute?

"**I** don't need your money. I have an anointing for wealth on my life." Preacher Wisdom was back at our church. "I'm already rich. To receive a harvest of my anointing, sow your financial seeds into my ministry. Break the curse of poverty!"

I believe this is what God says about preachers who swindle money from the flock.

In their greed they will make up clever lies to get hold of your money. But God condemned them long ago, and their destruction will not be delayed. 2 Peter 2:3 NLT

Wondering if Preacher Wisdom was making merchandise of us, I felt ashamed for the thoughts and pushed them away. Pastor Bill would call him out if he was a charlatan, wouldn't he? For God's Word says,

Be shepherds of God's flock that is under your care, watching over them—not because you must, but because you are willing, as God wants you to be; not pursuing dishonest gain, but eager to serve; 1 Peter 5:2 NIV

None of us should ever think that we can purchase God's anointing by sowing money into a preacher's ministry. When a sorcerer named Simon saw that the Holy Spirit was imparted through the laying on of the apostles' hands, he brought money and offered it to them.

But Peter replied, "May your money be destroyed with you for thinking God's gift can be bought! You can have no part in this, for your heart is not right with God. Repent of your wickedness and pray to the Lord. Perhaps he will forgive your evil thoughts, for I can see that you are full of bitter jealousy and are held captive by sin." Acts 8:20–23 NLT

Tyler picked up a book from Mom's table called *The Word-Faith Controversy: Understanding the Health and Wealth Gospel*, by Robert M. Bowman.

"Grandma, may I read your book?" he asked.

"Sure. You can take it home if you'd like."

The following evening, the kids and I reclined in our living room as I read to them.

"Mom?" Tyler asked a question as I opened our bedtime devotional. "Is it possible that those of us in the Word of Faith movement have fallen for the same temptation as Adam and Eve—wanting to be like God?"

"Well," I hesitated. "Our Word of Faith leaders have made some radical claims, but I don't think the majority of us believe we are gods." As I spoke, I felt a familiar anxiety, cognitive dissonance. I was clinging to contradictory and incompatible belief systems, and my conscience was trying to pierce through the darkness of my deceitful heart.

"**Y**ou must not think negatively about your bishop (Pastor Bill's new title)," admonished our guest minister, Preacher Green. "God has given me a message for you. Your bishop has a vision for the church, for the school, and for a new youth center. You need to get behind that vision."

What if our bishop's dream is getting in the way of the Lord's vision? I wondered.

When the sermon was over, Preacher Green said, "Bishop Bill, I want you to sit in this chair." Turning to the congregation, he instructed, "Each person who has thought or spoken negatively about Bishop, please line up in the center aisle of the church."

Bishop Bill sat on stage as a long succession of members came to him, one after another, kneeling and apologizing at his feet. I was perturbed, wondering whether I should have been in that line.

Though what happened on the cross is the central, most important event in Christianity, the ultimate purpose for which Jesus came to earth, one of our church's favorite preachers, *Apostle* Myles Munroe, alleged, "Our good news is not about Calvary...not even the resurrection....The good news is not Jesus....The good news is about a kingdom."

Myles claimed that the Christian church has been wrongly fixated on teaching what the world doesn't want to hear, such as the message of the cross and the blood of Jesus. He said we should be teaching that we are royalty, meant to *take dominion* over the earth, adopted to *rule a powerful government system*, and destined for success and wealth.[29]

Yet, the Bible says,

For the word of the cross is foolishness to those who are perishing, but to us who are being saved it is the power of God. *1 Corinthians 1:18 NASB*

The *New Apostolic Reformation* (NAR) is a movement within all WoF churches and in many Pentecostal churches that sets up a hierarchy of spiritual elitism where self-styled apostles and prophets are considered more exalted than others. These top positional titles have been sold by the late Charles Peter Wagner (whom many consider to be the founder of the NAR), as if money can buy rank in God's kingdom. Perhaps Paul would have rebuked the leaders of the NAR with words like these:

These people are false apostles. They are deceitful workers who disguise themselves as apostles of Christ. But I am not surprised! Even Satan disguises himself as an angel of light. So it is no wonder that his servants also disguise themselves as servants of righteousness. In the end they will get the punishment their wicked deeds deserve. *2 Corinthians 11:13–15 NLT*

While the NAR purports to restore the positions of the apostle and prophet, apostle was a title given to the original New Testament men who had seen Jesus directly, who were sent out as ambassadors for Christ, and who were chosen by God's Spirit to lay the church foundations. What house needs a second foundation set on top of the first? Are the leaders of this movement suggesting that the foundation laid by the apostles and prophets is no longer enough?

So then you are no longer strangers and aliens, but you are fellow citizens with the saints, and are of God's household, ***having been built on the foundation of the apostles and prophets****, Christ Jesus Himself being the corner stone, in whom the whole building, being fitted together, is growing into a holy temple in the Lord, in whom you also are being built together into a dwelling of God in the Spirit.* *Ephesians 2:19-22 NASB (Emphasis mine)*

Dominion Now / Kingdom Now doctrines intermingle with WoF tenets because both are focused on achieving elevated status, wealth, and power to control this temporary world. The NAR, dovetailing with Kingdom Now/ Dominion Now theology, alleges that the churches' commission in these last days is to take dominion over the earth. Through supernatural power, spiritual warfare against demons, signs, and wonders, as well as through a transfer of the world's wealth to the church, we are to seize the earthly kingdom from Satan. Then, supposedly, when the church is reigning over the earth, Jesus will return.

The Bible doesn't say that Christ's kingdom will take over the world until *after* the old earth and old heavens are destroyed. In fact, before the Day of the Lord, evil and deception (like these false teachings in the church) will continue to increase to such a degree that there will be a great apostasy (people turning away from God, refusing His truth), so much so that it will be hard to find faithful followers of Christ. Speaking of His return at the end of the age, Jesus asked His disciples,

"...when the Son of Man comes, will He find faith on the earth?" Luke 18:8b NASB

Regarding the return of Christ, Paul told the Thessalonians,

> *Let no one in any way deceive you, for it will not come unless* ***the apostasy comes first****, and the man of lawlessness is revealed, the son of destruction, 2 Thessalonians 2:3 NASB (Emphasis mine)*

Incidentally, the faith teachings may be part of the reason it will be hard to find true faith when Jesus returns. WoF preachers claim that God needed to have faith to create the world, that He is the biggest failure of all, and that He is governed by spiritual laws. How could anyone put faith in such a god?

Just as a spouse who doesn't keep his word cannot be trusted, should we trust a god who is not larger than faith, who makes mistakes, and who isn't sovereign? The faith teachings purport another god and stand against true faith in the God of the Bible.

"**M**om, do you think we should try to call things into existence?" Tyler sat in a rocking chair while Amber relaxed on the floor in front of the fireplace. She was petting Shadow—her newly adopted, black kitten that had replaced her cat from Kentucky. I reclined on the end of the couch because we had just finished devotions.

"Well, Tyler, God's Word says we're to speak those things which are not as though they are. We are supposed to call good things—like health for ourselves, deliverance for your dad, or finances to pay our bills—into existence."

"Are we?" Tyler hesitated a moment. "In Romans 4:17, God is the One who calls things into existence."

"No, that verse has been quoted in church so many times. *We're* the ones who are supposed to call things forth."

"Are you sure, Mom?"

The wood in the fireplace crackled and popped, shooting a burning ember onto the stone hearth. Amber jumped a little further from the fire, cuddling Shadow. I got up from the couch, grabbed the fireplace shovel, and tossed the glowing cinder into the fire while Tyler opened his Bible to the verse in question. We looked at it together.

> *As it is written: "I have made you a father of many nations." He is our father in the sight of God, in whom he believed—the* ***God*** *who gives life to the dead and calls into being things that were not. Romans 4:17 NIV*

I couldn't believe I hadn't seen it. We had essentially placed ourselves in the position of God in that verse. Having heard the twisted interpretation so frequently, my brain had become accustomed to the error. Even when I had read the Bible on my own, I'd automatically considered the verse to be about believers calling things into existence.

Amanda had been single for several years after Jerry's struggle with cancer, and Jeff had been raising Rose and Lilly alone for a year. After a few months of dating, they had a short engagement and were married.

At the wedding reception, Amanda introduced me to their photographer, Jeff's long-time friend. David was my age but had never been married. We talked for quite a while, but I was anxious to get away, concerned that God wouldn't want me in a relationship. If He wanted me to be a single mom forever, I was ready to obey. After the dinner, while David was taking pictures of the wedding party, the kids and I slipped away without saying good-bye.

That night, I dreamt God was arranging a marriage for me, like parents in some cultures do for their children. He asked, ***"How do you know I haven't picked this man [David] for you?"***

If God had given me the dream, I trusted that He would make it happen in His timing, which I sensed was not immediately. Because I had a slipped disc in my neck and could no longer practice dental hygiene, I was busy taking classes and didn't have spare time for a relationship.

A few days later, Tyler said, "I don't think God would want you to be alone. I think He'd want you to have a husband to love you."

"You think so?" I hoped my son was right.

"Excuse me, may I get past you?" asked the latecomer. He pointed to an empty seat in the middle of the row I was in. Only a few, scattered seats remained in the sanctuary at WoF Church.

We were singing our second song, and I'd been into the music so deeply that the gentle tap on my shoulder startled me. As we'd been repeating the soothing phrases of love to Jesus over and over, I'd been envisioning God on His throne in front of me. Swaying from side to side, I focused on the image in my mind. A prickly sensation enveloped me, as if there was static electricity in the air, and I believed the Holy Spirit was upon me. This was the feeling I'd been pursuing, the anointing which I believed would strengthen my Christian walk. I thought I'd entered the Most Holy Place, the glory realm.

"Oh!" I jumped like a frightened animal. "Yes, of course."

When the latecomer tapped my shoulder, I was jolted back to the physical realm, the spiritual sensations left, and I felt irritated. *How dare this inconsiderate person take me out of the Presence of the Lord!* The trance-like, peaceful vibes were gone. I couldn't understand why the spiritual energy hadn't filled me with love, or why my attitude plummeted and resentment surfaced so quickly. Had Uncle Pat been right about people falling into light trances during the music at Word of Faith Church?

Singing short phrases over and over is like repeating a mantra, which is a meditational technique to hypnotize oneself. Mantras are used by eastern mystics to empty their minds and enter altered states of consciousness. As if under a spell, this hypnotic state opens a portal to the spiritual realm, allowing evil spirits to influence the mind and to touch the person with tangible supernatural power.

Johanna Michaelsen—author, researcher, lecturer, and authority on the occult, tells us how she attracted an evil spirit guide, a counterfeit Jesus. In a trance, Johanna created an imaginary room in her mind. She says, "[T]he room was filled with a radiant light that emanated from the figure standing behind it...It was Jesus!...He was glowing with a holy radiance and smiling softly."

That night, Johanna asked the Lord to reveal the spirit. She then saw "the same radiance shining...but something was wrong...The hair was wild and matted, the forehead was covered with a coarse fur and the eyes were slanted, gleaming and wild...blood smeared the muzzle and oozed down long white fangs."[30] The spirit which had presented itself as Jesus appeared to be a werewolf.

While envisioning God on His throne in front of me and zoning out with the repetitive, tranquilizing music, had I accidentally fallen into a light trance and practiced the occult technique of visualization? Might the warm prickly presence, picked up in a church which had been infiltrated with the serpent's lies (as I would soon discover), have been a counterfeit Holy Spirit?

The late Dave Hunt, an internationally recognized expert on the occult who wrote numerous books on theology, apologetics, prophecy, cults, and other religions, and T.A. McMahan, president and executive director of The Berean Call said, "In visualizing 'God' or 'Jesus' or the thing being prayed for, the average Christian is not aware that he is following the same procedure that shamans insist opens a 'magic doorway' in the mind that leads to the sorcerer's world."[31]

In the Bible, there are many warnings against making images and bowing to them.

> *You must not make for yourself an idol of any kind* ***or an image*** *of anything in the heavens or on the earth or in the sea. You must not bow down to them or worship them, Exodus 20:4-5a. NLT (emphasis mine)*

It's easy to understand that we shouldn't trust in statues, pictures, amulets, good luck charms, scapulars, and crystals for protection or salvation, for that is how witchcraft works, but what about creating an image of God in one's mind and worshiping it?

According to Jesus, our thoughts are important. To hate a person is equal to murder, and to lust after a woman is adultery. Viewing pornographic pictures or creating nude images in one's mind is as evil as committing the sexual act. Might this principle apply when one visualizes God in her mind, as though one was worshiping a created graven image?

24 The Law of Attraction

If then the light that is in you is darkness, how great is the darkness! Matthew 6:23b NASB

"We got tired of defending Bishop Bill's fancy cars and extravagant lifestyle to our friends and relatives," said Nancy. "When he built his $700,000 home on the lake, it was the last straw."

"Are you going to church anywhere else?" I asked.

"We want no part of Christianity."

My heart began to ache for my friend, and I felt great concern for many people who had deserted the Gospel after attending WoF Church. How many others in congregations around the world have become disillusioned with God because positive confession techniques and misleading prophecies gave them false hope? How many have left the faith because of the apparent hypocrisy, manifest greed, self-indulgence, and manipulation they've witnessed within church?

While there are many people who truly love Jesus in 'Spirit-filled' and WoF churches, if each of these churches throughout our world were to have as many disillusioned members as my church had, there would be thousands upon thousands of lost people out there—souls swept out into the ocean by the tsunami of apostasy—no longer witnessing for the Lord, but rather against Him.

When hopes don't materialize, and unbiblical prayer techniques fail, there might be no recovery from the devastation that follows. What would it be like to arrive in one's eternal destination and discover oneself in a place far worse than anything fathomable on earth, forever, and ever, and ever? How would it feel to be the WoF leader who looks out over a multitude of condemned souls—sheep who looked to him for guidance—and realizes that he preached a counterfeit gospel, a phony Jesus who offered false security? In all ages, there have been leaders of God's people who've led their sheep in the wrong direction. God reprimands Israel's shepherds in the book of Jeremiah.

"I will send disaster upon the leaders of my people—the shepherds of my sheep—for they have destroyed and scattered the very ones they were expected to care for," says the LORD. This is what the LORD, the God of Israel, says to these shepherds: "Instead of leading my flock to safety, you have deserted them and driven them to destruction. Now I will pour out judgment on you for the evil you have done to them." Jeremiah 23:1–2 NLT

I don't ordinarily use the Message Bible because of various inaccuracies and some new age undertones, which may have been accidental on the author's part. I may receive criticism for doing so, but this version seems to hit the nail on the head regarding several verses, such as this one:

God enters the courtroom. He takes His place at the bench to judge His people. God calls for order in the court, hauls the leaders of His people into the dock: "You've played havoc with this country. Your houses are stuffed with what you've stolen from the poor. What is this anyway? Stomping on my people, grinding the faces of the poor into the dirt?" That's what the Master, GOD-of-the-Angel-Armies, says. Isaiah 3:13–15 Message Bible

I woke up one morning with these words in my mind. You may think you're okay without a husband but think about your children and their need for a father.

After the anguish of divorce, I placed protective walls around my heart to prevent future misery. Having my trust violated by the man who promised to cherish and love me caused a fear of relationships. My disappointment was so severe that I was reluctant to even allow myself to feel happiness. *If I don't get my hopes up, I won't be let down*, I thought.

When Amanda asked if she could give my email address to David, I listed some of my fears. "Tyler and Amber may have genetic tendencies toward alcoholism, and I want to set the best example for them. I'm afraid to be with a man who drinks. It would be hard for anyone to adjust to us. We homeschool and don't watch TV anymore."

"David doesn't watch much TV, and he barely drinks," she replied. "And he's a Christian."

"Alright, I suppose you can give him my email address."

After exchanging several emails with David, I figured I might as well lay everything on the table. If God was bringing us together, it would all work out. I explained my Christian views, that I didn't believe in being alone with men while dating, and that I wouldn't even kiss outside of marriage. Would he still be interested?

"Would it be OK if Jeff invited David over for Thanksgiving dinner at Dad and Mom's house?" asked Amanda.

I thought of my dream about God picking a husband for me, and I considered my children's need for a father. Since we had moved back to Wisconsin, God had allowed their need to remain unmet. "That would be fine."

Several weeks later, David and I met for Thanksgiving. We hadn't seen one another since Jeff and Amanda's wedding, which was many months earlier.

One of the first questions David asked was, "How would you feel about being with a man who drinks socially once in a while?"

I prayed before replying. "Whenever I saw a drink in Kevin's hand, I felt abandoned for alcohol. Seeing a drink in a man's hand would probably make me feel rejected."

"Alcohol means nothing to me. I could give it up forever," David replied.

With great relief, I felt comfortable going forward. Our first date was to a church service. We began to meet twice a month, sometimes at Jeff and Amanda's house in Green Bay, other times at my parents' house.

"Many pagans can produce magic wonders also, but we aren't supposed to follow signs," said Tyler, after doing some research. "Pharaoh's magicians were able to do magic feats, but the signs themselves were not proof of truth. The Antichrist will perform miracles that will lead many away from God." Tyler opened his Bible, and we looked at the verses together.

"For false Christs and false prophets will arise and will show great signs and wonders, so as to mislead, if possible, even the elect." Matthew 24:24 NIV

"It's easy to assume that we are not a part of the 'many' who will fall away in the last days, isn't it, Tyler?" I answered. "I believe God still does miracles in the earth, but it is a natural human tendency to look for exciting church services and miraculous signs, rather than steadily finding God in the Bible and in prayer-time."

As Christians, we are willing to recognize when other religions are involved in demonic practices, but can we consider whether our WoF teachings might be a 'Christianized' version of the occult? I had not yet investigated mystical religions, such as witchcraft, sorcery, Voodoo, and luciferianism, but I would eventually do so. I would also examine *thought actualization* and the *law of attraction* to see how they compared to WoF techniques and doctrine.

We learn from the Bible that some of the angels fell with Satan.

> *The great dragon was hurled down--that ancient serpent called the devil, or Satan, who leads the whole world astray. He was hurled to the earth, and his angels with him. Revelation 12:9 NIV*

We should be especially concerned when ethereal entities try to convince us that Jesus isn't God, that He is not the only way to Heaven, and that the cross isn't necessary. These deceptions are also purported by evil spirits at séances and in occult religions, such as witchcraft and satanism, the exact lies one can find in countless new age books which have been co-authored/channeled by spirit guides. The doctrines of demons in New Age Spirituality bear close resemblance to the teachings that have been brought into Pentecostalism. How is it that these precepts became absorbed into the church?

Please keep in mind that at this point in my life, I did not have the following information:

Phineas Quimby, an occultist who did not regard Jesus as God and didn't believe man needed salvation, founded the New Thought cult (mind science). He believed that positive thoughts attract good things, such as health, wealth, and success, while negative thoughts bring about bad things, like disease and poverty.

This 'law of attraction' is a major theme taught by a group of demonic spirit guides who collectively call themselves Abraham and have been channeled by the medium, Esther Hicks. This sorcerous teaching rests on the foundation which the serpent laid in the Garden of Eden—that human beings are gods, and the technique is used to tap into the power of demons. According to the law of attraction, the conscious thoughts and spoken words of people have creative power *because we are divine within*.

Quimby's mystical teachings captivated the heart of a preacher named E.W. Kenyon, who mingled occult beliefs with Christianity. This syncretistic blend fascinated Kenneth Hagin Sr., who fathered the WoF movement, which is the foundation of the New Apostolic Reformation. Thus, the demonic doctrines—which were based on the Serpent's lie that we can be like God—sprouted within many 'Spirit-filled' churches, and then passed into mainstream Christianity.

Other luciferian/satanic/new age teachings have slithered into WoF doctrine as well. Whereas New Age Spirituality teaches that Jesus had attained Christ-consciousness and that we all can do the same, WoF teachers tell us we are little Christs, or little messiahs. (Christ is Greek for the Hebrew word, Messiah). Whereas NAS proclaims we have a god within (self-deification), WoF televangelists say we are little gods. And whereas visualization is known to be the fastest way into the occult and to attain a demonic spirit guide,[32] WoF preachers teach us to envision health, wealth, success, etc.

New Year's Eve journal entry—

A homeschooled cousin of mine, who happens to be Tyler's age, has been a good companion for him. It's been a hard year for Amber, though, because she's been lonely for a friend. On top of that, her cat disappeared.

In children's church, she wrote this note about the upcoming year:

Three things I would like from God:
A friend
A puppy
A dad

While my life seems to be coming together, several others' fell apart this year. Cecelia's husband, Matt—who had seemed to be delivered by Counselor Susan, made choices that turned him away from her and destroyed their marriage. Perhaps, like many addicts, he had only traded his addiction to alcohol for a more secret obsession.

Pastor Ricky, in whose church I fell under the spiritual power and experienced 'holy laughter', ended up going to prison for molesting a young teenage girl. What kind of a spirit would cause such depravity? Is there a type of demonic anointing?

Incidentally, when the disciples were filled with the Holy Spirit and began speaking in foreign languages, they were accused of being drunk. This is not because they were acting foolish, but more likely because their excitement and euphoria are two emotions that can accompany drunkenness.

Except for those who were demon possessed and exhibited some of the following manifestations, the Bible records no instances of people being slain in the Spirit, rolling on the ground laughing, barking like dogs, hissing like snakes, shrieking, or shaking uncontrollably. The Holy Ghost is not a bartender who causes us to act foolish and drunk, which are works of the flesh. In contrast to worldly drunkenness, the infilling of the Holy Spirit brings sobriety and self-control.

Therefore do not be foolish, but understand what the Lord's will is. Do not get drunk on wine, which leads to debauchery. ***Instead****, be filled with the Spirit, Ephesians 5:17-18 NIV*

But the fruit of the Spirit is love, joy, peace, forbearance, kindness, goodness, faithfulness, gentleness and ***self-control****. Against such things there is no law. Galatians 5:22-23 NIV*

Be alert and of ***sober mind****. Your enemy the devil prowls around like a roaring lion looking for someone to devour. 1 Peter 5:8 NIV*

God is not a God of disorder *but of peace--as in all the congregations of the Lord's people. 1 Corinthians 14: 33 NIV*

"What about the gift of prophecy?" I asked. Bible fellowship at Aunt Mae's house had just ended. "Do you miss that?"

"Well," said Aunt Mae. "I've never been given a false prophecy at Evangelical Free Church. I think part of the problem is that we chase harder to experience the *gifts* of the Spirit than we seek the *Giver* of gifts. The Gospel is to be centered on Jesus, not on supernatural power."

"I guess you're right. When I look back at those times where I felt tangible spiritual energy in church, there was immediate gratification, but no lasting benefit."

"You know, Ariel, in the Bible, we do not find the apostles setting up meetings and announcing that one of the disciples was going to be moving in the gift of prophecy, healing, or miracles. The Holy Spirit fell on believers according to His own will, not according to the presumption of men."

David was a man of many thoughts and ideas. One day he said, "I was driving past a beautiful home, and it looks like a perfect place for the elderly. I've always had a vision of running a nursing home with a daycare in it."

"I've entertained the idea of running a bed and breakfast," I replied.

We were engaged in March and started taking marriage classes with Bishop Bill and his wife. We planned to be married in August, and I hoped to give him two children of his own. It looked as if God might grant me baby three and baby four after all.

25 The Antichrist Little Gods Doctrine

Children, it is the last hour [the end of this age]; and just as you heard that the antichrist is coming [the one who will oppose Christ and attempt to replace Him], even now many antichrists (false teachers) have appeared, which confirms our belief that it is the last hour. They went out from us [seeming at first to be Christians], but they were not really of us [because they were not truly born again and spiritually transformed]; for if they had been of us, they would have remained with us; but they went out [teaching false doctrine], so that it would be clearly shown that none of them are of us.
1 John 2:18-19 Amplified Bible

Grandma choked on the yogurt and blueberries I had just spooned into her mouth, her face turning beet red. Her swallowing muscles were becoming more paralyzed as the disease progressed, and she was losing weight, wasting away.

Wiping her mouth, I asked, "Are you okay, Grandma?"

She drew in a ragged breath and said in a raspy voice, "Are you okay, Grandma?"

After I finished feeding her, Mom and I set Grandma in her wheelchair and took her for a walk. The sun was shining, and the air was cool, crisp, and fresh smelling as we walked along a back road toward a small, nearby pond.

"Mom, I was thinking about one of the hallmarks of a cult that you mentioned years ago. It was about relying on extra-biblical information, such as the visions of a religious leader. Might we have put too much trust in the visions of Kenneth Hagin?"

"Well, our leaders are Spirit-filled Christians, so their visions are as valid as those of the Apostle John, the writer of the book of Revelation."

"But what if a lying spirit wanted to introduce deception into the church?"

"I suppose that's possible," she replied.

"The health and wealth teachings always brought an element of confusion to me. They don't seem to mesh with certain principles within the Scriptures."

Mom stopped pushing the wheelchair and adjusted Grandma's hat. "When I was on the Internet the other day, I came across a list of Scripture verses which contradict our WoF teachings."

"I'm beginning to wonder if our Health and Wealth doctrines might be cultic. It concerns me that we lift ourselves up as the ones who have power to make commands on earth, believing that Jesus no longer has the authority. According to my Bible, Jesus continued to cast out demons, heal the sick, and raise the dead, even *after* He had given authority to the 70 disciples."

"You have a good point," Mom responded. "The Bible doesn't say Jesus lost the authority when He shared it with His disciples."

"Our prosperity teachings and our leaders' visions make it appear as if the rest of the work of salvation—taking back our physical health and achieving material wealth—is up to us to complete because Jesus can't. And yet we know Jesus stated, 'It is finished' *before* He died."

"That's true," Mom replied. "But at least none of our WoF teachers claimed to be God."

"Oh, my goodness! We've got to get home and search the Internet! I believe they have!"

When we arrived at Mom's house, we helped Grandma into bed and headed up to Mom's computer to research WoF quotes. Mom sat down at her desk, and with a few clicks of her mouse, we came across this citation by Kenneth Copeland.

"The Spirit of God spoke to me and He said, 'Son, realize this. Now follow me in this and don't let your tradition trip you up.' He said, 'Think this way: a twice-born man whipped Satan in his own domain.' And I threw my Bible down, like that, and I said, 'What?' He said, 'A born-again man defeated Satan. The firstborn of many brethren defeated him.' He said, **'You are the very image and the very copy of that one.'** I said, 'Goodness, gracious sakes alive!' And I began to see what had gone on in there. And I said, 'Well now you don't mean, you couldn't dare mean that I could have done that same thing?' He said, 'Oh yeah. If you'd had the same knowledge of the Word of God that He did, you could've done the same thing, cause you're a reborn man too.'"[33]

"That's not true," said Mom. "Only God, the second Person of the Trinity, could become the perfect sacrificial Lamb of God. Kenneth was born with the sinful spirit of Adam, and his blood was tainted the first time he sinned."

"Right," I agreed. "And he wasn't born of a virgin, nor was he the only begotten Son of God. He wasn't the Word who was with God in the beginning, creating all things."

"He wasn't born on the exact day or in the correct town of the Old Testament prophecies either. It makes you wonder whether Kenneth knows what the Bible says about the Messiah."

Next, Mom found a video of Kenneth saying "[W]hen I read the Bible where He (Jesus) says, 'I AM,' I just smile and say, 'Yes, I AM too!'"[34]

"Wow, Mom. When Jesus said the words 'Before Abraham was, **I am,'** He meant He was God. A mere man who makes such claims would be committing blasphemy."

We watched another video clip of Kenneth where he said, "You don't have a god in you, you are one!"[35]

Mom then found a portion of one of Creflo Dollar's tapes, *Made after his Kind*, dated Sept. 15, & 22, 2002, in which he told church members that "Horses produce horses, and dogs produce dogs, and cats produce cats, and fish produce fish, and God produced gods!"

"I don't believe it." I remarked when Mom paused the video. "God produced the animals, too, and they aren't gods. Where does the Bible say God has DNA, or that He used His genetic material to produce man?"

Mom pressed play, and Creflo continued. "Now I gotta hit this thing real hard in the very beginning because I ain't got time to go through all this, but I am going to say to you right now ***you are gods***, little "g". You are *gods* because you came from God... The only human part about you is this physical body that you live in."[36]

After watching the video of Creflo Dollar, we watched a clip by Joyce Meyer as she said, "You know, I was listening to a set of tapes by one man and he explained it like this... He said, 'Why do people have such a fit about God calling...His man...little gods? If He's God, what's He going to call them but the god-kind?'"[37]

Mom paused the video. "He called us mankind, not god-kind in the Bible."

(Allow me to interject a few Bible verses, and then the conversation will resume.)

In his hand is the life of every creature and the breath of all ***mankind****. Job 12:10 NIV (Emphasis mine)*

Then the LORD God formed a ***man*** *[not a god] from the* ***dust of the ground*** *[not God's DNA] and breathed into his nostrils the breath of life, and the man became a living being. Genesis 2:7 NIV (Emphasis mine)*

"Behold, I belong to God like you; I too have been ***formed out of the clay****." Job 33:6 NASB (Emphasis mine)*

For He Himself knows our frame; He is mindful that ***we are but dust****. Psalm 103:14 NASB (Emphasis mine)*

"You're right." I knelt next to Mom so I wouldn't have to bend my neck to see the computer.

Mom pressed play, and Joyce continued. "I mean, if you, as a human being have a baby, you call it a human kind. If cattle has (sic) another cattle, they call it cattle-kind. So, I mean, what's God supposed to call us?"

Mom stopped the video again. "God didn't say, 'Let us make man after our own *kind*.' He said, 'Let us make man after our own *image*'."

"Right. Neither did He say, 'Let us make gods after our own image,'" I replied.

On Biblestudytools.com, I found a well-respected commentary by Matthew Henry, a theologian and pastor who was an expert in Greek and Hebrew. I looked up his notes regarding Genesis 1:27, the verse about man being made in God's image.

"Man was not made in the likeness of any creature that went before him, but in the likeness of his Creator; yet still between God and man there is an infinite distance. **Christ only is the express image of God's person**, as the Son of his Father, having the same nature. It is only some of God's honour that is put upon man, who is God's image only as the shadow in the glass, or the king's impress upon the coin."[38] (Emphasis mine)

In a sermon on itunes, TD Jakes said,

"When God created Adam, He created him from the dust of the earth. God put his mouth on him; blew in the breath of life. He became a living soul. God said, 'I wanted to see what I looked like, so I made you in my image. You have my DNA. You [are] out of me. You're a derivative of me."[39]

If that isn't adding to the Bible, I don't know what is. God never said that we have His DNA or that we are a derivative of Him. Though our WoF teachers continually tell us that we are gods, the Scriptures clearly state that there is only one God.

> *For You are great and do wondrous deeds;* ***You alone are God****. Psalm 86:10 NASB (emphasis mine)*

> *"You are My witnesses," declares the Lord, "And My servant whom I have chosen, so that you may know and believe Me* and *understand that I am He. Before Me there was no God formed, and* ***there will be none after Me****." Isaiah 43:10 NASB (emphasis mine)*

> *"****I am the Lord, and there is no other****;* b***esides Me there is no God****. That men may know from the rising to the setting of the sun* that *there is no one besides Me.* **I am the Lord, and there is no other**," Isaiah 45:5-6 NASB (emphasis mine)

> *Know therefore today, and take it to your heart, that the LORD, He is God in heaven above and on the earth below;* ***there is no other****. Deuteronomy 4:39 NASB*

> *Now to the King eternal, immortal, invisible,* ***the only God****, be honor and glory forever and ever. Amen. 1 Timothy 1: 17 NASB*

> *Well, we all know that an idol is not really a god and that* ***there is only one God****. 1 Corinthians 8:4b NLT*

As with cults, WoF preachers are well-known for demoting Jesus. In a video by Mark Chironna, these premises were made:

1.) In Genesis 1:3, God said, 'Let there be light.'

2.) Jesus said, 'I am the Light of the world.'

Mark concludes, "When God **the Father** said, 'Let there be, what came out of His mouth was His Son.'"[40]

Genesis 1:3 does not say "God, the Father said, "Let there be light." Jesus, as part of the triune Godhead, created light with the Father.

Then God said, "Let there be light"; and there was light. Gen. 1:3 NASB

Besides that, the Bible says Jesus existed before anything was created, which would include light.

*Christ is the visible image of the invisible God. He **existed before anything was created** and is supreme over all creation, He **existed before anything else**, and he holds all creation together. Colossians 1:15, 17 NLT (Emphasis mine)*

Justin Peters, an ordained minister who is widely regarded as one of the foremost authorities on the WoF movement, has a YouTube video that shows a conversation where Paula White is hosting Larry Huch.

"Jesus Christ is not the only begotten Son of God. He is not," said Larry Huch.

Paula White shakes her head, as if in agreement, saying "He's the first fruit."[41]

Yet, the Bible says,

*"For God so loved the world, that He gave **His only *begotten Son**, that whoever believes in Him shall not perish, but have eternal life." John 3:16 NASB (Emphasis mine)*

*Begotten-literal only child, unique Son of God

Kenneth Hagin also diminishes Jesus' incarnation by stating, "The believer is as much an incarnation of God as Jesus Christ."[42]

Those who claim Jesus was not the only begotten Son of God, as well as those who claim we are as much an incarnation of God as Jesus, make it look like Jesus was just a man, not superior to believers, not God incarnate in the flesh. He who denies that Jesus (God incarnate) has come in the flesh has the spirit of the antichrist.

By this you know the Spirit of God: every spirit that confesses that Jesus Christ has come in the flesh is from God; and every spirit that does not confess Jesus is not from God; this is the spirit of the antichrist, of which you have heard that it is coming, and now it is already in the world. 1 John 4:2-3 NASB

"**I** saw Joyce Meyer on TV the other day," said Mom, "and she was saying that Jesus went to hell, and the demons had Him on the floor and were standing on His back. She claimed they were mocking Him, laughing at Him, and having a big party."[43]

"I've always enjoyed her practical advice, but the Bible doesn't say those things," I replied. "If Jesus was going to be in hell for three days, why would He tell the thief on the cross next to Him that they would be together in Paradise that same day?" (Luke 23:43)

"The stories about Jesus going to hell and being born again must be an attempt to make it appear as if He needed to *attain* divinity," Mom replied. "That way, being born again can be about becoming gods."

In WoF theology, alleging that Jesus' work of redemption was to return man to godhood, man supposedly needs to realize that he became deified at the time he was born again. If we reject this or any of the above WoF beliefs, the bedrock of the movement that we stand upon begins to crumble. Elevating ourselves to the status and power of godhood is the *cornerstone of the WoF teaching that justifies all its other practices and 'prayer' techniques.*

Stripping Jesus of His deity and reducing His unique position as the Son of God enables us to believe that we can ascend to a position just as glorified as His. Then we can believe our spoken words are like those of God, containing creative power, enabling us to bring about those things which we name and claim. We cannot adhere to the softcore branches of prosperity, health, success, and word-power on the WoF tree without subscribing to those hardcore, idolatrous roots by which the movement is anchored.

We can irreverently find what we want in the Word of God, foolishly mishandling and trampling on that which is most holy. Our lusts and inclinations confirm our bias wherever we look, as we infer our own ideas into the Scriptures while we filter out those things that oppose our personal passions.

These intentional heresies aren't a minor variation of inconsequence, but rather, they are *blasphemous doctrines, contrary to our foundational Christian beliefs.

*Blasphemy–the act or offense of speaking sacrilegiously about God or sacred things; profane talk.[44]

But there were also false prophets in Israel, just as there will be false teachers among you. They will cleverly teach destructive heresies and even deny the Master who bought them. In this way, they will bring sudden destruction on themselves. Many will follow their evil teaching and shameful immorality. And because of these teachers, the way of truth will be slandered. In their greed they will make up clever lies to get hold of your money. But God condemned them long ago, and their destruction will not be delayed. 2 Peter 2:1–3 NLT

What sorrow awaits them! For they follow in the footsteps of Cain, who killed his brother. Like Balaam, they deceive people for money. And like Korah, they perish in their rebellion. When these people eat with you in your fellowship meals commemorating the Lord's love, they are like dangerous reefs that can shipwreck you. They are like shameless shepherds who care only for themselves. They are like clouds blowing over the land without giving any rain. They are like trees in autumn that are doubly dead, for they bear no fruit and have been pulled up by the roots. They are like wild waves of the sea, churning up the foam of their shameful deeds. They are like wandering stars, doomed forever to blackest darkness. Jude:11-13 NLT

Teachers and preachers in the WoF movement are preaching a different gospel than the apostles taught, bringing a curse upon themselves, according to the verse below. We must love them enough to expose the error. In his letter to the Galatians, Paul actually uses the word anathema, doomed to hell.

I marvel that ye are so soon removed from him that called you into the grace of Christ unto another gospel, for there is not another; but there are some that trouble you and would pervert the gospel of the Christ. But even if we, or an angel from heaven, were to preach any other gospel unto you than that which we have preached unto you, ***let him be anathema****. As we said before, so do I say now again, If anyone preaches any other gospel unto you than what ye have received,* ***let him be anathema****. Galatians 1:6–9 Jubilee (Emphasis mine)*

In the next verse, we see that if a person is righteous in every way, and his only sin is greed, as may be the case with some preachers, this would be enough to keep him from spending eternity with God. The Lord can save him, but he must not look to a rich, prosperity-promoting, counterfeit Jesus for salvation.

You can be sure that no immoral, impure, or greedy person will inherit the Kingdom of Christ and of God. For a greedy person is an idolater, worshiping the things of this world. Ephesians 5:5 NLT

26 Witchcraft Incantations

"But for the cowardly and unbelieving and abominable and murderers and immoral persons and sorcerers and idolaters and all liars, their part will be in the lake that burns with fire and brimstone, which is the second death." Revelation 21:8 NASB

hristians pray with a spirit of humility, making supplication to the Lord. Their prayers take on the form of asking. In witchcraft, our ‘prayers’ are in the form of commands and demands.”

When I listened to a former witch explain the difference between Christian prayer and witchcraft spells, I realized how similar our ‘prayers’ were to witchcraft invocations. Unfortunately, there were more resemblances between the WoF movement and the craft.

“At the core of witchcraft, we find a fascination with knowing the future and a desire to manipulate areas which are beyond our rightful jurisdiction,” the former witch continued. “Witchcraft seeks to control the physical world around itself by taking charge of spiritual forces and using forbidden power through spells and incantations.”

“What exactly are spells and incantations?” asked the show host.

“They are words spoken with intention and filled with sorcerous power to make things happen.”

Perhaps I had found the reason why it felt like God was displeased during prayer times of commanding, demanding, rebuking, and the insertion of my name into Bible verses about wealth. Had I invoked the precious name of the Lord Jesus in witchcraft-type incantations? Had I exploited the Holy Scriptures of God, using His Word in ways He never intended?

The sun was just peeking over the horizon as the little black and white Shih-tzu, a tiny ball of fur, danced on the blacktop parking lot at Sam’s Club. She followed her former owner to our car, and Amber scooped the puppy into her arms. A half-hour later, my daughter ran up our spiral staircase to Tyler's room, where he lay sleeping.

"Look Tyler. Our new puppy!"

Tyler opened his eyes to see Snuggles, doing the doggie paddle in the air, as Amber dangled the dog above his face.

"When I heard that you hadn't even kissed before the wedding ceremony, it meant a lot to me." Colleen, a young teen-ager from David's side of the relation, stood before us at the head table during our wedding reception. "It makes me want to wait until I get married too."

(14 years later, David and I caught up with Colleen at her grandmother's funeral, and she said, "Waiting until marriage makes the wedding night so much more special.")

Though David and I don't believe everybody needs to abstain from alcohol, the presence of alcoholic beverages was absent at our reception and will be absent in our home. Going into marriage, I knew that my relationship with Jesus must always supersede my relationship with my husband.

In my dream one night, there were many prophets giving 'Words from the Lord.' All were proclaiming a time of great financial prosperity. After they spoke, one lone prophet said, "God's people won't be extremely rich."

Then the Lord spoke. **The last prophet is the real prophet of God.**

When I couldn't sleep after my dream, I read in the book of 1 Kings. To entice the wicked King Ahab to war, God granted a lying spirit to put words in the mouths of false prophets.

> *And finally a spirit approached the LORD and said, 'I can do it!'*
> *'How will you do this?' The Lord asked.*
> *And the spirit replied, 'I will go out and inspire all of Ahab's prophets to speak lies.'*
> *'You will succeed,' said the LORD. 'Go ahead and do it.'*
> *"So you see, the LORD has put a lying spirit in the mouths of all your prophets. For the Lord has pronounced your doom." 1 Kings 22:21–23 NLT*

The following night, I came across these verses:

A horrible and shocking thing has happened in this land—the prophets give false prophecies, and the priests rule with an iron hand. Worse yet, my people like it that way! But what will you do when the end comes? Jeremiah 5:30–31 NLT

Then the LORD said, "These prophets are telling lies in my name. I did not send them or tell them to speak. I did not give them any messages. They prophesy of visions and revelations they have never seen or heard. They speak foolishness made up in their own lying hearts." Jeremiah 14:14 NLT

"I have not sent these prophets, yet they run around claiming to speak for me. I have given them no message, yet they go on prophesying." Jeremiah 23:21–22 NLT

I wondered how we could know whether a prophet's word is true. I started thinking about how many times the words 'Thus saith the Lord' had prefaced prophetic promises given to other Christians and to myself in the various Spirit-filled churches, conferences, and ladies meetings I had attended.

Sick people were told they would recover… and then they died. Successful pregnancy was guaranteed… before the miscarriage. Restoration of marriage was just around the corner… until the spouse insisted on divorce. The lame were told they would walk again, deliverance from addiction was close at hand, large sums of money would wipe out the debt, the next revival was coming to our church.

Though I never said, "Thus sayeth the Lord," I gave prophecies I believed were from God. Were the recipients counting on my predictions? What does it mean to take the Lord's name in vain?

I came to realize my need to repent. More importantly, I began to understand the urgency of sounding the alarm for others. If our friends and family members are surrounded with occult fires that threaten their eternity, we ought to be doing everything possible to expose the errors in the WoF movement. To do so may risk the reputation of our leaders, but dare we remain silent as a great holocaust of souls is taking place?

"My name is Marlene, and I'm the Sunday School teacher here."

The game room at Evangelical Free Church was bustling with activity as we entered for the first time, and the instructor, an energetic woman with short, brown hair, approached us and introduced herself.

While Marlene and I were becoming acquainted, her daughter came up to Amber and said, "Hi, my name is Breanna. Would you like me to show you around?"

"Amber's been looking for a new friend since we moved back to Wisconsin almost two years ago." I watched as Breanna took Amber by the hand and led her off to the games.

Marlene turned to me and smiled, "We homeschool, and my daughter's been praying for a new friend."

"So do we, and so has mine." I returned the smile.

Though Amber's third prayer request had been granted, life was not bringing about baby number three for David and me. After three miscarriages, my doctor suggested we give my 40-year-old body some time to rest. Devastated, I began to wonder if I needed to give up my dream for two more children.

One Sunday afternoon, during my nap, I dreamt about revival. In my dream, the anointing of God didn't come upon one individual and bring that person into the glamorous forefront of a stage, but rather, God's Spirit was scattered upon many people. Collectively, there was a great luminosity surrounding God's children, and this light was an obvious contrast to the world's darkness, which was steadily growing more evil. Those children of God—upon whom the Spirit of the Lord had been dispersed—didn't have noticeable financial wealth, nor did they appear powerful or glorious. They were plain and humble, representative of a people who were willing to sacrifice everything for their Lord.

When I awoke, I wondered, *Might it be possible that our view of revival is wrong? Could it be that the kind of revival we've been expecting—like those with supernatural happenings that are televised on TBN—isn't coming to WoF Church? If not, there's nothing to hold me in this congregation.* (Recall that the Bible does not say there will be a great end-times revival, but rather, a great apostasy).

I needed to eliminate the Pharisaic attitude that my WoF beliefs were the greater truths and that opposing positions were wrong. Just as Kevin's addiction to alcohol had made his life all about him, my addiction to the power, prestige, and purse of the WoF teachings had been corrupting my faith.

How good it had felt to repeat after the guest minister 'I am confident', 'I am a good person', 'I am rich', 'I am successful', and 'I receive favor wherever I go.'

Rather than looking forward to the next time I would get drunk, I looked to the next Ladies' conference, the next powerful televangelist who would pump our congregation up, or to the next prophetess who would give me a prophecy.

New Year's Eve Journal Entry—

What a humbling blow to realize how much darkness I've embraced while being certain I was right! I am reminded once again that I need to maintain a continual attitude of repentance, daily asking God where I might still be wrong, and seeking Him to remove my selfish nature.

"I think it's time for us to leave Word of Faith Church," said David.

I wished we didn't need to withdraw from our church family, but I knew that the sermons carried unbiblical themes. "I'm beginning to see that the Word of Faith message is antagonistic to the Gospel of Jesus," I admitted. "Bishop Bill and his wife did such a wonderful job in our marriage counseling, though."

"Yes, they did," David replied. "Bishop Bill expects a final meeting before anyone leaves, right?"

"He does, and I really don't like confrontation."

Our trial period at Evangelical Free Church had gone well, and an appointment with Bishop Bill needed to be made. While we don't need to—and shouldn't—get into endless debates about every small, peripheral Christian tenet, we do need to protect the Scriptures and defend essential Christian doctrines. May the Lord forgive David and me for supporting a church that promotes false doctrine.

"God tells me when someone is supposed to move on, and He hasn't told me that you should leave," said Bishop Bill, "so I'm very surprised to hear this." David and I sat across the table from Bishop Bill in the church conference room.

We want to get away from the Word of Faith movement," David replied.

"I can see how the Word of Faith teachings have hurt people," admitted Bishop Bill. "That's why I'm moving away from them."

I was afraid to ask why church bulletins continued to promote Kenneth Copeland conferences and why Bishop hadn't corrected any of the erroneous doctrines which he had been teaching from the pulpit.

"The local Assembly of God just fired their pastor for having an affair with a woman from his congregation," Bishop Bill divulged. (It was a frequent occurrence for our members to switch to the Assembly of God). "Where will you go to church?"

"Well, Amber made a good friend at Evangelical Free Church, and we feel God is leading us there," I explained.

"You do know that Evangelical Free Church doesn't believe in the gifts of the Spirit, don't you?" challenged Bishop Bill.

The tension in my neck caused the nerve to burn. I considered the Holy Spirit power that filled the apostles with courage, empowering them to share the Gospel in public despite floggings, beatings, imprisonment, and threats to their lives. I remembered the boldness that enabled them to face death for their beliefs. I thought of the Holy Spirit power that filled the martyrs with strength as they walked to their stakes and as they sang hymns to the Lord while their flesh was burned from their bones. My heart yearned to be like them. I despised the occultic power that enslaves many people under the strong delusion of demons, which masquerades as Jesus and pretends to be the Holy Spirit.

"We feel God is calling us there, and we want to be in the center of His will," David said.

On our way out of the church, David and I walked past the picture frame with the revival prophecy from Miss Televangelist in the foyer. I still didn't realize that many of the people who left our Wisconsin church had received false prophecies. While I understood that Satan's worldly counterfeit to the gift of prophecy is fortune telling, I didn't comprehend that he has a counterfeit gift of prophecy *within* Pentecostal churches, where many vague prophecies are given, and most prophetic words fail. How I wish this wasn't true!

"**M**om, what do you think about all the failed prophecies our family has had over the years?"

We sat on a bench in my parent's backyard, and Mom turned toward me. "Well, it seems our prophets and prophetesses are no more accurate than fortune tellers."

"Do you believe the gifts of the Spirit are still available today?"

"I'm not sure, Ariel. It doesn't seem like we've seen the real thing."

"We've seen plenty of the counterfeit." I opened my notebook with all the prophetic words that had been spoken over Kevin and me in Word of Faith Church, the Assemblies of God, Full Gospel Tabernacle, a Pentecostal ladies' group, and a few other churches where I'd attended conferences. Of 27 entries, not even one had come to pass.

"Look at this one." I pointed to a prophecy from Pastor Bill which said, 'He's going to deliver you, and you're going to experience some freedoms that you've never had. It's going to be better than it was before.'

"I guess the wording was a bit ambiguous," Mom said. "It doesn't exactly say that Kevin would be delivered from alcohol."

"That's true, Mom, but I can't think of <u>any</u> freedoms that made his life better than it was before. In fact, he's become more ensnared as the time went by."

"Yes, he has."

"Look at this one." I pointed to a prophecy in the middle of the page. "Church Leader Judy spoke this word 15 years ago. Kevin and I were supposed to have an exemplary marriage and teach marriage classes while we were young."

"There's one from me." Mom pointed at a prophecy she'd given. "I'm sorry, Ariel. I thought I was hearing from God."

As a mosquito buzzed around us, I considered several 'prophetic words' I had given to others. "I told one leader at WoF Church that he was going to be a pastor someday, and he doesn't even go to church anymore." The mosquito landed on Mom's neck, and I brushed it away. "I used to be enthralled with the spiritual energy at supernatural services because it made me feel so good. Sadly, there were always a few depressing days that followed, and waiting for the false prophecies to manifest was so disheartening."

"None of the prophecies in the Bible *ever* failed. It doesn't seem like our gift of prophecy is the same. I wonder if we've misunderstood something."

"I don't know if I'm ready to let go of the possibility that spiritual gifts are still in operation in this day and age." I slapped a mosquito off my arm. "It's just that there are so many forgeries. Do you think our adversary might be falsifying the gifts in our churches?"

"I'm not sure." Mom sighed.

"It seems like the types of prophetic words we're seeing in church and on Elijah's list resemble the fortune tellers and diviners which the Bible warns against." I scratched my arm, and my ankle began itching. "We'd better get inside before we get eaten alive."

When I researched commentaries regarding prophecy, as it occurred in the early church, I discovered that it is less about telling the future ahead of time and more about explaining Scriptures under the influence of the Holy Spirit.

Let love be your highest goal! But you should also desire the special abilities the Spirit gives—especially the ***ability to prophesy****. 1 Corinthians 14:1 NLT (Emphasis mine)*

According to *Benson's Commentary on the Old and New Testaments* on the word prophecy in this passage, "The word here does not appear to mean foretelling things to come, but rather opening and applying the Scriptures, and discoursing on divine things in an edifying manner."[45] I've included several other commentary citations, in Appendix C, on the above Bible verse because it's good to read more than one expert in case a certain commentator is biased. In this case, Joseph Benson and the other commentators on Biblehub.com share similar interpretations.

While several people in the New Testament predicted future events accurately, the *gift of prophecy* was more of an ability to open the Scriptures, to exhort others, and to teach. This endowment was used in writing the prophetic book of Revelation, as well as the entire New Testament. Since the canon is now closed and no new revelation is to be added to Scriptures, the prophetic gift was much more necessary for the New Testament writers.

My readers may have recognized my fallacious beliefs easier than I did because I've reordered some of the events to keep subjects, like divine health, in one section. Also, I moved contrasting pieces of information closer to one another to help readers see the sharp dichotomy between the doctrines of the WoF movement and Orthodox Christianity.

Though I placed critical truths near their counterfeit deceptions, I didn't come across some relevant information, like the 'little gods doctrine' until after I left Bishop Bill's church. When David and I met with Bishop Bill for the last time, I didn't know my 'Spirit-filled' prayer techniques were veiled witchcraft incantations and wasn't aware of the occult origins of the WoF movement.

It is hard to dig oneself out of the pit of sacrilegious and idolatrous quagmire after being a tenacious adherent of the WoF teachings for many years. Many Bible verses had been distorted and taken out of context in such a way that they appeared to confirm the WoF teachings. I needed to stop listening to and/or reading the materials of anyone—even my favorite preachers—who taught the positive confession, prosperity-seeking, success-oriented, health and wealth focused messages.

When I discovered that the WoF movement was based on occult teachings, I sent a letter to Pastor Bill. I received a reply filled with prosperity verses. I've sent further messages but have not received replies from him.

WoF books often top the bestselling lists, convincing people of the importance of having their best life now, rather than looking toward eternity for their finest life. Trinity Broadcasting Network (TBN) is the largest 'Christian' television network in the world, and its message is largely antichrist. When one isn't in the WoF movement, it is easy to see that the televangelists on TBN are scamming their audiences. How does this affect unbelievers, who tune in to the channel seeking to discover what Christianity is about?

Cloaked with a Christian veneer, this false gospel worms its way into Christian churches and bookstores, and people are gobbling it up as though they were starving. For instance, Joel Osteen, the author of seven New York Times bestsellers and senior pastor of America's largest congregation, has put out a book in 2015, titled '*The Power of I am: Two Words that will change Your Life Today*.'

Why are the words 'I am' considered powerful? God told Moses to say that 'I AM' sent him. In other words, God called Himself 'I AM.' Calling oneself by God's name, I AM, would be blasphemous for anyone other than God.

"You must not misuse the name of the LORD your God. The LORD will not let you go unpunished if you misuse his name." Exodus 20:7 NLT

According to Jesus, in the last days, many will come in His name, saying, "I Am," and we are not to follow these people.

He said, "Be careful that you are not deceived, because many will come in my name and say, 'I AM' and, 'The time has come.' Don't follow them." Luke 21:8 International Standard Version

One has only to look at the names of occult, metaphysical books to find titles like, *The Power of I Am: Aligning the Chakras of Consciousness, The Power of I Am: Creating a New World of Enlightened Personal Interaction, The Power of I Am and the Law of Attraction*, and *I Am: The Power of Discovering Who You Really Are.* Millions of mystics in New Age Spirituality and people in the Word of Faith movement are claiming the words 'I am', intentionally using God's holy name in their sorcerous positive confession claims.

27 Kundalini

Be of sober spirit, be on the alert. Your adversary, the devil, prowls around like a roaring lion, seeking someone to devour. 1 Peter 5:8 NASB

"Did you know witch doctors and shamans speak in tongues?" asked Tyler. We stood in our driveway facing the farmhouse on a warm, breezy day after returning from a walk.

"No, I've never heard that. I have heard that Mormons speak in tongues, though."

Tyler scratched the surgical scar behind his ear. "Do you think there is any chance people could be allowing evil spirits to blaspheme God when they speak in tongues?"

"I don't know," I replied, recalling how my 'gift of tongues' occasionally took on a harsh, rebuking tone. "I've always thought I could tell the difference between the spirits, but my feelings have often led me wrong in other areas."

"How can we tell when the person is speaking a real language versus talking gibberish?" Tyler watched a few of our neighbor's chickens stray into our front yard, pecking for bugs in the grass.

As I considered his question, I recalled the words of Anna, an elderly missionary to Africa, who spoke at my favorite ladies' meeting in Kentucky. She had said, "I keep praying that the Lord will give me the gift of Kenyan tongues. It's so hard to learn a new language at my age."

I realized that in 30 years of being around Pentecostals, I had heard one unverifiable, third-hand story about a woman who was gifted with the Hebrew language. I'd never personally known anyone (and I know many missionaries to other lands) who had been given a true, foreign language.

In my church, we were taught to speak in tongues by copying our pastor as he spoke unintelligible syllables. As he babbled faster and faster, eventually the student wouldn't be able to keep up and would begin making up their own words. Then, Pastor Bill would say, "That's how you speak in tongues."

The absence of this gift in my own life can't confirm that tongues have ceased, but it made me wonder, *If God doesn't seem to be giving the gift of tongues to the missionaries who need it most, why should I believe He's given them to me? What about people who've used their gift of interpretation to translate those tongues in church, speaking forth prophecies that didn't come to pass and doctrines that contradicted the Bible?*

"You know, Tyler," I resumed, "real languages have a unique sound to them, compared with strings of syllables that sound like babble."

"I wonder what Paul meant when he mentioned tongues of angels."

"I'm not sure," I replied. "I'll have to look that up in my commentaries."

(If you are interested to see what the commentaries on Biblehub say regarding 1 Corinthians 13:1-3, see Appendix B, Tongues of Angels).

> *If I speak with the tongues of men and of angels, but do not have love, I have become a noisy gong or a clanging cymbal. If I have the gift of prophecy, and know all mysteries and all knowledge; and if I have all faith, so as to remove mountains, but do not have love, I am nothing. And if I give all my possessions to feed the poor, and if I surrender my body to be burned, but do not have love, it profits me nothing. 1 Corinthians 13:1-3 NASB*

Interestingly, none of the commentators seemed to indicate that the Holy Spirit speaks through our mouths using a language that only angels understand. Rather, to show the importance of walking in love, Paul seems to be saying that even if he could speak in the best way possible, going beyond natural means of communication and being able to share thoughts supernaturally, as angels do, this would be valueless when compared with walking in love.

To make his point that love is more important than the charismata, we notice that Paul is exaggerating, taking the circumstances to extreme positions (removing mountains, giving his body to be burned, or speaking as angels do). Did Paul remove any mountains or give his body up to be burned? If not, what of communicating as angels do?

Tyler continued our conversation. "That prophetess at the Assembly of God said I'd be proclaiming the Gospel from the rooftops. Do you think that was from God?"

"I'm not sure. Her prophecy about divine order in our home didn't happen. Over the years, I've heard at least a hundred prophecies that failed." I was quiet a moment. "And I couldn't discern they weren't from God."

"No one informed Amanda and Jerry that Pastor Bill's prophecy was false," replied Tyler, "and Jerry didn't win his battle with cancer."

"And none of us warned her when prophets claimed she would get pregnant. Some of the sincerest Christians, whose lives demonstrated holiness, gave false prophecies. I wonder why none of us demonstrated the supernatural gift of discernment. Why haven't we seen any of these sign gifts in their true form, as the early church experienced?"

"Maybe now that we have the Scriptures, God wants us to look to them to gain natural discernment."

A red-tailed hawk circled above, and the rooster alerted his hens. "Look," I pointed. "The rooster is chasing his hens under the porch."

"Yeah, he looks out for them."

"If we have as much of the Holy Spirit as Paul and the apostles," I said, "we should know beyond a shadow of a doubt if someone is being false. When Ananias and Sapphira [Acts 5:1-11] lied to Peter, he discerned it immediately, and they dropped dead."

"Do you think the early church might have had a different measure of the Holy Spirit than we do?"

"Perhaps," I replied. "The New Testament was in the process of being written, so they needed Him for accuracy, and Christianity was just getting started, so they needed the Lord to validate the movement."

"God gave the writers of the Old Testament a great measure of the Holy Spirit, too. They seemed certain that their words were from the Him."

"You know, Tyler, all people who are saved receive a measure of the Holy Spirit, just maybe not to the same degree as the early church."

"Do you think it's because we aren't as single-minded as the they were?" asked Tyler. "They dedicated themselves to prayer and fasting together for days on end and were willing to face severe persecution, even when their friends were martyred."

"Right. And Paul faced shipwrecks, beatings, and sleepless nights for the sake of the Gospel. Believers sold their property and gave the proceeds to the general fund. They also didn't have all the distractions [computers, smartphones, TVs] that we have, so they might have been reading the Scriptures more than we do."

The hawk had flown away, and we could see him circling above my cousin's cornfields as their rooster warned his hens.

"Do you remember playing the telephone game?" I asked.

"You mean where one person tells a story to another, then that person passes it on to the next, and so on, until the whole thing doesn't sound like the original?"

"Yes," I replied. "God always expected the highest degree of precision where His Word was concerned. Perhaps the gift of languages was given so the Gospel could be spoken firsthand, in the original language of the hearers. That way, it wouldn't be changed through various interpretations, and the Holy Spirit could give the most accurate rendition to each nation."

"But what about the verse where Paul says that he speaks in tongues more than others?"

[I thank God, I speak in tongues more than you all; however, in the church I desire to speak five words with my mind so that I may instruct others also, rather than ten thousand words in a tongue. 1 Corinthians 14:18-19 NASB]

"Well, as a missionary in foreign lands, Paul would have spoken in tongues more than most people. If, for instance, he was given the Latin language, he would have preached and prayed in Latin when he was among the Romans. However, back in Jerusalem where Aramaic was known, he probably didn't use his Latin tongue, for it wouldn't have edified the church."

Regarding the above verse (1 Cor. 14:18), *Barnes' Notes on the Old and New Testaments* says, "'I [Paul] **am able to speak more foreign languages than all of you**.' How many languages Paul could speak, he has nowhere told us. It is reasonable, however, to presume that he was able to speak the language of any people to whom God in his providence, and by his Spirit, called him to preach. He had been commissioned to preach to the "Gentiles," and it is probable that he was able to speak the languages of all the nations among whom he ever traveled. There is no account of his being under a necessity of employing an interpreter wherever he preached."[46] (Emphasis mine)

For more commentary citations on the above Bible verse, please see Appendix A, Section 3.

"**I** can't figure out what I want to do for a career," Amber said. "It seems like everyone my age has already decided."

"If you're not sure yet, it's better to take your time than to make the wrong decision," I advised.

Once I was married and living in town, it was easier to take Amber to a homeschool co-op, where she became involved in dramas and was able to get experience in speech, basketball, and ultimate frisbee. David and I were blessed with two sons by the time I was 44. We bought a home nearer to town and began taking care of disabled adults, which was difficult, though very satisfying and rewarding. In a sense, I had my 'bed and breakfast', and David was helping run a 'nursing home combined with a daycare.'

In the meantime, Kevin remarried and then divorced. His health declined, and he lost his job. I continued to pray that he would get sober and give his life to the Lord, and that if he were to have an accident, no one else would be injured.

2008

"Did you hear about the diabetic girl who passed away?" David asked, as we cuddled on our couch. "Her parents were looking for spiritual reasons for her illness, rather than taking her to the doctor."

I recalled the story at WoF church about the baby who grew limbs and wondered if the girl's parents had heard similar fantastical stories in their church. As I thought back over my own religious history, I could understand why they would stand in faith believing their child could have divine health.

Years earlier, Tyler and I were speeding down an icy, sled hill when we hit a large bump and were airborne for several seconds. Upon landing, I felt my tailbone crack. All the surrounding muscles seized up, and I immediately began confessing Scriptures and commanding my body to line up with the Word of God. Though the area swelled and was so painful that I couldn't sleep on my back, nor could I sit for several months, I denied there was anything wrong and insisted on using my WoF 'prayer' techniques. (After many years of pain, I ended up in physical therapy, and it took two years of exercises to correct the problem because I'd waited so long).

Another time, Tyler was in gym class with other homeschoolers and tore his Achilles tendon. When he complained on our two-mile walk, I told him, "You need to show your faith by walking on it like normal. Don't let yourself limp." We did our spiritual warfare and positive confession, but his tendon got worse. If I had taken him for medical attention, maybe it wouldn't have become a chronic problem for him.

“You mean the girl in Weston [Wisconsin]?” I asked.

“Yes.” David combed my hair with his fingers.

"I can see how that would happen. When Tyler had ear problems, I believed that taking him to the doctor was an act of doubt. He could have become disabled or died if I had waited longer.”

“They tried to resurrect her, didn’t they?” asked David.

“Yes.” I laid my head on my husband’s chest. “I might’ve done the same thing at one time. I wonder if her parents think their faith wasn’t strong enough to bring her back to life. Wouldn’t that be the saddest way to live—harboring needless guilt because you were deceived?”

The pain in my neck took a turn for the worse, and my sessions with the ‘invisible therapist’ (which had continued since Pastor Bill prayed over me) didn’t seem to be helping. I investigated the phenomenon and discovered an exact description of what I’d been experiencing. In Kundalini kriyas, the body is moved and stretched, allegedly by the ‘higher self’, into yoga-like poses. The movements are spontaneous, like the first yawning stretch of the morning.

In the *Encyclopedia of New Age Beliefs,* John Ankerberg and John Weldon said, “In Hindu mythology and occult anatomy, the goddess Kundalini is thought of as a female serpent lying dormant at the base of the spine.... when aroused... she uncoils, travels up the spine...”[47]

I’d received this ‘healing power’ in WoF Church. Would the Holy Spirit use signs and wonders to authenticate a message which advanced luciferianism and that undermined and distracted from the Gospel by promoting prosperity and success, not to mention the channeled teaching of positive confession and the antichrist ‘little god doctrine’ of demons? When one considers the rescinded healings, the failed prophecies, and the demonic manifestations which I’d witnessed in some of the WoF Church services, as well as the depravity and greed of ministers who transfer their ‘anointing’, it seemed like the power that moved my body could not have been the anointing of the Holy Spirit.

When healing comes through the hand of demons, rather than from the hand of God, there is always a price to pay. Evil spirits never leave you in better shape than you were. The headache may be gone, but might something worse be planted in its place? Perhaps a disease would manifest in later years. Not only had I subjected myself to demonic power when I allowed those who preached a luciferian message to lay their hands upon me, but I had placed Tyler in the same vulnerable position.

Because we live in a fallen world, the disease that entered Tyler's head and destroyed the bone up to his brain may have been caused by purely natural means. However, there was an occasion where he had two ear infections, and a man at church asked if he could pray for him. Greg used the sorcerous prayer method of positive confession and the witchcraft technique of demanding when he ordered sickness to leave Tyler's body. Though Tyler had been inconsolable for an hour, he stopped instantly when Greg laid his hands on him and commanded the infection and pain to leave.

As mentioned earlier, those with the biggest demonic anointing often have serious sin in their lives, and Greg later ended up divorced because of a drug addiction. While we shouldn't see a demon behind every rock, nor should we presume that each illness is caused by evil spirits, neither should we think that we can play with the fire of the Kundalini serpent power or any other demonic 'anointing' without being burned.

There are many evil spirits who can perform signs and wonders. The Apostle John said,

> *They are demonic spirits who work miracles and go out to all the rulers of the world to gather them for battle against the Lord on that great judgment day of God the Almighty. Revelation 16:14 NLT*

Regarding the tale of the Trojan horse, Wikipedia says,"[A]fter a fruitless 10-year siege, the Greeks constructed a huge wooden [Trojan] horse and hid a select force of men inside. The Greeks pretended to sail away, and the Trojans pulled the horse into their city as a victory trophy. That night, the Greek force crept out of the horse and opened the gates for the rest of the Greek army, which had sailed back under cover of night. The Greeks entered and destroyed the city of Troy, ending the war."[48]

Is it possible that Satan and his forces might have created a Trojan horse to invade Pentecostal churches from within? In his book, *Trojan Church: The New Age Corruption of the Evangelical Faith,* Dr. Gregory Reid (author and retired private investigator with over 20 years' experience as a contract criminal justice trainer on the occult) said, "The church no longer understands that Satan is quite capable of imitating all the gifts of the Holy Spirit, such as tongues, healing, prophecy, and words of knowledge."[49]

Author and preacher, Andrew Strom, (author of *Kundalini Warning: Are False Spirits Invading the Church?)* voices his concern that Hindu Kundalini is masquerading as the Holy Spirit. This false spirit produces laughter, barking, hissing, shrieking, weeping, euphoric experiences, etc., and is spread from one congregation to the next, like a contagion. Andrew asks, "[W]hy then was it so different from the Bible and yet so similar to the New Age — and the spirits the Hindu gurus operated under?"[50]

When we bring luciferian philosophy into our churches and use occult methods, is it any wonder that we have the same spiritual demonstrations as some sects of the mystical religion of Hinduism, such as uncontrollable laughter or weeping, shaking, screaming, involuntary body movements, and feelings of heat or electricity, all passed off as Holy Spirit drunkenness? Sometimes, during Hindu events, people fall to the ground and appear to be unconscious—slain in the spirit, as if in a trance. In the Bible, when believers were baptized in the Holy Spirit, there is not one recorded instance where they fell backwards, as if asleep or in a trance.

In his book, *Occult ABC,* the late Kurt E. Koch Th. D, (Protestant pastor, theologian, lecturer, and missionary) recorded a conversation during one man's deliverance from demonic possession. The demon was asked when it entered the man, and it replied, "When he was slain in the spirit."[51]

When one realizes that the occult has entered the church, it seems as if all the pieces of the puzzle fall into place. It makes sense that false prophecies abounded in churches where supernatural experiences were sought and occult techniques were taught, why demonic manifestations occurred, and why ministers who fell into depravity manifested more supernatural 'anointing' than those who lived with integrity—not only in my experience, but in the history of the Pentecostal movement. One can understand why there was tangible power to make people feel healed or delivered, and why these often failed afterwards, causing people to turn from God. Our mortal enemy is more seductive than we anticipated.

While I was beginning to realize the evil source behind the power in services with Hindu Kundalini manifestations, I came across the testimony of Miss Televangelist (who rebuked my sister for crying during her miscarriage, and whose healing of a little boy with glasses was rescinded). When the Pentecostal minister, A.A. Allen, laid hands on her, she was *slain by spiritual power*. She was out, lying on her back for the rest of the service. Not only did this happen **before** she was saved, but she was given the ability to foretell that her neighbor's house was about to burn down due to electrical wiring problems.

While the 'spirit guides' of Hinduism and NAS give the gift of divination to those who aren't saved, the gift of prophecy was never given to an unbeliever in the New Testament. In Acts 16:16-18, we learn of a servant girl who was a soothsayer, until Paul cast the demon out of her. I wondered if the minister who laid hands on Miss Televangelist carried a power that was not of God, so I looked him up.

According to Wikipedia, the Pentecostal preacher, A. A. Allen, was one of the first men to call poverty a spirit. He died from liver failure brought on by acute alcoholism. His body was found in a room with scattered pills and liquor bottles, and there was enough alcohol in his blood to put a man into a coma. [52] Does this sound like a man who was filled with the Holy Spirit? In Ephesians 5:18, God instructs us not to be drunk with wine, but *instead* to be filled with the Holy Spirit.

The house of Miss Televangelist's neighbor did burn down the day after she divined it. Demons can occasionally make good predictions because they see behind the scenes, perhaps being able to detect a smoking electrical wire before people notice.

In John MacArthur's book, *Strange Fire, The Danger of Offending the Holy Spirit with Counterfeit Fire,* he mentions disturbing phenomena which Hagin wrote about in a booklet, *Why Do People Fall Under the Power*. I ordered Ken's booklet to read it firsthand.

When supernatural power first began to occur in his meetings, one woman levitated—strictly a demonic manifestation—while she was dancing, and another fell into a deep eight-hour trance—a sorcerous practice that opens a person's mind to the influence of evil spirits. Hagin's wife and two close relatives wondered, 'Is this God?'

The following morning, as these three were praying with Ken, a spirit told him to lay the finger of his right hand on each of their foreheads to convince them that the power came from God. When he did so, the three of them were knocked flat on their backs. As if glued to the floor (like happened to me in Pastor Ricky's church), they could not get up. When these people acknowledged that the manifestations were of God, Ken touched each one, and they were released.[53] The supernatural force, in this instance, seems like a bully sitting on a younger child, demanding the victim admit the intimidator is superior. Is this how God operates?

In the Garden of Eden, God gave Adam and Eve freedom to believe and do according to their own will. He allowed them to choose the serpent's knowledge over His advice and to disobey His one rule. Jesus never demanded that people believe in His godhood, and the Holy Spirit did not force Kevin to place God and family ahead of alcohol. While the Lord allows consequences to come upon us for our sins, He doesn't coerce people to believe one way or another.

On the other hand, I've listened to many testimonies where demons become oppressive if their victims begin to turn toward Christianity. When we see manipulation, such as people being held down by spiritual forces until they make a certain admission, we should question whether the 'anointing' is of God. Unfortunately, because of the signs and wonders which occurred in Ken's meetings, he gained popularity, which helped usher in the WoF movement with its luciferian, little gods doctrine.

Some of the godliest people I know are continuationists (those who believe the gifts of the Spirit are in operation today). Many of these believers reject the WoF/NAR movements, but some of these Christians are deceived by the supernatural Kundalini demonstrations. They are not aware that the occult phenomenon of being slain in the spirit, drunken laughter, and ecstatic tongues (glossolalia, gibberish, not real human languages) are given by the spiritual powers of pagan, mystical religions, but not by the Holy Spirit in the Bible.

Many continuationists are Word of Faith/Kingdom Now dominionists who believe there are super apostles and 'anointed ones' who are spiritually elite, making idols of certain preachers. Some of these self-styled 'apostles' kick elderly women in their faces with biker boots to heal them, leave their wives to marry their mistresses, speak one false prophecy after another, have women stand before them naked so they can prophesy over them, and indulge in homosexual liaisons.

Jesus never kicked people or grabbed them by their arthritic legs and slammed them up and down. Neither did the apostles. None of them became drunkards, had affairs, or practiced homosexuality. Rather, the infilling of the Holy Spirit made them kind, gentle, holy, pure, and sober-minded.

One of these NAR so-called prophets told of a vision where he was in Heaven and saw Jesus absorbing people into His heart. Hinduism and New Age Spirituality teach that people will eventually be absorbed into Brahman (an impersonal god force) once they work out their bad karma. Since these are demonic doctrines that are opposed to Christianity, might this vision have come from an evil spirit to bring deceptive Hindu philosophy into Christianity?

Despite the above, many devoted followers give these 'super apostles' and 'super prophets' grace. This should not be the case. Paul told Titus and Timothy,

An elder must live a blameless life. He must be faithful to his wife, and his children must be believers who don't have a reputation for being wild or rebellious. Titus 1:6 NLT

An overseer, then, must be above reproach, the husband of one wife, temperate, prudent, respectable, hospitable, able to teach, 1 Timothy 3:2 NASB

Once I learned of the Kundalini serpent power, I quit going to services where these exhibitions occurred, and I stopped speaking in tongues when I realized that these are counterfeited in occult religions where demonic power is evident. Apparently, ecstatic babbling (glossolalia), not to be confused with the biblical gift of an unlearned foreign language (xenoglossia), has been a manifestation of the mystery religions as a way of bypassing the mind to commune with demons.[54]

I wondered how it came to be that we Pentecostals, who supposedly had the gift of discernment, didn't recognize the enemy's diabolical philosophies when they infiltrated our churches. If we truly had the same measure of God's Spirit as the apostles possessed, then many false preachers should have dropped dead—like Ananias and Sapphira—when they introduced the serpent's lies that sabotaged our churches.

Since many, though not all, Pentecostal denominations were the first to allow the luciferian Word of Faith movement into our midst, I wondered whether it might be possible that the satanic realm was involved in the inception of our movement to deceive the elect. Our focus was effectively taken off Jesus and put onto the spiritual gifts. In the end times, we are told of a great apostasy where people who appear to be Christians will leave the faith.

But the Spirit explicitly says that in later times ***some will fall away from the faith****, paying attention to deceitful spirits and doctrines of demons, 1 Timothy 4:1 NASB (Emphasis mine)*

Let no one in any way deceive you, for it [the day of the Lord's return] will not come unless the apostasy comes first... 2 Thessalonians. 2:3a NASB

This would explain the demonic manifestations, the depravity of so many of our leaders, the desertion of the Christian faith by disappointed WoF believers, and the Antichrist theology that has undermined the Gospel. Since demons lie, impersonate Jesus, and imitate the Holy Spirit's power, how do we know that we aren't playing with the wrong kind of spirits?

When I took a good, hard look at why my tongue speaking never seemed to edify or strengthen me, why I wasn't less edified when I stopped practicing this 'gift', and why there was no supernatural discernment to help us Pentecostals recognize the evil nature behind the WoF/NAR teachings, I naturally wondered if we might have been wrong about tongues, prophecy, interpretation of tongues, and words of knowledge. I wanted to avoid a knee jerk reaction, however, and not immediately dismiss the gifts of the Spirit.

In Kentucky, Kevin's life was falling apart. Though he needed a walker to ambulate in his house, he regularly managed to drive to the liquor store and use the drive-through window. When I was 47, I received the dreaded phone call.

"Ariel, it's Dana. Kevin had an accident and may not make it through the night. They've resuscitated him and flown him by helicopter to Vanderbilt's trauma center in Nashville."

"Was anyone else injured?"

David, Tyler, and Amber stopped talking when they heard my alarmed voice. Seth, age five, was playing with his food, and Logan, age three, sat contentedly on David's lap.

"No," replied Dana. "It was a one car accident. He flipped his truck several times and landed in the lanes of oncoming traffic. I'm getting ready to head down there right now."

Kevin was on a ventilator for almost a week, unconscious. Early in the second week of his recovery, he began moving the right side of his body. By the third week, he was starting to move his left side. He had a long road to recovery and no health insurance to cover the helicopter ride, hospital expenses, or rehabilitation. Nursing homes and rehab centers refused to take him without insurance.

I shuddered to think of how it would have been for me if I was still married to him. I would have been facing financial devastation and would not have been able to support Tyler's dream of becoming a physician, nor would I have been able to encourage Amber to go to college. I would have been forced to work full-time to pay a $400,000 debt, as well as to cover the expenses of Kevin's caregiver while I was at work. After work, I would have had to come home and shoulder the entire household responsibility, as well as care for a man who needed full assistance with everything.

Our home, in which David and I cared for disabled adults, had a vacant bedroom, a wheelchair ramp, shower grab bars, and a handicapped toilet. More importantly, God had done a lot of work in my heart so that I'd completely forgiven the one who had deeply hurt me. Much to the relief of Dana, who couldn't find anywhere for Kevin to live, David and I offered to take him in and rehabilitate him.

While Tyler was on spring break from his pre-med program at the local university, he, Amber, and I headed to Nashville to bring Kevin to Wisconsin.

"**I** wonder how David is managing with the boys." Tyler shouted.

It was difficult to hear him. The loud, whomp, whomp, whomping of the medical helicopter, which was landing above the hospital, made conversation difficult as I pushed Kevin's wheelchair to our van. Amber brought a wheeled-pole with an IV bag alongside her father, and Tyler pulled a cart loaded with a commode, a walker, and a few of Kevin's personal items.

"He took the boys to the Hobby Lobby this morning to look at toy trains, and it sounded like they had a nice time," I hollered back to Tyler.

Colorful flowers and blooming dogwood trees adorned the beautifully landscaped campus at Vanderbilt University Hospital. Since Tyler would be applying at medical colleges the following year, he and Amber had spent the day exploring the Vanderbilt School of Medicine while I worked with Kevin's occupational, speech, and physical therapists, as well as with his nurses. They taught me how to change his IV bag, flush his PICC line (catheter that is inserted into a vein so medications can be delivered directly into the blood), give his injections, and remove his neck brace to shave him.

"**Y**ou've shown me that it's possible to live without drinking and smoking," said Kevin.

"Do you think you'll go back to alcohol?" I set out the supplies to flush his PICC line.

"Not if I can help it."

"Would you be interested in turning your life over to Jesus?"

"Yes," he replied. Whether Kevin was serious when he prayed with me, I cannot say.

Tyler and Amber had a year to get to know their dad while he was sober. We took Kevin to many doctor appointments, as well as to physical, occupational, and speech therapy, and he had a partial recovery from the traumatic brain injury. To top it off, when Amber took her dad to speech therapy, she discovered a career.

Between Kevin's traumatic brain injury and the brain damage caused by his overuse of alcohol throughout the years, it seems he is incapable of making right decisions or having empathy for others. Sadly, as soon as he moved out of our home, Kevin returned to drinking. He's been in and out of jail for driving under the influence, lived in homeless shelters and on the streets, and has never acknowledged that his drinking has hurt us.

Though he'd always claimed he could quit anytime and wanted to enjoy drinking a little longer, there came a point when Kevin discovered that he was trapped. As a frog placed in cold water slowly gets used to the rising temperature until it is boiled to death, an addiction is a slow fade of one's will power and sanity, until it destroys relationships, finances, and ultimately, the individual.

Dear Reader, is there any sin that comes between you and the Lord? Have you been putting off Jesus for one more day, believing that you can wait a little longer before surrendering your life to Him? If so, I urge you to ask Him to be the Lord of your life today.

> *Remember what it says: "Today when you hear his voice, don't harden your hearts as Israel did when they rebelled." Hebrews 3:15 NLT*

Since leaving the WoF/NAR movements, my life has greatly improved. Ironically, except for my college years, I was never as poor as when I was naming and claiming wealth and filling the pockets of WoF preachers. When I stopped practicing the unbiblical type of 'spiritual warfare' of binding supposed spirits named Cancer, Depression, Disease, and Lust, etc., as well as rebuking the devil and 'loosing the Holy Spirit', I certainly didn't see my life fall apart. If anything, it has come together.

My mind has been more renewed as I've meditated on and learned the Scriptures than it ever was when I felt the prickly sensations, heat, and tingling which I thought were God's presence. Rather than experiencing spiritual highs followed by low times, I've learned to appreciate the Holy Spirit's fruit of steadiness and temperance.

In our human relationships, we communicate back and forth, and we can see, feel, touch, and hear one another. One must wonder where we should draw the line between a relationship of experience—the give **and take** of communication—with God versus learning to know Him through His Word alone. I want as much of the Lord as I can possibly have. Does God still give impressions, dreams, and words of direction to those He is in relationship with?

Various prophets and people in Biblical history have been able to experience God's presence in tangible ways, and one can hardly blame many of the sincere Christians in Charismatic and Pentecostal denominations who desire a tangible, intimate relationship with Jesus, who are willing to spend hours in worship and prayer, hoping to hear His voice. (I'm not trying to justify looking outside of the Scriptures for experiences, but rather, sharing the heart of true believers in these Full Gospel churches).

I've known numerous genuine, devoted, Pentecostal Christians who were well-versed in the Bible, who put the Scriptures into practice, and who were growing in holiness and humility, being transformed into the image of Christ. (Most of these were in churches which didn't promote the WoF heresies). During worship, many of these committed believers lifted their hands in surrender and did their best to commune with the Lord. They were bold evangelists, who often reached out to their neighbors and friends with the Gospel message. Many have given up worldly riches and comforts to be missionaries in foreign lands.

As time has passed, I've noticed that quite of few of these Christ-followers have been leaving 'Spirit-filled' denominations. Some still believe that the charismata continue in today's church, while others have become cessationists. I began to wonder if we, like the Corinthians, might have placed the charismata and supernatural experiences on a pedestal, making them into idols.

Our greatest gift is Jesus, and He (not the Holy Spirit) is to be our central focus. While we should have been putting to death the desires of our flesh and pursuing the miraculous transformation of our hearts, many of us sought spectacular signs, wonders, and prophecies that would relieve our pain and/or excite our flesh.

More important than possessing the spiritual endowments of the early church is the way of love. (1 Cor. 12:31-1 Cor. 13:3) With this in mind, I sought to understand the cessationist point of view. If you are interested in the viewpoints of continuationists and cessationists, see my Afterward.

Just as Kevin didn't know he'd have an accident, none of us knows our last day. Time is short. We must be on guard, reading God's Word with all diligence and imploring our friends and family members to do the same. We need to be aware of the occult methods of our enemy. We must get the word out, sharing the information we find in books like this one, for souls are hanging in the balance, unaware of their perilous position.

The end-times deception—so severe, dense, and dark that it would deceive even the elect, if that were possible—is upon us. It is like a disease that is contaminating one person after another as each gets inoculated with the serpent's venomous knowledge. And if we become seduced by the appealing supernatural experiences of our mortal enemy, it is difficult to discern the truth.

For now we see in a mirror dimly, but then face to face; 1 Corinthians 13:12a NASB

In these last days, as the rise of occult energy is occurring, fellowship with other Christians is extremely important to keep us aware of the traps of our mortal enemy. It is easy to fall victim to the snares of Satan, especially when we hear them in church, read them in books by 'Christian' authors, watch them in 'Christian' movies, and sings songs which are written by worship teams who bask in the Kundalini serpent spirit.

Besides the WoF/NAR deceits, there are several other movements *within* Christianity that try to seduce us with enticing occult methods. Hinduism, with its embrace that smothers, is attempting to put out the Light of Chrisendom by introducing sorcerous, 'prayer' techniques that allege to bring us into the presence of God while excluding Jesus as our mediator. It is not only critical that we stay on top of orthodox Christian doctrines, but we must be cognizant of the mystical deceptions that are currently sabotaging mainstream Christianity. Understanding the ways of our mortal enemy, which will be the subject of my next book, can help prevent us from falling into the great end-times deception.

"Behold, I send you out as sheep in the midst of wolves; so be shrewd as serpents and innocent as doves. Matthew 10:16 NASB

Epilogue

Three ambulances, five rescue vehicles from different counties, and a fire truck were lined up on both sides of the narrow country road for the Special Olympic fundraiser. A square 10 by 10-yard hole had been cut through the lake's thick ice. Four news vehicles with local radio and television station logos, a sheriff's car, and nearly 50 snowmobiles were parked on the ice. People lined all sides of the water hole as an emcee asked questions of the participants. Admiration for my sister, Amanda, filled our hearts as we stood with Rose watching her step-mother, now married to Jeff for 12 years, do the polar bear plunge. (Lilly, Amanda's other daughter, was at work that day).

Tyler, now married to a sincere Christian woman, was able to recover 85% of the hearing in his right ear. He earned his MD at the School of Medicine and Public Health, University of Madison and is currently a resident pathologist at the University of Wisconsin Hospital and Clinics. He and his wife have recently adopted a 7-year-old girl and would like to adopt a playmate for her soon.

Amber recently attained her bachelor's degree in Communication Sciences and Disorders and is in her final year of grad school to become a Speech Language Pathologist. She and Breanna have been good friends for 13 years.

David and I continue to care for disabled adults in our country home as we homeschool Logan and Seth. The burning pain in my neck has diminished to a great degree with a medication that reduces nerve inflammation.

If you would like to know when my next book, *Shrewd as Serpents: Exposing the Enemy's Tactics to Prevent Deception in the Church*, is published, please send your email address, and I will contact you.

I can be reached on Facebook at https://www.facebook.com/ariel.abornski.9, through my blog at https://christiantouch.blogspot.com/, and by email at Ariel.abornski@gmail.com. If you enjoyed this book, please consider leaving a review on Amazon and Goodreads. I'd be eternally grateful if you would also consider sharing it on your social feed. Together, we can bring souls out of the deception.

Shrewd as Serpents

Exposing the Enemy's Tactics to Prevent Deception in the Church

Since Satan and his cohorts were cast to the earth, our mortal enemy has been scheming the destruction of our souls. Similarly, when Maitreya enters the lives of a single mother and her daughter, Rebecca has no idea of his sinister plan. Will she be mesmerized by his smooth talk and subtle deceptions?

Afterward – Continuationism and Cessationism

I must admit that I was very hesitant to write this section, for it is likely to find criticism with continuationists and cessationists, who may not like it that I present both sides of the argument. When people only listen to one side of the discussion, they become surer they are right, even though they might be deceived, and the more certain one is, the more extreme one's position becomes. Perhaps the truth lies somewhere in the middle of both lines of reasoning.

In all my years as a continuationist, I had gone along with the only side of the debate which had been presented to me: that the charismatic gifts of the Spirit were for the church in these days. I followed my personal experiences and opinions, assuming cessationists were closed-minded legalists who put God in a box. I felt that they depersonalized God, didn't understand what an intimate relationship with Jesus was, didn't realize that God communicates in prayer as well as through the Scriptures, and that they quenched the Holy Spirit and denied His power. These judgments were based on my one-sided knowledge and my unwillingness to seek the other perspective.

The Holy Spirit, who was promised to all believers through the end of the age, has many functions, and we are instructed to be filled with Him continually. But what does it mean to be filled with God's Spirit? Is this limited to experiencing the Charismata, which is only a small portion of the Holy Spirit's work?

In addition to the charismatic sign gifts, we have the gifts of serving, teaching, exhortation, leadership, mercy, helps, Apostles, prophets, teachers, pastors, and evangelists. The Holy Spirit leads us to Jesus, illuminates the Scriptures, transforms our hearts, fills us with love for others, comforts us in sorrows, counsels us, and develops the fruit of peace, joy, love, patience, kindness, goodness, faithfulness, gentleness, and self-control. He convicts us of sin, righteousness, and judgment, fills us with boldness to witness, and strengthens us to resist sin. Paul tells us that we are to be led by the Spirit.

So I say, let the Holy Spirit guide your lives. Then you won't be doing what your sinful nature craves. Since we are living by the Spirit, let us follow the Spirit's leading in every part of our lives. Galatians 5:16, 25 NLT

Though the Charismata may seem like a peripheral tenet that shouldn't divide Christians, they are being heavily counterfeited by evil spirits, and signs and wonders follow those who teach the antichrist 'little gods doctrine'. We may not, however, be able to deduce that the sign gifts are no longer occurring just because there are Satanic imitations of them.

Love impels me to bring these issues to light so my brothers and sisters in Christ can be aware of the subtle deceptions that our enemy uses to get into our churches. Some of the preachers with the most powerful 'anointing' have demonstrated the depravity that is common in the gurus of Hinduism, whose Kundalini power comes from the evil one. We must consider the fact that every sign and wonder is not from God. Paul told the Thessalonians,

The coming of the lawless one will be in accordance with how Satan works. He will use all sorts of displays of power through signs and wonders that serve the lie, 1 Thessalonians 2:9 NIV

Jesus told the people that they should not be looking for signs.

"An evil and adulterous generation seeks after a sign; and a sign will not be given it, except the sign of Jonah." Matthew 16:4a NASB

It is not my goal to prove or disprove that the sign gifts are in operation in these days. Rather, I believe we shouldn't take a myopic view, focusing on the Charismata to the point where we exclude more important aspects of Christianity. Neither should we elevate experiences, signs, and wonders to the point where we allow the Kundalini serpent power into our churches.

If the Holy Spirit decides to give the sign gifts in these days, I wouldn't want to limit Him, nor would I desire to give credit to the Kundalini for every sign and wonder. When the Pharisees accused Jesus of operating by the power of the devil, He warned them that it is blasphemous to label the power of the Holy Spirit as demonic.

"I tell you the truth, all sin and blasphemy can be forgiven, but anyone who blasphemes the Holy Spirit will never be forgiven. This is a sin with eternal consequences." He told them this because they were saying, "He's possessed by an evil spirit." Mark 3:28-30 NLT

In the book of the Acts of the Apostles, written by Luke, we find that most (though not all) miracles were done by the apostles. It seems his intention was to document the acts of the apostles and not necessarily to follow the deeds of everyone in the churches. However, because most signs and wonders that Luke recorded were performed by the apostles, some say that these were done to authenticate the apostles and their message. Maybe we see less signs and wonders because God sovereignly planned it that way, that the Charismata were intended to boost Christianity while it was in its infant stage. The writer of the book of Hebrews asks,

how will we escape if we neglect so great a salvation which had its beginning when it was spoken through the Lord and was confirmed to us by those who heard, while ***God was testifying*** *at the same time by signs and wonders and various miracles and distributions of the Holy Spirit according to his will. Hebrews 2:3-4 LEB (Emphasis mine)*

We do know, from history, that there have been no signs and wonders movements that come anywhere near to those of Jesus and the apostles. The lives of these were permeated with holiness and the fruit of the Spirit, the healings were immediate and consisted of the most challenging conditions, and the miracles were never rescinded afterwards.

According to cessationists, the sign gifts of tongues, interpretation of tongues, healings, discernment, words of knowledge, prophecy, and miracles have ceased to operate in the same way they did in the Apostolic Age (when the Apostles laid the foundations of the church and the prophetic gift was used to explain the Scriptures and to write the New Testament). S*oft cessationists* believe that God has continued to do miracles and heal people throughout the centuries, but most agree that we don't find people *gifted with a supernatural anointing* to do miracles or perform healings on a routine basis. *Hard cessationists* believe miracles, healings, and all charismata ceased at the end of the Apostolic Age.

Having witnessed firsthand how Pentecostal Christianity has furthered Satan's kingdom and brought the influence of the Antichrist system through the WoF/NAR movements into our midst, I decided to study its history. When I examined Pentecostalism, I was surprised to discover that it did not go all the way back to the day of Pentecost.

Ronald Kydd, associate professor of church history at Tyndale Seminary in Toronto, Canada, wrote a book on the Charismata in the first 300 years of the common era. He tells us, "about AD 260 evidence for the presence of spiritual gifts is nonexistent. It looks as though by then they had ceased to be a part of the day-by-day experience of the Christians of the time....The Christian community grew phenomenally in size; it became increasingly wealthy; it climbed the social ladder; its level of education rose; it developed its organization, and it formalized its worship. While all this was going on, the gifts of the Spirit just quietly slipped away....The evidence indicates that the gifts were still around. However, there is no question but that their importance was on the wane..."[55]

Perhaps the changes in the church were the reason the gifts of the Spirit decreased significantly. It may be that we do not have the level of faith as the early church, where people were willing to be inconvenienced to the greatest degree, where they sold their properties to give into the common purse, and where they faced persecution and death regularly.

The early church certainly didn't have all the distractions which we have, such as TVs, computers, smartphones, sporting events, etc. They were in continual prayer and fellowship with one another, daily studying the Scriptures together. They may have had more physical work, but they didn't have all the worldly ambitions that are part of our culture, such as the American dream. In addition to that, they didn't have to contend with the Theory of Evolution, which causes many to doubt the supernatural realm. Might our unbelief contribute to the scarcity of spiritual gifts?

And because of their unbelief, he couldn't do any miracles among them except to place his hands on a few sick people and heal them. Mark 6:5 NLT

And He did not do many miracles there because of their unbelief. Matthew 13:58 NASB

Justin Martyr (Christian apologist, 100-165 AD), Origen (Christian apologist and theologian, 184-253 AD), and Augustine (Christian theologian and philosopher, 354-430 AD) believed tongues manifested only as the Church was getting started to authenticate Christianity. (This doesn't necessarily mean they felt the same way about the other gifts, such as discernment, miracles, and healings).

It is important to note that Justin Martyr, whose travels exposed him to many churches within the Roman empire, did affirm other gifts of the Spirit. (According to Wikipedia, Justin Martyr "travel[ed] throughout the land, spreading the knowledge of Christianity as the 'true philosophy,'...)"[56]

Justin tells Trypho (possibly a Jewish rabbi), "For the prophetical gifts remain with us, even to the present time. And hence you ought to understand that [the gifts] formerly among your nation [Israel] have been transferred to us [Christians],"[57] and "it is possible to see amongst us women and men who possess gifts of the Spirit of God."[58]

John MacArthur, (pastor, author, and president of The Master's University and Seminary), tells us, "The historians and theologians of the early church unanimously maintained that tongues ceased to exist after the time of the apostles. The only exception of which we know was within the movement led by Montanus, a second century heretic..."[59]

I found one Greek church father who spoke of tongues as though he'd seen them during his lifetime. According to the historian, Eusebius, Irenaeus (theologian, Christian apologist, and Bishop of Lyon who lived approximately 130-202 AD) said "For some drive out demons with certainty and truth, so that often those who have themselves been cleansed from the evil spirits believe and are in the church, and some have foreknowledge of things to be, and visions and prophetic speech, and others cure the sick by the laying on of hands and make them whole, and even as we have said, the dead have been raised and remained with us for many years. And why should I say more? It is not possible to tell the number of the gifts which the church throughout the whole world, having received them from God in the name of Jesus Christ....

"Just as also we hear many brethren in the church who have gifts of prophecy, and who speak through the spirit with all manner of tongues, and to bring the hidden things of men into clearness for the common good and expound the mysteries of God."[60]

A later church father who wrote about the fact that tongues were no longer present in his days (354-430 AD) was Augustine of Hippo. Regarding 1 John 3:19–4:3 in HOMILY VI, he comments on 1 John 3:23-24, "In the earliest times, 'the Holy Ghost fell upon them that believed: and they spake with tongues,' which they had not learned, 'as the Spirit gave them utterance.' These were signs adapted to the time. For there behooved to be that betokening of the Holy Spirit in all tongues, to shew that the Gospel of God was to run through all tongues over the whole earth. That thing was done for a betokening, and it passed away.

"In the laying on of hands now, that persons may receive the Holy Ghost, do we look that they should speak with tongues? Or when we laid the hand on these infants [young believers], did each one of you look to see whether they would speak with tongues, and, when he saw that they did not speak with tongues, was any of you so wrong-minded as to say, These have not received the Holy Ghost; for, had they received, they would speak with tongues as was the case in those times?

"If then the witness of the presence of the Holy Ghost be not now given through these miracles, by what is it given, by what does one get to know that he has received the Holy Ghost? Let him question his own heart. If he love his brother, the Spirit of God dwelleth in him. Let him see, let him prove himself before the eyes of God, let him see whether there be in him the love of peace and unity, the love of the Church that is spread over the whole earth.... Question thine heart. If love of thy brethren be there, set thy mind at rest. There cannot be love without the Spirit of God: since Paul cries, "The love of God is shed abroad in your hearts by the Holy Spirit which is given unto us."[61]

According to Augustine, one shouldn't feel as though he/she didn't have the Holy Spirit if tongues were not endowed. Rather, one should believe he/she had the Holy Spirit if he/she loved peace and unity, the Church, and his/her brothers and sisters in the Lord.

The Bible doesn't record tongues as having ended because they were still occurring when the New Testament was being written. For this reason, one won't find a Bible passage to prove tongues stopped. Neither can we find a verse to confirm the holocaust, but this doesn't mean that the holocaust didn't happen. Even so, there cannot be absolute proof that tongues have already ceased.

Scientists have occasionally claimed that a certain species has become extinct, only to discover that the animals existed in an unknown area. Because the historians and church fathers were not omniscient, as with scientists, we cannot claim with 100% certainty that this endowment ceased. We must recognize, however, that scientists are most often correct when they assert that an animal no longer exists, and the church fathers and historians may have been correct with regard to the existence of tongues.

The Bible revealed that tongues would cease, and according to respected historical records, evidence strongly points in their cessation. The Scriptures do not tell us this gift would be resurrected again.

> *Love never fails; but if there are gifts of prophecy, they* ***will be done away****; if there are tongues, they will* ***cease****; if there is knowledge, it* ***will be done away****. For we know in part and we prophesy in part; but when the perfect comes, the partial will be done away. 1 Corinthians 13:8-9 NASB*

Please note that, at this juncture, I am making a point about tongues only here. Interestingly, the Greek verb in the verse above that is used to describe what will happen to knowledge and prophecy, (they ***will be done away when the perfect comes***) is different from the verb used to describe what will happen to tongues (**they will cease**).

According to an article on Gotquestions.com, "Paul uses one Greek verb about the completion of prophecy and knowledge, and a completely different Greek verb about the cessation of tongues. The implication is that prophecy and knowledge will be "rendered inoperative or abolished" by an external force, but the gift of tongues will cease on its own. So, when the perfect comes, prophecy and knowledge are actively ended, but tongues will already have ended [on their own]."[62] For commentary citations on 1 Corinthians 13:8-9, see Appendix D.

Most theologians consider 'when the perfect comes' to mean when we are in heaven, in a state of perfection where we will be able to clearly understand those things that are veiled in this life. Since we haven't reached that state of perfection yet, it may be that God gives us a word of knowledge, a prediction, or the gift of prophecy to explain the Scriptures or foretell an event in the same way the soft cessationist believes that God occasionally does miracles and healings. Not that we find certain people are gifted in words of knowledge or prophecy (as in foretelling), but perhaps God might use these at His discretion.

Let us not miss the main meaning of the verses (1 Cor. 13:8-9) above. The charismata, such as *words of knowledge, prophecy, tongues,* and *interpretation of tongues* are transient and temporal. Some of these (tongues and interpretation of tongues) appear to have ceased, and others have not been seen in same measure as in the early church. Love, more important than all the gifts, lasts forever. We are not to be like the Corinthians, overvaluing and priding ourselves in that which doesn't last, while love, which is imperishable, takes a sideline.

As to the gift of healing, early in Paul's ministry, he raised Eutychus from death. Cloths, which touched his body, were given to those who were ill, and they recovered. However, later in his life, he tells us that Epaphroditus was so sick that he almost died (Philippians 2:25-27), and that he left Trophimus sick at Miletus (2 Timothy 4:20). Had Paul's gift of healing been fading?

By the fourth century AD, John Chrysostom, an important Church Father, wrote sermons on various New Testament passages. Regarding whether the charismata were in operation during his lifetime (349 - 407 AD), he says, "This whole place is very obscure: but the obscurity is produced by our ignorance of the facts referred to and by their **cessation**, being such as then used to occur but now **no longer take place**."[63]

As an apple doesn't fall far from the tree, children tend to act like their parents. You know a tree by its fruit, whether good or evil, and bad fruit indicates rotten roots. It saddens me to bring up some of the fruit of the Pentecostal movement, for I can affirm that there are many godly pastors and dedicated Christians within Pentecostalism whose deeds are excellent, and whose lives speak of the inner transformation of the Holy Spirit. Large numbers of people hear the true Gospel, have genuine conversions, and are set free from sin in these churches. Some are even delivered from demons in Pentecostal, Full Gospel, and Charismatic congregations. That said, let us explore history.

After approximately 1650 years where the gifts of the Spirit were widely known to have decreased and tongues were not being heard that we know of, Charles Parham (the 'Father of Pentecost') began to advance the charismata. In 1901, he promoted speaking in tongues and baptism in the Holy Spirit, as if those who were born again did not have the Holy Spirit initially, and as though the gifts were to be restored to the same extent that the early church experienced. The spiritual manifestations which occurred in his meetings were supposedly a *latter rain* of God's Spirit. Thus, Pentecostalism was birthed, later considered to be the *first wave* of the Holy Spirit.

Unfortunately, several serious incidents marred Parham's ministry. A woman was beaten to death by five of his followers as they tried to exorcise a demon of rheumatism from her, and a young girl died because her parents sought healing through his ministry, rather than taking her to a doctor.[64] Does it sound like these people were following and hearing the Holy Spirit more than other Christians?

In the mid 1960's to the 1980's, the *Charismatic Renewal* began, which would eventually be considered a *second wave* of the Holy Spirit. In 1983, the term *Third Wave* was coined by C. Peter Wagner, as if another round of God's Spirit was coming.[65]

In the 1990's, Wagner went on to define the New Apostolic Reformation (NAR), in which he promoted the idea of a second apostolic age wherein the offices of apostles and prophets were to be restored. He charged money to hand out various titles, such as *Vertical Apostle, Horizontal Apostle*, and *Territorial Apostle,* to name a few.[66] In church history, the gift of prophecy was not something Christians learned in prophetic schools (as is being promoted today), and the office of a prophet was never a title which they paid for.

The sordid details of top leaders in the above movements have been detailed in *Defining Deception: Freeing the Church from the Mystical-Miracle Movement* by Costi Hinn and Anthony Wood. I will tell you that many of the main 'ministers' who moved in supernatural manifestations had lives riddled with adultery, affairs, alcoholism, homosexual liaisons, etc. Are these sins limited to a few Pentecostal leaders?

In most of the Pentecostal churches which I attended and visited, I regret to say that serious sins affected the leaders and pastors. In addition to Pastor Ricky, who molested a 12-year-old girl, our youth pastor at Full Gospel Tabernacle had an affair while out on the mission field. In my Wisconsin hometown Assembly of God, the main pastor had an affair with a member of the congregation, and a guest minister at WoF church, Roberts Liardon, fell into a homosexual relationship shortly after giving a sermon to us.

On top of that, several of my favorite televangelists have succumbed to the above sins. While no denomination is completely free of pastors who fall, sexual problems seem more predominant in those who are looking for experiences and in those who do not have the Holy Spirit to empower them. Might we Pentecostals have a problem with sensuality, and might our passions be part of the reason we are drawn toward experiencing signs, wonders, and spiritual gifts?

Unfortunately, those of us in 'Spirit-filled' Christianity are acutely aware that many of our revered preachers have often fallen to depravity, rather than rising to holiness and being conformed to the image of Christ by the sanctifying work of God's Spirit. Can one who is *filled* with the Holy Spirit ignore the Lord's conviction and fall into utter immorality? If the fruit of the Spirit includes holiness, sober mindedness, temperance, self-control, and steadiness, it seems as if those in regular denominations may have more of God's Spirit than some in Pentecostal churches.

But I say, ***walk by the Spirit, and you will not carry out the desire of the flesh****....Now the deeds of the flesh are evident, which are: immorality, impurity, sensuality, idolatry, sorcery, enmities, strife, jealousy, outbursts of anger, disputes, dissensions, factions, envying, drunkenness, carousing, and things like these, of which I forewarn you, just as I have forewarned you, that* ***those who practice such things will not inherit the kingdom of God****. Galatians 5:16, 19-21 NASB (Emphasis mine)*

Over the past 12 years, I've developed many friendships with cessationists at Evangelical Free Church. I've learned that they are not closed-minded legalists who put God in a box. Rather, many of them have an intimate, abiding relationship with Jesus. They realize that God communicates in prayer as well as through the Scriptures, and they welcome the Holy Spirit's direction. However, they do not believe we should be led by dreams and visions apart from the Scriptures, and that if we feel prompted in our hearts, we must always go to God's Word to be sure we aren't being led astray.

Thomas was not with Jesus when He first appeared to the disciples after His resurrection, and this apostle wanted the same experience in order to believe. He said,

"Unless I see in His hands the imprint of the nails, and put my finger into the place of the nails, and put my hand into His side, I will not believe." (John 20:25b NASB)

After appearing to Thomas, Jesus said to him,

"Because you have seen Me, have you believed? Blessed are they who did not see, and yet believed." (John 20:29 NASB)

In this temporary life which will be over in the blink of an eye, if the Holy Spirit doesn't give out the charismata in the same capacity as in the early church, and if He doesn't mean for us to seek supernatural experiences, signs, and wonders, but prefers us to rely on the completed canon of the Scriptures (which the early church didn't possess), can we be satisfied to walk in a greater gift, love, which endures forever?

Perhaps the Lord is calling us to walk through the darkest times with the Light of the Scriptures to guide us, asking us to place our faith in Jesus without seeing His pierced hands and without experiencing the charismata (which are only a small portion of the Holy Spirit's work) in the exact way the early church did. Soon, we will be in Heaven, where our knowledge will be perfect and where the gifts of the Spirit will not be needed. We will see Jesus face to face and will have all eternity to bask in His true presence.

We must search to know the Scriptures more than to experience gifts, for signs and wonders will be used by the antichrist to deceive many and to cause great apostasy. Jesus told the Pharisees,

> *"A wicked and adulterous generation asks for a sign! But none will be given it except the sign of the prophet Jonah. For as Jonah was three days and three nights in the belly of a huge fish, so the Son of Man will be three days and three nights in the heart of the earth." Matthew 12:39–40 NIV*

Appendix A – Foreign Language Tongues

Section 1

For if you have the ability to speak in tongues, you will be talking only to God, since people won't be able to understand you. You will be speaking by the power of the Spirit, but it will all be mysterious. 1 Corinthians 14:2 NLT

I searched commentaries on Biblehub.com regarding the above verse to discover its true meaning. *Cambridge Bible for Schools and Colleges* states, "*For he that speaketh in an* unknown *tongue*] The word *unknown* is not in the original. The word translated *tongue* **signifies a *human language*** ....Because the language is not the language of those to whom he is speaking, and therefore what he says is hidden from them."[67]

According to *Barnes' Notes on the Old and New Testaments*, "He [Paul] did not undervalue the power of **speaking foreign languages** when foreigners were present, or when they went to preach to foreigners; ....It was only when it was needless, when all present spoke one language, that he speaks of it as of comparatively little value.[68]

Benson Commentary states, "it is plain that the inspired person, who uttered, in an unknown language, a revelation made to himself, must have understood it, otherwise he could not increase his own knowledge and faith [be edified] by speaking it."[69]

Jamieson-Fausset-Brown Bible Commentary tells us, "its [tongues] legitimate use **was in an audience understanding the tongue of the speaker**, not, as the Corinthians abused it, in mere display.[70]

In *Matthew Poole's Commentary,* "the writer believes the restored language of Hebrew was being spoken in the company of those in Israel, where Aramaic was most commonly spoken. Therefore, the language would be mysterious to those present, not unto man, but unto God, who being the Author of all languages, must necessarily know the significancy (sic) of all words in them..."[71]

John Gill's Exposition of the Entire Bible seems to agree with Matthew Poole's Commentary, saying, "that the Hebrew tongue...is here meant, and that not without reason; seeing the public prayers, preaching, and singing of psalms among the Jews, were in this language; in imitation of whom, such ministers, who had the gift of speaking this language, read the Scriptures, preached, prayed, and sung psalms in it, which were no ways to the edification of the people, who understood it not; upon which account the apostle recommends prophesying, praying, and singing, in a language that was understood: otherwise he speaketh not unto men; to the understanding, profit, and edification of men: but unto God: to his praise and glory, and he only knowing, who knows all languages, and every word in the tongue what is said; excepting himself, unless there should be any present capable of interpreting..."[72]

The *Geneva Study Bible* says, "the Corinthians used tongues in the congregation without an interpreter. And although this thing might be done to some profit of him that spoke them, yet he corrupted the right use of that gift because there came by it no profit to the hearers. And common assemblies were instituted and appointed not for any private man's commodity, but for the profit of the whole company."[73]

Cambridge Bible for Schools and Colleges states, "*For he that speaketh in an* unknown *tongue*] The word *unknown* is not in the original. The word translated *tongue* **signifies a *human language*** ....Because the language is not the language of those to whom he is speaking, and therefore what he says is hidden from them."[74]

<u>Section 2</u>

Regarding this Bible verse:

> *For if I pray in a tongue, my spirit prays, but my mind is unfruitful. 1 Corinthians 14:14 NASB*

John Gill's Exposition of the Entire Bible says of this verse, "For if I pray in an unknown tongue....In the Hebrew tongue, which the greatest part of the Jewish doctors insisted...and the custom was used by such as had the gift of speaking that language, even though the body and bulk of the people understood it not:

my spirit prayeth; I pray with my breath vocally; or else with affection and devotion, understanding what I say myself, and so am edified; or rather with the gift of the Spirit bestowed on me: but my understanding is unfruitful; that is, **what I say with understanding to myself is unprofitable to others**, not being understood by them."[75]

Section 3

Regarding this Bible verse:

> *I thank God, I [Paul] speak in tongues more than you all; 1 Corinthians 14:18 NASB*

Benson's Commentary on the Old and New Testaments says, "More than the whole society taken together. The apostle had this **great variety of languages given him by inspiration, that he might be able immediately to preach the gospel to all nations, without spending time in learning their languages**. But it must be remembered that the knowledge of so many languages miraculously communicated, was a knowledge for common use, such as enabled the apostle **to deliver the doctrines of the gospel clearly and properly**;"[76]

Barnes' Notes on the Old and New Testaments says, "'I [Paul] **am able to speak more foreign languages than all of you**.' How many languages Paul could speak, he has no where told us. It is reasonable, however, to presume that he was able to speak the language of any people to whom God in his providence, and by his Spirit, called him to preach. He had been commissioned to preach to the "Gentiles," and it is probable that he was able to speak the languages of all the nations among whom he ever traveled. **There is no account of his being under a necessity of employing an interpreter wherever he preached.**"[77]

John Gill's Exposition of the Entire Bible says, "for he [Paul] had this gift in a very eminent manner, and oftentimes made use of it, and was frequently under a necessity of so doing; **he could speak with more tongues than any of those that had them**, and spoke them oftener than they did; **having occasion for them through his travelling into different countries, and preaching the Gospel to people of divers languages**;"[78]

Cambridge Bible for Schools and Colleges says, "St Paul, no doubt, had the gift of interpretation. Yet apparently he did not often exercise in public, whatever he may have done in private, the gift of speaking with tongues unknown to his hearers."[79]

Section 4

Regarding this Bible verse:

> *however, in the church I [Paul] desire to speak five words with my mind so that I may instruct others also, rather than ten thousand words in a tongue. 1 Corinthians 14:19*

Barne's Notes says, "It is probable that in the Christian assembly, usually, there were few who understood foreign languages. Paul, therefore, **would not speak in a foreign language when its only use would be mere display**."[80]

According to trusted commentators, it appears that the tongues at Pentecost were true human languages.

Appendix B – Tongues of Angels

Might **some** tongues be the languages of angels? This next verse is often cited to show that the Holy Spirit might give us languages of angels, not knowable by man unless there is a person present with the gift of interpretation.

> *If I speak with the tongues of men and of angels, but do not have love, I have become a noisy gong or a clanging cymbal. If I have the gift of prophecy, and know all mysteries and all knowledge; and if I have all faith, so as to remove mountains, but do not have love, I am nothing. And if I give all my possessions to feed the poor, and if I surrender my body to be burned, but do not have love, it profits me nothing. 1 Corinthians 13:1-3 NASB*

Barnes' Notes on the Old and New Testaments says, "And of angels - The language of angels; such as they speak. Were I endowed with the **faculty of eloquence and persuasion** which we attribute to them; and the power of speaking to any of the human family **with the power which they have**. The language of angels here seems to be used to denote **the highest power of using language, or of the most elevated faculty of eloquence and speech**. It is evidently derived from the idea that the angels are "superior" in all respects to human beings; that they must have endowments in advance of all which man can have. It may possibly have reference to the idea that **they must have some mode of communicating their ideas one to another**, and that this dialect or mode must be far superior to that which is employed by man. Man is imperfect. All his modes of communication are defective. We attribute to the angels the idea of perfection; and the idea here is, that even though a man had a far higher faculty of speaking languages than would be included in the endowment of speaking all the languages of human beings as people speak them, and even had the higher and more perfect **mode** of utterance which the angels have, and yet were destitute of love, all would be nothing."[81]

Jamieson-Fausset-Brown Bible Commentary says, "though I speak, that is, if I could speak, or admit I did speak, with the tongues used in all the nations of the world, and with the tongues of angels; by which some understand the best and most excellent ways of expressing ourselves. **Angels have no tongues, nor make any articulate audible sounds, by which they understand one another**; but yet there is certainly a society or intercourse among angels, which could not be upheld without some way amongst them to **communicate their minds and wills each to other**."[82]

John Gill's Exposition of the Entire Bible says, "and of angels; **not that angels have tongues in a proper sense, or speak any vocal language, in an audible voice, with articulate sounds**; for they are spirits immaterial and incorporeal; though they have an intellectual speech, by which they celebrate the perfections and praises of God, and can discourse with one another, and **communicate their minds** to each other;"[83]

Meyer's New Testament Commentary says, "The tongues of *angels* here spoken of are certainly only an **abstract conception**, but one in keeping with the poetic character of the passage..."[84]

The Pulpit Commentary says, "Though I speak with the tongues of men and of angels. The case is merely **supposed.** The tongues of men are human languages, including, perhaps, the peculiar utterance of ecstatic inspiration with which he is now dealing. It is, perhaps, with reference to this latter result of spiritual exultation, at any rate in its purest and loftiest developments, that he adds the words, "and of angels."....**The words are meant to express the greatest possible climax. The most supreme powers of utterance, even of angelic utterance** - if any of the Corinthians had or imagined that they had attained to such utterance - are nothing in comparison with the universally possible attainment of Christian love. It is remarkable that here again he places "tongues," even in their grandest conceivable development, on the **lowest** step in his climax."[85]

Benson Commentary says, "*Though I speak with the tongues of men and angels* — That is, all the languages which are spoken upon earth, and with the ***eloquence of an angel***....by the *tongues of angels,* the apostle doubtless meant the ***methods***, whatever they are, by which angels ***communicate their thoughts*** to each other, and which must be a much more excellent language than any that is spoken by men."[86]

Appendix C – What is Prophecy?

egarding this Bible verse:

> *Let love be your highest goal! But you should also desire the special abilities the Spirit gives—especially the* ***ability to prophesy****. 1 Cor. 14:1 NLT (Emphasis mine)*

The *Matthew Henry Concise Commentary* says, "Prophesying, that is, **explaining Scripture**, is compared with speaking with tongues."[87]

Barnes' Notes on the Old and New Testaments says, "the prophet spoke more from the impulse of **sudden inspiration, from the light of a sudden revelation at the moment**...and his discourse was probably more adapted, by means of **powerful exhortation, to awaken the feelings and conscience of the hearers**."[88]

John Gill's Exposition of the Entire Bible says, "regarding the word prophecy, it is "**not so much the gift of foretelling future events**, though there was such a gift bestowed on some persons in those times, and, in certain cases, was very profitable to the churches; but a **gift of preaching the word, or explaining the prophecies of the Old Testament, and of praying and singing of psalms**, all which, as appears from some following parts of this chapter, were included in it; and that not in an ordinary, but in an extraordinary way; a person possessed of this gift could at once, without the use of means, or help of study, preach the word, and open the more difficult parts of Scripture; he had an extraordinary gift of prayer, which he could make use of when he pleased, and at once compose and deliver out a psalm, or hymn, in the public congregation."[89]

Jamieson-Fausset-Brown Bible Commentary says, "it is therefore more probable, that he speaketh of an **ability to open the Scriptures, either by immediate**

revelation, (as to which they could use no means but prayer and a holy life), **or by ordinary meditation, and study of the Scriptures**."[90]

Geneva Study Bible says, "Prophecy was about '**the gift of teaching and applying the doctrine**...."[91]

Cambridge Bible for Schools and Colleges says, "The gift of prophecy...was not confined to the prediction of future events.... the prophet was "not only a *fore*-teller but a ***forth*-teller**," **one who communicates the moral and spiritual truths which he has received by direct revelation from God**.[92]

While we do see several prophetic foretellings of future circumstances in the New Testament, according to the above commentary excerpts, the word used regarding the gift of prophecy was most often used to explain and preach the Scriptures. The Old Testament is similar. The prophets spent the majority of their time admonishing the people to turn from sin, exhorting them to live godly lives, and warning them of coming judgment if they refused to repent.

Appendix D – Cease vs. Will Be Done Away With

egarding these Bible verses:

> *Love never fails; but if there are gifts of prophecy, they* ***will be done away****; if there are tongues, they will* ***cease****; if there is knowledge, it* ***will be done away****. For we know in part and we prophesy in part; but when the perfect comes, the partial will be done away. 1 Corinthians 13:8-9 NASB (Emphasis mine)*

Jamieson-Fausset-Brown Bible Commentary tells us about the verb which Paul uses to describe what will happen to prophecy and knowledge. "They "shall fail ... vanish away—The same Greek verb is used for both; and that different from the Greek verb for "faileth." Translate, "Shall be done away with," that is, shall be dispensed with **at the Lord's coming**, being superseded by their more perfect heavenly analogues; for instance, knowledge by intuition. Of "tongues," which are still more temporary, the verb is "shall cease." **A primary fulfilment of Paul's statement took place when the Church attained its maturity; then "tongues" entirely "ceased," and prophesyings" and "knowledge," so far as they were supernatural gifts of the Spirit, were superseded as no longer required when the ordinary preaching of the word, and the Scriptures of the New Testament collected together, had become established institutions**."[93]

John Gill's Exposition of the Entire Bible tells us, "but the gift of speaking with diverse tongues will cease, **indeed it has already**;" (John Gill lived from 1697-1771 and is one of many theologians through the ages who believed the supernatural gift of tongues had ceased).[94]

Bengel's Gnomen gives us the Greek verbs as well as their interpretation. **"καταργηθήσονται**, *they shall be done away with*) This is the expression in the case of prophecies and knowledge; but regarding tongues, **παύσονται**, *they shall cease.* Tongues are a most charming thing, but the least lasting; they were the first gift on the day of Pentecost, Acts 2, **but they did not continue in the primitive church so long as the other miraculous gifts**..."[95]

Acknowledgments

Special appreciation to my husband, David, and my family members, Tyler, Amber, and Liz, for patiently supporting this endeavor. I'd like to thank Pastor Gene, David and Janet, Amanda and Dave, Aunt Mae, Amy, Louise, Dana, and Karen for reading my manuscript, editing assistance, and your valuable input.

Notes:

1. Josh McDowell and Bill Wilson, *The Best of Josh McDowell, A Ready Defense,* (Nashville, Atlanta, London, Vancouver, Thomas Nelson Publishers, 1993) p. 56
2. Ibid., 26-27
3. David Henke, *Religious Dysfunction, Last accessed on 10/02/18, Retrieved from:* https://www.watchman.org/articles/cults-alternative-religions/religious-dysfunction/
4. Last accessed on 10/02/18, Retrieved from *https://en.wikipedia.org/wiki/Christian_countercult_movement*, David Breese, as cited on Wikipedia article titled: Christian Countercult Movement
5. Walter Martin, Jill Martin Rische, and Kurt Van Gorden, *The Kingdom of the Occult*, 1st. Ed, Nashville, Thomas Nelson, 2008, p. 193
6. David Spangler, *Reflections on the Christ*, 3rd Ed. (Findhorn, Moray, Scotland, Findhorn Publications, 1981), p. 41
7. Helena Blavatsky, *Helena Blavatsky Collection: Isis Unveiled, The Secret Doctrine, The Key to Theosophy (Timeless Wisdom Collection*, 2015), Kindle Location 55963
8. Walter Martin, *The Kingdom of the Cults*, 5th Ed, (Bloomington, Bethany House Publishers, 2003), p. 24
9. Kenneth Hagin, *The Believer's Authority, 2nd Ed.* (USA, Rhema Bible Church, 1996) p. 35-36
10. Myles Munroe, "*This Is Your Day*," Benny Hinn, July 12, 2004
11. Dave Hunt & T.A. McMahon, *The Seduction of Christianity*, (Eugene, OR, Harvest House Publishers, 1985), p. 33
12. Last Accessed on 10/02/18, Retrieved from, https://www.georgemuller.org/quotes/category/worldliness
13. Last accessed on 10/02/18, as cited on http://www.againstallheresy.com/modern-day-heretics-2/heretic-kenneth-copeland/, (Kenneth Copeland, Praise-a-Thon program on TBN (April 1988).
14. Last accessed on 10/02/18, as cited on http://www.againstallheresy.com/modern-day-heretics-2/heretic-kenneth-copeland/, (Kenneth Copeland, *Our Covenant with God* (Fort Worth, TX: KCP Publications, 1987), 8–11
15. Last accessed on 10/02/18, as cited on http://www.againstallheresy.com/modern-day-heretics-2/heretic-kenneth-copeland/, (Kenneth Copeland, *Image of God in You III* (Fort Worth, TX: Kenneth Copeland Ministries, 1989), audiotape #01-1403, side 1.
16. Last accessed on 10/02/18, as cited on http://www.againstallheresy.com/modern-day-heretics-2/heretic-benny-hinn/, (Benny Hinn, *Our Position in Christ #2—The Word Made Flesh*, Orlando: Orlando Christian Center, 1991, videotape #255).
17. Last accessed on 10/02/18, as cited on http://www.againstallheresy.com/modern-day-heretics-2/heretic-benny-hinn/, (Benny Hinn Praise-a-thon TBN November 6, 1990).
18. Last accessed on 10/02/18, as cited on http://www.againstallheresy.com/modern-day-heretics-2/heretic-benny-hinn/ , (Benny Hinn, TBN, 1990)
19. Last accessed on 10/02/18, as cited on http://www.againstallheresy.com/modern-day-heretics-2/heretic-kenneth-hagan/, (Kenneth M. Hagin, *Zoe: The God-Kind of Life* (Tulsa, OK: Kenneth Hagin Ministries, Inc., 1989), 35–36, 41.
20. Last accessed on 10/02/18, as cited on http://www.rapidnet.com/~jbeard/bdm/exposes/copeland/general.htm, (*Following the Faith of Abraham I*, 1989 audiotape, #01-3001, side 1)
21. John Foxe, *Foxe's Book of Martyrs*, Kindle edition, (Amazon Digital Services LLC, 2012) p. 304
22. Walter Martin, Jill Martin Rische, and Kurt Van Gorden, *The Kingdom of the Occult,* (1st. Ed, Nashville, Thomas Nelson, 2008), p. 37
23. Dietrich Bonhoeffer, *The Cost of Discipleship* (1949), P. 87
24. Terry Nance, *God's Armor Bearer, Vol. 1* (USA, Focus on the Harvest, 1990), p. 11, 12, 13, 29, 30, 31,
25. Marsha West, *Touch Not My Anointed*, Jan. 25, 2018, Last accessed on 10/02/18, Retrieved from: https://bereanresearch.org/touch-not-anointed/
26. Josh McDowell *Why True Love Waits,* (Wheaton, IL, Tyndale House Publishers, Inc., 2002 revised edition), p. 136
27. Focus on the Family, *Risk Factors for Premarital Sex*, Last accessed on 10/02/18, Retrieved from: https://www.focusonthefamily.com/family-q-and-a/parenting/risk-factors-for-teen-premarital-sex
28. Alavi, Hamid Reza. "*The Role of Self-Esteem in Tendency towards Drugs, Theft and Prostitution.*" *Addiction & Health* 3.3-4 (2011): 119–124. Print. Last accessed on 10/02/18, Retrieved from: https://www.ncbi.nlm.nih.gov/pmc/articles/PMC3905528/

29. Last accessed on 10/02/18 from YouTube video: Simplysaved, *The Kingdom Message of Jesus* ~ Dr. Myles Munroe, May 26, 2016, https://www.youtube.com/watch?v=-NdlghU52lw&feature=youtu.be
30. Johanna Michaelsen, *The Beautiful Side of Evil,* (Eugene, OR, Harvest House Publishers, 1982), p.75, 77
31. Dave Hunt & T.A. McMahon, *The Seduction of Christianity*, (Eugene, OR, Harvest House Publishers, 1979), p. 160
32. Dave Hunt, *Occult Invasion*, (Eugene, OR, Harvest House Publishers, 1998), p. 181
33. Last accessed on http://www.thebiblepage.org/avoid/copeland.shtml on 10/02/18, Kenneth Copeland, "*Substitution and Identification*" (Kenneth Copeland Ministries, 1989), tape #00-0202, side 2
34. Last accessed 10/02/18, Retrieved from https://www.allaboutreligion.org/Faith-Healing.htm (Kenneth Copeland, "*Believer's Voice of Victory*", broadcast on TBN, recorded July 9, 1987)
35. Last accessed on 10/02/18, Retrieved from https://www.allaboutreligion.org/Faith-Healing.htm, (Kenneth Copeland, "*The Force Of Love*", audiotape #02-0028, Kenneth Copeland Ministries, 1987.)
36. Last accessed 10/02/18 on YouTube video published by Biblical Christianity on 03/04/18 titled, *Creflo Dollar: you are gods HERESY - Justin Peters*, https://www.youtube.com/watch?v=HYPAzsxiCdk
37. Last accessed 10/02/18 on YouTube video published by Dyinta on 11/19/09 titled *Joyce Meyer False Teaching,* https://www.youtube.com/watch?v=yrP3OLCH9Gl&feature=related
38. Accessed on 08/19/18, https://biblehub.com/commentaries/mhcw/genesis/1.htm
39. Accessed on 04/11/18, TD Jakes "*Mega Care, 1*" The Potter's Touch, iTunes podcast, lightsource.com, August 17, 2008, the quote can also be found at https://www.zedekiahlist.com/cgi-bin/quotes.pl?&id=96541976
40. Last accessed on 10/02/18, Retrieved from YouTube video: BARNUMandBENTLEY, *Mark Chironna's Created "Anointed One"*, 08/25/09, https://www.youtube.com/watch?v=hahgpvJbJ-M&feature=youtu.be,
41. Accessed on 04/11/18 from YouTube video: Justin Peters, *FALSE TEACHERS EXPOSED: Word of Faith/Prosperity Gospel* | Justin Peters/SO4J-TV", 10/28/15, https://youtu.be/ptN2KQ7-euQ
42. Kenneth Hagin, *Zoe: The God-Kind of Life* (Tulsa, OK: Kenneth Hagin Ministries, Inc., 1989, 35-36, 41 as cited by Hank Hanegraaff, *Christianity in Crisis,* (Eugene, OR, Harvest House Publishers, 1993), p. 108
43. Accessed on 10/20/18, Retrieved from YouTube Video by Kaycee Watchman, *Jesus went to hell died spiritually and got born again in hell. Part 1,* Published on July 15, 2013, https://www.youtube.com/watch?v=nFG7cXOLiQQ
44. https://en.oxforddictionaries.com/definition/us/blasphemy
45. Accessed on 08/14/18, https://biblehub.com/commentaries/1_corinthians/14-1.htm
46. Accessed on 08/16/18, https://biblehub.com/commentaries/1_corinthians/14-18.htm
47. John Ankerberg & John Weldon, *Encyclopedia of New Age Beliefs,* (Eugene, OR, Harvest House Publishers, 1996). p. 606
48. https://en.wikipedia.org/wiki/Trojan_Horse
49. Dr. Gregory Reid, *Trojan Church: The New Age Corruption of the Evangelical Faith,* (USA, Xulon Press, 2008), p. 176
50. Andrew Strom, *Kundalini Warning: Are False Spirits Invading the Church?* (Revival School, Second edition, 2015), p. 19-20
51. Kurt Kock, *Occult ABC,* (Grand Rapids, Kregel Publications, 1986), p. 33
52. Accessed on 08/15/18, https://en.wikipedia.org/wiki/A._A._Allen
53. Kenneth Hagin, *Why Do People Fall Under the Power,* (Tulsa, Rhema Bible Church, 1981), p. 9-12
54. John MacArthur, *Strange Fire, The Danger of Offending the Holy Spirit with Counterfeit Fire,* (Nashville, Nelson Books, 2013), p. 150
55. Ronald A. N. Kydd, *Charismatic Gifts in the Early Church: The Gifts of the Spirit in the First 300 Years, (*Peabody, MA, Hendrickson Publishers Marketing, LLC, 1984, 2014), p. 59-60
56. Accessed on 09/03/18, https://en.m.wikipedia.org/wiki/Justin_Martyr
57. Justin Martyr Dialogue, 82: Roberts and Donaldson, The Ante Nicene fathers, 1:2:40
58. Dialogue, 87: Roberts and Donaldson, the ante Nicene fathers, 1: 243
59. John MacArthur, 1 Corinthians, *MacArthur New Testament Commentary* (Chicago: Moody Press, 1984) p. 361 as cited by Costi W. Hinn and Anthony G. Wood, *Defining Deceptions: Freeing the Church from the Mystical-Miracle Movement*, (El Cajon, CA, Southern California Seminary Press, 2018), p. 142
60. https://play.google.com/store/books/details?pcampaignid=books_inapp_quotesharing&id=pFghCgAAQBAJ, *Eusebius*, The Ecclesiastical History, (Aeterna Press, 2015), p.177
61. *Philip Schaff, Augustine of Hippo,* Nicene and Post Nicene Fathers, First Series, Vol. VII: St Augustine: Homilies on the Gospel of John, Homilies on the First Epistle of John, Soliloquies
62. Accessed on 08/14/18, article titled, *What is the meaning of "perfect" in 1 Corinthians 13:10?* https://www-gotquestions-org.cdn.ampproject.org/v/s/www.gotquestions.org/amp/perfect-1Corinthians-13-

10.html?usqp=mq331AQCCAE%3D&_js_v=0.1#referrer=https%3A%2F%2Fwww.google.com&_tf=From%20%251%24s&share=https%3A%2F%2Fwww.gotquestions.org%2Fperfect-1Corinthians-13-10.html

63. John Chrysostom, *The Homilies of St. John Chrysostom*, Bible Hub, accessed on 08/02/18, https://biblehub.com/commentaries/chrysostom/1_corinthians/12.htm

64. John MacArthur, *Strange Fire, The Danger of Offending the Holy Spirit with Counterfeit Fire,* (Nashville, Nelson Books, 2013), p. 24-25

65. Costi W. Hinn and Anthony G. Wood, *Defining Deceptions: Freeing the Church from the Mystical-Miracle Movement*, (El Cajon, CA, Southern California Seminary Press, 2018), p. 48-49

66. Ibid., p. 52-53

67. Accessed on 08/15/18, https://biblehub.com/commentaries/1_corinthians/14-2.htm

68. Accessed on 08/15/18, https://biblehub.com/commentaries/1_corinthians/14-2.htm, Albert Barnes and James Murphey, *Barnes' Notes on the Old and New Testaments*, 1834

69. Accessed on 08/15/18, https://biblehub.com/commentaries/1_corinthians/14-2.htm, Joseph Benson, *Benson's Commentary on the Old and New Testaments*, (Carlton and Phillips, G. Lane and C.B. Tippet, 1846-1854)

70. Accessed on 08/15/18, https://biblehub.com/commentaries/1_corinthians/14-2.htm, Robert Jamieson, Andrew Fausset, David Brown, *Jamieson-Fausset-Brown Bible Commentary*, 1871

71. Accessed on 08/15/18, https://biblehub.com/commentaries/1_corinthians/14-2.htm, Matthew Poole, *Matthew Poole's Commentary on the Holy Bible*, (New York, Robert Carter and Brothers, 1853)

72. Accessed on 08/15/18, https://biblehub.com/commentaries/1_corinthians/14-2.htm, *John Gill's Exposition of the Entire Bible*, 1746-1748

73. Accessed on 08/15/18, https://biblehub.com/commentaries/1_corinthians/14-2.htm, *Geneva Study Bible: Bringing the Light of the Reformation to Scripture*, 1599

74. Accessed on 08/15/18, https://biblehub.com/commentaries/1_corinthians/14-2.htm, John Perowne, *Cambridge Bible for Schools and Colleges*, 1891

75. Accessed on 08/14/18, https://biblehub.com/commentaries/1_corinthians/14-14.htm, *John Gill's Exposition of the Entire Bible*, 1746-1748

76. Accessed on 08/16/18, https://biblehub.com/commentaries/1_corinthians/14-18.htm, Joseph Benson, *Benson's Commentary on the Old and New Testaments*, (Carlton and Phillips, G. Lane and C.B. Tippet, 1846-1854)

77. Accessed on 08/16/18, https://biblehub.com/commentaries/1_corinthians/14-18.htm, Albert Barnes and James Murphey, *Barnes' Notes on the Old and New Testaments*, 1834

78. Accessed on 08/16/18, https://biblehub.com/commentaries/1_corinthians/14-18.htm, *John Gill's Exposition of the Entire Bible*, 1746-1748

79. Accessed on 08/16/18, https://biblehub.com/commentaries/1_corinthians/14-18.htm, John Perowne, *Cambridge Bible for Schools and Colleges*, 1891

80. Accessed on 08/16/18, https://biblehub.com/commentaries/1_corinthians/14-19.htm, Albert Barnes and James Murphey, *Barnes' Notes on the Old and New Testaments*, 1834

81. Accessed on 08/14/18, https://biblehub.com/commentaries/1_corinthians/13-1.htm, Albert Barnes and James Murphey, *Barnes' Notes on the Old and New Testaments*, 1834

82. Accessed on 08/14/18, https://biblehub.com/commentaries/1_corinthians/13-1.htm, Robert Jamieson, Andrew Fausset, David Brown, *Jamieson-Fausset-Brown Bible Commentary*, 1871

83. Accessed on 08/14/18, https://biblehub.com/commentaries/1_corinthians/13-1.htm, *John Gill's Exposition of the Entire Bible*, 1746-1748

84. Accessed on 08/14/18, https://biblehub.com/commentaries/1_corinthians/13-1.htm, Heinrich August Wilhelm, Meyer, *Meyers New Testament Commentary*, (Funk and Wagnalls, 1884)

85. Accessed on 08/14/18, https://biblehub.com/commentaries/1_corinthians/13-1.htm, H.D.M. Spence, *Pulpit Commentary*, (Funk and Wagnalls, 1909-1919)

86. Accessed on 08/15/18, https://biblehub.com/commentaries/1_corinthians/13-1.htm, Joseph Benson, *Benson's Commentary on the Old and New Testaments*, (Carlton and Phillips, G. Lane and C.B. Tippet, 1846-1854)

87. Accessed on 08/14/18, https://biblehub.com/commentaries/1_corinthians/14-1.htm, *Matthew Henry Concise Commentary*, 1706

88. Accessed on 08/14/18, https://biblehub.com/commentaries/1_corinthians/14-1.htm, Albert Barnes and James Murphey, *Barnes' Notes on the Old and New Testaments*, 1834

89. Accessed on 08/14/18, https://biblehub.com/commentaries/1_corinthians/14-1.htm, *John Gill's Exposition of the Entire Bible*, 1746-1748

90. Accessed on 08/14/18, https://biblehub.com/commentaries/1_corinthians/14-1.htm, Robert Jamieson, Andrew Fausset, David Brown, *Jamieson-Fausset-Brown Bible Commentary*, 1871

91. Accessed on 08/14/18, https://biblehub.com/commentaries/1_corinthians/14-1.htm, Geneva Study Bible: Bringing the Light of the Reformation to Scripture, 1599

92. Accessed on 08/14/18, https://biblehub.com/commentaries/1_corinthians/14-1.htm, John Perowne, *Cambridge Bible for Schools and Colleges*, 1891

93. Accessed on 08/14/18, https://biblehub.com/commentaries/1_corinthians/13-8.htm, Robert Jamieson, Andrew Fausset, David Brown, *Jamieson-Fausset-Brown Bible Commentary*, 1871

94. Accessed on 08/14/18, https://biblehub.com/commentaries/1_corinthians/13-8.htm, *John Gill's Exposition of the Entire Bible*, 1746-1748

95. Accessed on 08/14/18, https://biblehub.com/commentaries/1_corinthians/13-8.htm, Johann Albrecht Bengel, Bengel's Gnomen of the New Testament, (Edinburgh, T and T. Clark, 1759)

Made in the USA
Middletown, DE
19 March 2019